IMPROVING PSYCHOLOGICAL SERVICES FOR CHILDREN AND ADOLESCENTS WITH SEVERE MENTAL DISORDERS: CLINICAL TRAINING IN PSYCHOLOGY

PHYLLIS R. MAGRAB

AND

PAUL WOHLFORD

COEDITORS

AMERICAN PSYCHOLOGICAL ASSOCIATION
WASHINGTON, DC

DEDICATION

Dedicated to Kimberly Anne Young, who was at the beginning of this journey. Now others must take the steps for her and carry forward her warmth, goodness, and strength.

They that love beyond the world cannot be separated by it.

—William Penn

This book is based on papers given at the National Conference on Clinical Training in Psychology: Improving Psychological Services for Children and Adolescents With Severe Mental Disorders, held on May 18-20, 1988, in Herndon, VA. The conference was sponsored by the National Institute of Mental Health through an interagency agreement with the Bureau of Maternal and Child Health and Resources Development, and it was coordinated by Phyllis R. Magrab.

ISBN Number: 1-55798-080-2

Library of Congress Catalog Card Number: 89-082675

First Edition

Published by
American Psychological Association
1200 Seventeenth Street, NW
Washington, DC 20036

Copies may be ordered from:
APA Order Department
PO Box 2710
Hyattsville, MD 20784
Order No.: 428-0120

Printing: Malloy Lithographing, Ann Arbor, MI
Cover Design: Sans Serif Graphics, Alexandria, VA
Composition: Kylee Magrab
                        Vernice M. Thompson

Printed in the United States of America.

TABLE OF CONTENTS

FOREWORD

The National Institute of Mental Health's (NIMH) Education and Training Branch has responsibility for clinical training of mental health professionals concerned with treatment of three priority populations: seriously mentally ill children and adolescents, adults, and racial/ethnic minorities. At a meeting on May 1, 1987, NIMH invited open discussion of a proposed 3-year plan to improve clinical training of mental health professionals for providing services to priority populations. During the meeting, it became clear that not only did economic issues have to be considered but also many other important factors had to be reconciled and that a good, consensus-based policy resolution would require a long process. Because additional funds were made available for NIMH clinical training in the FY 1988 budget (for the first time in 7 years), it was possible to plan for systematic program improvement, including having several conferences designed to discuss factors affecting training and to make policy recommendations.

In 1987, laying the foundation for subsequent activities, two interdisciplinary conferences were sponsored by NIMH, the Western Interstate Commission for Higher Education (WICHE), and the National Association of State Mental Health Program Directors (NASMHPD), which culminated in the report Interdisciplinary Collaboration Between State Mental Health and Higher Education (WICHE, 1987). The primary purpose of these conferences was to explore ways to increase the collaboration between the university-based mental health professional educational programs and the array of state and local mental health programs serving the public sector. Over the last two years, this basic concept has been refined through various conferences and now is simply referred to as "public-academic linkages for clinical training."

While certain clinical training issues are common to all disciplines, it is also true that each discipline, like psychology, has dynamic factors in its growth and development that make it unique. Therefore, in 1988, three national conferences on clinical training specifically in psychology were held, one on each of three priority populations:

- Training Psychologists to Work with the Seriously Mentally Ill, April 6-8, 1988, University of Houston (Johnson, in press).

- Clinical Training In Psychology: Improving Psychological Services for Children and Adolescents with Severe Mental Disorders, May 18-20, 1988, Georgetown University (reported in this volume).

- Improving Training and Psychological Services for Ethnic Minorities, June 8-10, 1988, University of California, Los Angeles (Myers, Wohlford, Echemendia, & Guzman, in press).

At each conference, 40 to 60 national leaders intensively examined training issues and, inductively, recommended policy directions. Each conference was large enough to be representative of the country's best programs (many of which had been supported by NIMH), and at the same time, focused enough to allow in-depth discussion.

The agenda of each conference covered a matrix of training issues, focusing primarily on what constitutes the best training models for providing professionals with the skills and experiences necessary to serve the needs of a specific population. In addition, each agenda considered level of training (master's, predoctoral academic, predoctoral internship, postdoctoral fellowship), type of setting and client (dual diagnosis, homeless, etc.), and type of support mechanism (student stipend, faculty support, faculty development, curriculum development, etc.). Each conference was given the charge to make specific sets of recommendations to:

- NIMH for funding priorities, clinical training policies, and administrative procedures.

- American Psychological Association (APA) boards and committees for improving the quality of training in given areas.

- Other institutions, such as states, and so forth.

On June 15, 1988, just after the third conference, representatives from the three conferences met at APA headquarters and drafted an executive summary of recommendations to NIMH for funding priorities and general policies (see Section I).

On August 12, 1988, at the APA convention in Atlanta, 35 psychologists representing the steering committees of the three conferences met to discuss all three conferences' implementation of the conferences' recommendations to NIMH and to APA boards and committees. There was great agreement in the general and even specific recommendations across the three conferences, although some topics were discussed by only one conference. The most salient recommendation emerged independently from each of the three conferences:

- More young psychologists should be recruited to make their careers in the public service sector for the priority populations.

The August 12 conferees also concurred with other recommendations in the June 15 executive summary concerning the importance of adding racial/ethnic minorities as a fifth NIMH clinical training priority population and the importance of institutional faculty development, curriculum development, and continuing education.

Moreover, the August 12 conferees themselves displayed qualities that were observed in the process and products at each of the three conferences: cooperation, helping, and sharing rather than competitiveness and secretiveness. Concretely, this was seen in all three conferences' endorsing the sharing of new curricula and curricular materials via faculty development programs or some type of new national curriculum clearinghouse. The cooperativeness was perhaps due to a general recognition that those in the public service sector constitute a special subset of the whole profession. This recognition also led to the conclusion that the three conferences should unite for the explicit purpose of helping each other to implement all the recommendations.

The implementation of the recommendations of the three conferences involves four steps: First, to work with appropriate offices of the APA to ensure that policy recommendations to NIMH are followed up. This occurred; the FY 1989 and FY 1990 NIMH clinical training announcements reflect input from the three conferences. Second, to seek a broader base for implementation of recommendations to APA boards and committees by disseminating the conferences' published proceedings and by having public discussions at the 1989 APA convention. The latter did occur; the recommendations of each conference were presented at three separate symposia reporting on the conferences. Third, to publish the recommendations in the American Psychologist following the 1989 convention. Fourth, to establish a structure or committee, with representatives of all three conferences, to meet regularly to oversee the implementation of the recommendations.

The recommendations made by the three conferences, as reported in each and summarized at the June and August 1988 follow-up meetings, provide important guidelines for future development and expansion of training in the area of treatment of the severely mentally ill in the United States. The recommendations are pertinent both to federal and state agencies responsible for service delivery who use psychologists to provide services and to institutions and individuals responsible for training working and future psychologists.

Very significantly, the fresh recommendations from three 1988 conferences on clinical training in psychology contributed to the corresponding multidisciplinary clinical training conferences held in 1989 and planned for 1990:

- Clinical Training for Services to the Long-Term Seriously Mentally Ill: A Multidisciplinary Review and Assessment, September 22-24, 1989, University of Cincinnati (Paulson, 1990).

- National Conference on Multidisciplinary Services for Seriously Disturbed Children and Adolescents, September 6-8, 1989, Georgetown University (Magrab, 1990).

- National Conference on Multidisciplinary Clinical Training and Services for Seriously Mentally Ill Ethnic Minorities (planned for Spring, 1990).

In spite of the fact that the NIMH clinical training budget in recent years has fluctuated*—inhibiting the implementation of some recommendations developed by the clinical training conferences—progress has been made. The field of psychology has responsibly pointed out what psychology itself should be doing, as well as what federal and state agencies should do, to improve training for psychologists who wish to provide services to seriously mentally ill adults, children and adolescents, and ethnic minorities. This ability to articulate its training priorities, along with the willingness to make recommendations for change and assist in implementation, has moved the field forward and provided a good foundation for growth and change.

PAUL WOHLFORD
Chief, Psychology Education Program
National Institute of Mental Health

---

*NIMH's clinical training budget increase, from $15 million in FY 1987 to $16.8 million in FY 1988, was the first increase in 7 years. However, in FY 1989, the budget was again reduced, this time to $12.8 million. Nevertheless, it was possible to fund a total of 39 new training grants, including 18 in psychology, because of savings from terminated grants. Just before this goes to press, the FY 1990 budget became final: again it was increased, this time to $13.6 million. In summary, the budget pattern over the past 4 years is: up, down, up.

References

Johnson, D.L. (Ed.). (1990). Training psychologists to work with the seriously mentally ill. Washington, DC: American Psychological Association.

Magrab, P.R., & Wohlford, P. (Eds.). (1990). Improving psychological services for children and adolescents with severe mental disorders: Clinical training in psychology. Washington, DC: American Psychological Association.

Magrab, P.R. (Ed.). (1990). National conference on multidisciplinary services for seriously disturbed children and adolescents: Conference report. Washingon, DC: Georgetown University Child Development Center.

Myers, H.F. (Ed.). (1990). Improving training and psychological services for ethnic minorities. Washington, DC: American Psychological Association.

Paulson, R. (Ed.). (1990). Clinical training for services to the long-term seriously mentlly ill: A multidisciplinary review and assessment. Cincinnati, OH: University of Cincinnati, School of Social Work.

Western Interstate Commission for Higher Education (WICHE). (1987). Interdisciplinary collaboration between state mental health and higher education. (M. Davis and A. M. Sanchez, Eds.) Boulder, CO: Author.

SECTION I

POLICY RECOMMENDATIONS

Policy Recommendations to NIMH from the Three National
Conferences on Clinical Training in Psychology, 1988*

To address the National Institute of Mental Health's clinical training priorities, 140 leading psychologists participated in three National Conferences on Clinical Training in Psychology in the spring of 1988. Sponsored by the three host universities and by NIMH's Division of Education and Service Systems Liaison, each conference focused on one of the three NIMH clinical training priorities:

- Seriously Mentally Ill (schizophrenia, mood disorders), April 6-8, 1988, University of Houston, Dale L. Johnson, Coordinator

- Children and Adolescents with Severe Mental Disorders, May 18-29, 1988, Georgetown University, Phyllis R. Magrab, Coordinator

- Training of Racial/Ethnic Minorities Students, June 8-10, 1988, UCLA, Hector Myers, Coordinator

The participants were nationally recognized psychology program directors in academic, internship, and state/community service settings in the three priority population areas. They represented a wide cross-section of relevant divisions, boards, and committees of the American Psychological Association (APA) and related organizations. The three conferences made major recommendations regarding NIMH clinical training grant priorities for FY 1989.

Seriously mentally ill adults, children, and adolescents constitute underserved priority populations, and racial/ethnic minority and disadvantaged students need special support. However, racial/ethnic minority adults and children, soon to be one quarter of the U.S. population, constitute another underserved priority population that NIMH should acknowledge. Indeed, this fact is documented not only by the last President's Commission on Mental Health, but also by many other reports, including NIMH's 1987 Conference on Minority Mental Health Services Research.

A major reason why millions with serious mental disorders in the above priority populations do not receive adequate services continues to be a shortage of well-trained personnel, including psychologists.

Therefore, all three conferences were in agreement on the following recommendations:

1. Very high priority should be given to the restoration of <u>Clinical Training Grants that Include Trainee Stipends</u>; these grants should follow the Community Support Program (CSP) or Child and Adolescent Service Systems Program (CASSP) model, with academic-state/community collaboration and should support trainees at least at three levels: academic doctoral, predoctoral internships, and postdoctoral fellowships. Academic doctoral support is critical to the development of mental health professionals qualified to respond to the needs of the underserved priority populations.

2. <u>Faculty Development</u> ranks high in priority for funding, with the stipulation that such new faculty development awards be much more flexible than the present Individual Faculty Scholar Awards. Specifically, such awards should permit short-term as well as long-term training, they should be given as institutional training grants as well as to academic faculty, they should encourage exchange of academic faculty and state/community staff, and so forth.

*Letter to National Institute of Mental Health, January 15, 1988, from Dale L. Johnson, Phyllis R. Magrab, and Hector F. Myers.

3. Also, Model Curriculum Research and Development, Continuing Education, and Model State-Academic Interdisciplinary Linkage Programs deserve some modest level of funding.

Additional, more detailed recommendations from each of the three conferences are being refined to present to NIMH and the American Psychological Association later.

Executive Summary: Recommendations to NIMH
from the 1988 National Conference on Clinical Training in Psychology:
Improving Psychological Services for Children and
Adolescents with Severe Mental Disorders*

Mental Health Service Needs of Children, Adolescents, and Families: Implications for Training

1. As the recent Office of Technology Assessment (OTA) study and many other studies have pointed out, millions of children and adolescents with severe mental disorders still do not receive adequate services.

2. A major reason continues to be the shortage of well-trained personnel.

3. Minority children and adolescents are particularly underserved.

Recommendations to NIMH for Clinical Training Policy:

I. General Policies: NIMH should continue to urge national leaders to:

A. Attract more students in clinical child psychology and related areas to seek careers in the public service sector to provide services to children, adolescents and families; there should be special incentives for minority students. Specifically, trainee stipends should be continued, with payback to assure that trainees begin their careers in the public sector. Special federal-state incentives should be created to draw students who are already experienced in state/community programs.

B. Strengthen linkages between state/community service settings and academic/internship training programs; the CASSP model should be used to stimulate stronger linkages by new, creative, flexible funding.

C. Encourage academic/internship faculty to develop their skills and curricula in the latest community-based services and clinical research; create academic-state exchange programs; create special incentives for minority faculty.

D. Restore greater integrity and confidence in the clinical training grants process by providing pre-1981 staffing for purposes of consultation/technical assistance and standing review committees.**

---

*This conference was held at the Ramada Renaissance Hotel, Herndon, Va., May 18-20, 1988. It was conducted by the Georgetown University Child Development Center's CASSP Technical Assistance Program, and it was supported by NIMH's Education and Training Branch and CASSP. The 56 participants were leaders in clinical child psychology and related areas such as pediatric psychology, school psychology, and applied developmental psychology; state CASSP directors; NIMH staff; and several graduate students. Included were training program directors in academic, internship, and state/community service settings. The participants represented a wide cross-section of relevant divisions, boards, and committees of the American Psychological Association and related organizations. In short, the conference constituted an excellent representation of clinical child psychology and its related specialties.

**The conference was evenly divided on whether the standing review committees for clinical training should be disciplinary committees to review all areas (child, minorities, etc.), or multidisciplinary committees in each area. Nevertheless, the conference was in unanimous agreement that standing review committees should be restored to assure a higher quality of review than is possible with ad hoc committees.

E. Like the Congressionally mandated 1987 study of personnel for aging, there should be a systematic study to assess the numbers and kinds of trained personnel, including but not limited to clinical child psychologists, to render quality services to children and adolescents with severe mental disorders.

F. High quality clinical training for children and adolescents with severe mental disorders should not be narrowly confined, but it should be construed to include training for services to the seriously emotionally disturbed (SED), as in the CASSP definition, but also to the less seriously emotionally disturbed, and even prevention programs.

G. A multidisciplinary clinical training-state-CASSP conference should be conducted next year, in 1989, for implementing federal-state-academic models of clinical training for service to children and adolescents with severe mental disorders.

H. Finally, to implement these recommendations in a thoughtful, meaningful way, the implementation should be subject to a dialogue between NIMH and a small committee representing the conference.

II. Specific Recommendations for the NIMH Clinical Training Budget:

A. Unanimously, the conferees recommended that the highest priority is the restoration of <u>Clinical Training Grants that Include Trainee Stipends</u>; these grants should follow the CASSP model, with academic-state/community collaboration and support trainees at least at three levels:***

  1. Academic doctoral support is critical to attract new students into the field.

  2. Predoctoral internship support is critical because little or no reimbursement is available for training for comprehensive child-service activities such as family consultation/home visit, consultation with schools, court appearances, and so on.

  3. Postdoctoral fellowship support is critical because attaining clinical competence in the various subspecialties within the general clinical child domain seems to demand training beyond doctorate.

B. The conferees ranked <u>Faculty Development</u> as second in priority for funding, with the stipulation that such new faculty development awards be much more flexible than the present Individual Faculty Scholar Awards. Specifically, such awards should permit short-term as well as long-term training, institutional training grants as well as individual awards, to be available to internship supervisors as well as academic faculty, encourage exchange of academic faculty and state/community staff, and so on.

C. Third in importance, the conferees ranked both <u>Curriculum Development</u> and <u>Continuing Education</u> as equally deserving of some modest level of funding.

***Support at other levels, for example, master's level training, was not addressed at this conference. Also, no attempt was made to rank-order the three levels of training.

SECTION II

THE CONTEXT OF CLINICAL TRAINING: DIMENSIONS AND
COMPLEXITIES OF THE SERVICE NEEDS OF CHILDREN AND
ADOLESCENTS WITH SEVERE MENTAL DISORDERS

Chapter 1
NIMH Clinical Training Policy:
The Context of the 1988 Conferences

J. Stockdill
Division of Education and Service Systems Liaison
National Institute of Mental Health

Almost three years ago, plans were made for a major reorganization of NIMH research, training, and service demonstration programs. In October 1985, this reorganization was implemented--with one of the major changes being the bringing together of service demonstration, services technical assistance and knowledge transfer, and clinical training programs into one division. Dr. Shervert Frazier was Director of NIMH at that time, and his basic rationale for this decision was that clinical training should be closely tied to service needs and priorities as had been identified by our Community Support Programs and Child and Adolescent Service System Programs. As the Director of this revamped division, I worked with Sam Silverstein and others to outline some assumptions that we felt should guide NIMH clinical training policy.

The major assumptions included the following:

Assumptions Underlying Division of Education and Service Systems Liaison's Three-Year Strategy:

(1) A general assertion of simply "increasing the supply of mental health manpower" could no longer serve as the basic rationale for Federal support of clinical training grants. For the foreseeable future, the rationale for Federal support needs to be one of improving the quality of education and/or improving the distribution of human resources by priority and geography. If we are going to affect the quality of education, there needs to be an emphasis on faculty development.

(2) A federally funded mental health clinical training program must display a strong sense of public responsibility by focusing on the needs of individuals whose services are funded predominantly through public tax dollars. This means that the priority populations should be severely mentally ill adults and seriously emotionally disturbed children in publicly funded programs.

(3) A successful clinical training program requires effective collaboration and linkages among service providers, educators, researchers, and the governmental entities responsible for the severely mentally ill. Linkages with community service providers and the support of the state mental health authority should be a required feature of every federally funded clinical training grant.

(4) Within the severely mentally ill population, special attention must be paid to subgroups, such as racial and ethnic minorities, homeless persons, persons in the criminal justice system, and the dually diagnosed.

(5) A high priority should be given to training for the provision of psychosocial rehabilitation services to those with severe psychiatric disabilities. Staff development and in-service training activities should be directed at clearly identifying the roles, functions, skills, and competencies required for the provision of these services, including vocational rehabilitation.

(6) The federal grants should be of significant size to make a significant difference in the training and education program being supported. There is no longer a good rationale for small awards that support only a few stipends in a given institution.

(7) A high priority should be given to research and development grants to assure the continued development of research-based model curricula for working with high priority population groups.

Dr. Frazier generally agreed with these principles, and in fiscal year 1986 we developed what we called an "omnibus" announcement for the field that had individual training grant programs related to SED children and adolescents, severely mentally ill adults, and minority and disadvantaged students. We also had a separate program announcement on curriculum development with the same general population priorities and a priority on prevention. The response to both the omnibus announcement and the curriculum development announcement was quite good, with psychology putting the greatest priority on children.

In FY 1987, there was a cut in clinical training funds, and we had no new announcement. However, in FY 1988--with an acting Institute Director--we planned for new announcements for FY1988 for an extensive period of time with great fluctuations in direction. One month we would be doing an announcement on seriously emotionally disturbed children with options for faculty development, student stipends, and curriculum development under it--and the next month we would have a faculty development announcement with a priority on children under it. I wanted a priority on new centers for interdisciplinary training on priority populations--such as seriously emotionally disturbed children--but no one else seemed to like that approach.

To make a long story short, we finally settled on just two announcements (RFA's)--one in relation to minority and disadvantaged students, and the other in relation to faculty development. Each had the same special emphasis--priorities on seriously emotionally disturbed children, severely mentally ill adults, and the geriatric populations. The faculty development announcement emphasizes an individual faculty development approach. The response to this announcement has not been extensive except in psychiatry. At present these applications have not yet been reviewed.

FY 1989 is a big turnover year for clinical training grant funds. Even if we do not get a budget increase, we could have significant resources for new and competing grants. A few things being discussed in relation to next year's request for applications are as follows:

(1) Maintain the same priority populations for training emphasis--but allow disciplines the flexibility to decide how to use those funds--faculty development (individual or institutional), student stipends, curriculum development, and so on.

(2) Have close coordination between research and training. Put a heavy emphasis on the translation of research results into education. All proposed training programs would have to have a significant science base.

(3) Put a priority on academic and public service linkages. Include research in the public service sector as part of clinical training.

I hope you will think about the following questions as you consider clinical training to improve services for children:

- Is there a great need for child psychology faculty development?

- Will emphasis on research in clinical faculty development take away from community experience role models?

- Is there a great need for Federal support for curriculum development?

- Would interdisciplinary continuing education on children be a better investment of Federal funds?

- What would be some creative psychology department/state or community linkages to improve children's services?

- How do we meet the special needs of minority children?

Chapter 2
National Responsibilities To Improve Training for Psychological Services for Children, Youth, and Families in the 1990s

Paul Wohlford*
Chief, Psychology Education Program
National Institute of Mental Health

The purposes of this chapter are to provide a framework for the rest of this book, to present the rationale for including certain issues, and to indicate what issues will remain unfinished, to be addressed in the future. National responsibilities will be described in three domains:

- The National Institute of Mental Health (NIMH) and other federal agencies,
- The American Psychological Association (APA) and related organizations, and
- State and local governments, collectively, and related organizations.

After describing the scope of children's psychological problems and service needs, I shall present the state and local governments' complex and changing responsibilities for services to all seriously mentally ill adults and children. Next I shall describe NIMH's support of clinical training for children's services and recommend changes that may simultaneously help to bridge the gap between the public service system and academic training programs, and to improve both clinical training and public services for the seriously mentally ill. Finally, in anticipation of many of the following chapters, I shall discuss the critical evolution of certain key issues in training for children's services, concluding with a model for training to assure adequate breadth and depth of training in the preparation of an individual clinician.

The Scope of Psychological Problems and Service Needs of Children, Youth, and Families

It is generally known and accepted that children, youth, and their families have enormous unserved and underserved psychological problems. From the 1969 Joint Commission on the Mental Health of Children (Joint Commission, 1969), to the 1978 President's Commission on Mental Health, to the 1986 U.S. Congress, Office of Technology Assessment (OTA) report, many reports have amplified the same theme: Many of the 65 million children and youth under age 18 (from 5% to 15%) have serious emotional disorders, which impair their present functioning and future potential. Just a small proportion of these children (probably from 10% to 15%) are currently receiving adequate treatment, services, or both. Although the general problem is clear, the specific data to document exactly the what, the who, and the why of the problem, are frustratingly absent. We do not have accurate data about children's psychological problems and needs.

The President's Commission on Mental Health summarized the problem as follows:

> Because diagnostic criteria vary so widely, different surveys of general populations show that the overall prevalence of persistent, handicapping mental health problems among children aged three to fifteen ranges from 5 to 15 percent. These conditions include emotional disorders, the so-called conduct disorders, and impairments or delays in psychological development. (President's Commission on Mental Health, 1978, p. 8)

Mental health diagnostic codes used with adults are usually not appropriate for children; DSM-III and DSM-III-R have failed to improve this situation (Garmezy, 1978).

---

*The opinions expressed in this article are those of the author and do not necessarily reflect the opinions, official policy, or position of the National Institute of Mental Health.

NIMH's definitions in this area range from the Child and Adolescent Service System Program's (CASSP) definition, "seriously emotionally disturbed children and adolescents," which intentionally follows PL 94-142's definition, to the clinical training announcement's definition, "mental disorders of children and adolescents," or "severe mental disorders." Perhaps some resolution to the issue of definition will be gained through implementing recommendations of NIMH's recent report on Research on Children and Adolescents with Mental, Behavioral and Developmental Disorders (Institute of Medicine, 1989). In the next chapter of this book, Friedman and Duchnowski illuminate the important issues and implications of the definition problem.

One difficulty with diagnostic codes for children is the developmental nature of the children themselves--that is, children are a changing entity. The emotional problems of infants and very young children often involve physical symptoms or developmental disabilities, and these youngsters are seen in pediatric settings. When children are a bit older, ages 3 to 6, their emotional vulnerabilities are more often manifested as behavior problems, such as temper tantrums at home and hyperactive behavior disorders in nursery school. Problems of children ages 6 to 12 often appear in school settings as learning disorders. On reaching puberty, many children with mental disorders are at high risk for acting out disorders, including dropping out of school, delinquency, sexual acting-out, running away, and substance abuse, as well as the adult varieties of neuroses and psychoses. Though the extent of children with psychological problems is not known with precision, it is clear that these children do not receive adequate services.

The above developmental transitions illustrate the complexities of both defining the problem and delivering needed services to children, youth, and their families. While many children are seen in traditional mental health facilities, such as child guidance clinics, community mental health centers, psychiatric hospitals, and so on, the majority of children with psychological disorders are not. And that is part of the problem. A matrix is needed to describe the parameters of this complex problem.

A useful matrix for children's psychological services should be comprehensive and should include not only the at-risk population (e.g., infants) and the problem or disorder (e.g., mother-infant bonding) but also the setting, the mode of intervention, the target persons besides the children, and the professionals or others to do the intervention. It is assumed that a problem focus and an interdisciplinary/multidisciplinary approach is most effective. The matrix in Table 1 is intended to be illustrative rather than exhaustive. At-risk populations are presented at major developmental stages: infancy (years 0-3), preschool (years 3-6), school age (years 6-12), adolescence (years 12-18), and finally, family-marital issues, can affect all family members. The psychological services matrix may have a third dimension superimposed--that of types of mental disorders and service settings where appropriate personnel are needed. First, "pure" mental disorders are seen in traditional mental health service settings, such as child guidance clinics. Second, mental disorders are mixed with other problems, such as primary health, educational, or social problems. Third, developmental crises or other high-risk situations call for preventive interventions to avoid later mental disorders. In conclusion, most children in need of direct services and preventive services are found outside of traditional mental health service settings and should probably be treated there.

In Chapter 5, Shore provides a useful historical context for principles of service delivery to children that psychology has played a major role in developing, based on an ecological model. These principles of service delivery are: comprehensive services, multidimensional services, services in different settings, different roles for service providers, and multidisciplinary services; finally, all service elements must be interconnected, integrated, organized, and funded. These principles of service delivery, which provide the foundation for the recently created CASSP program, are discussed in greater detail by Friedman and Duchnowski in Chapter 3 and by Hanley in Chapter 4. The overarching issue of this book is how we should train psychologists to provide services based on these principles of service delivery.

Functional Analysis of Psychological Services for Children

It has not been sufficiently recognized that providing services to children and families requires special skills that go beyond adult work. Psychological disorders of childhood and the corresponding

TABLE 1

Matrix of Illustrative Children's Mental Disorders and Service Settings

Age of at-risk population	Frequent mental disorder	Setting	Intervention/target persons (besides children)	Other professionals besides clinical child psychologists to do intervention
New mothers, fathers, infants (0-3)	Bonding, child abuse, etc.	Primary health	Parent counseling/parents, nurses, pediatricians	Pediatric psychologists, nurses, pediatricians, home visitors, etc.
Infants, older children (0-3, 3-18)	Developmental, Neuropsychological disorders	Primary health and mental retardation facilities	Parent counseling/parents, health care and MR staff	Developmental psychologists in mental retardation facilities
Preschool children (3-6)	Hyperactive behavior disorders	Day care, nursery schools, kindergartens, Head Start	Family psychoeducational methods/families, teachers, other staff	School psychologists, other mental health professionals
Young and older children (3-18)	Neurotic and psychotic disorders	Child guidance clinics; mental health clinics and hospitals	Individual, family, and other therapy/families	Other mental health professionals
School-age children (6-12)	Learning disabilities, psychoeducational problems	Schools	Psychoeducational, other methods/teachers, families	School psychologists, other mental health professionals
Adolescents (12-18)	Juvenile delinquents, school dropouts, runaways, substance abuse, etc.	Juvenile justice, schools, welfare agencies, etc.	Group, milieu, individual counseling/agency staff, families, teachers	Social welfare workers, other mental health professionals
Parents, children of all ages	Marital, family problems	Mental Health clinics, homes, etc.	Marital counseling/spouses, clergy	Other mental health professionals

From "Clinical Child Psychology: The Emerging Specialty" by Paul Wohlford, 1979, The Clinical Psychologist, 33, p. 26. Copyright 1979 by Pergamon Press. Reprinted by permission.

assessment procedures and treatment methods for children are often quite different from those used with adults. Frequently, it is more difficult and complicated to work with a whole family than with an individual adult. The parents of a disturbed child may have mental disorders, substance abuse problems, or both, which contribute to their child's disorders and which may complicate the provision of services to the family. Or the parents may be in need of supportive services or peer support groups of other parents like themselves who are coping with one or more seriously emotionally disturbed children.

Services to children, youth, and families embrace different functions in different settings and may involve different levels of expertise. Professional child psychology should be recognized as a specialty within clinical psychology; nevertheless, it is a broad field that itself includes several very different subspecialties, from school psychology to pediatric psychology, as illustrated in Table 1.

During the discussion at the Georgetown conference, Nadine Lambert recommended a sensible nomenclature to describe the field:

> Psychology; within it is nested:
>> Professional Psychology; within it is nested:
>>> Professional Child Psychology; within it are nested:
>>>> Clinical Child Psychology,
>>>> Pediatric Psychology,
>>>> School Psychology,
>>>> and perhaps others, such as Applied Developmental Psychology.

Within each subspecialty, one may specify functional tasks of evaluation, treatment, research, and so on, and specify different levels of expertise in rendering these services. After a functional analysis is completed, what constitutes competence for each function should be specified. Then, standards can be established on the basis of competent performance for each of the functions, as we shall discuss below.

Some may argue that the above analysis will increase the stratification of the field of psychology and hence be detrimental. This argument, however, fails to recognize that the increased specialization has already occurred. To counteract the narrowness of this specialization and stratification, special efforts should be made in training and service settings to have the psychologists work as a part of teams, occasionally teams of other psychologists, but usually not. Usually the teams will be multidisciplinary . The team concept is not new in primary health settings, preschool and school settings, and mental health settings in the public sector. However, for the team concept to work well, it must be specially nurtured; it should be based on a cognitive-systems understanding and an affective-personal respect among team members for each other's contributions to the team effort. That is, everyone should recognize that professionals of different disciplines and levels of expertise can all contribute to the optimal services for children and their families, including pediatricians and public health nurses, PhD clinical psychologists and MA school psychologists, paraprofessional teacher aides and BA teachers, and so on (Wohlford, 1975).

Assessing Competence in Psychological Service Functions

Competency-based standards should be created and applied in all disciplines working with children. With regard to some functions and levels, other professions or disciplines may function as well as (or better than) professional child psychology, for example, in evaluations of scholastic performance or in family therapy. Some functions, however, such as psychological evaluation and research, will continue to be unique to professional child psychology. Of the many thousands who work directly with disturbed children, psychologists are a minority; nevertheless, psychologists should take the lead role in creating these standards (see Chapter 7, by Pion & Sechrest).

Professional competence to render quality service to children, youth, and families goes hand in hand with training to attain that competence and with standard-setting or credentialing to confirm that competence has been attained or maintained. Given the present state of the art in assessing competence in work with children and families, probably the best means of quality control is on-the-job supervision during training. Again, this probably true for all disciplines working with children, from teachers to psychologists. If trainees are unsuited to work with children and families, they should be dismissed as early as possible. If people lack certain necessary experience or skills, the best time to provide it is during formal preservice training, rather than in on-the-job-training.

The next question is, what constitutes adequate training for work with children? For example, if new PhDs successfully completed a general clinical psychology training program in which they gave children IQ tests and had a brief rotation through a child guidance clinic, would they be competent to work with children? If children are referred to them, what should they do?

Society's chief protection in that situation is the individual psychologist's own interpretation of the APA Code of Ethics, which states:

> Principle 2. Competence. The maintenance of high standards of competence is a responsibility shared by all psychologists in the interest of the public and the profession as a whole. Psychologists recognize the boundaries of their competence and the limitations of their techniques. They only provide services and only use techniques for which they are qualified by training and experience. (American Psychological Association, 1990, p. 390)

Ethically, in the above example, the new adult-trained PhDs who were asked to see children should refer the family to an appropriately trained and experienced clinical child psychologist. However, it is my impression that this frequently doesn't occur. Children and their families are not given enough protection.

Another situation is not uncommon: New PhD clinical psychologists completing a general program with little exposure to children apply for jobs in clinics where they would primarily work with children, and the new psychologists' clinical faculty, with full knowledge of their background and the position, write strong recommendations. If this clinic has the resources to provide adequate on-the-job supervision of the new psychologists' work with children, then this could be one of five acceptable alternatives ensuring professional competence (Tuma, 1975). However, with the present demand for child clinicians outstripping the supply, such a clinic might not have adequate resources to provide such supervision. Then the new psychologists might flounder and might do harm. If so, have APA ethics been violated? Yes, by the new psychologists and by the faculty who gave endorsements.

It is hard to estimate the prevalence of these situations, but apparently it is growing with the increasing demand for clinical child psychologists. It is necessary to sensitize both clinical training faculty and students to the demands of work with children and families and the ethical issues involved. In conclusion, the long-term solution will require action at every level to upgrade and to expand professional child psychology training programs as discussed later in this volume. Specifically:

1. NIMH and other federal agencies should

    a. assess the expected shortages of mental health personnel for comprehensive services to children, youth, and their families now and in the years 1995, 2000, 2010, and 2020;
    b. determine clinical competencies in providing services to children; and
    c. increase its support for clinical training for children's services.

2. APA and related organizations should upgrade the standards for training, accreditation, and credentialing for children's services. In particular, besides general clinical psychology, professional child psychology should be recognized as another specialty, with subspecialties of clinical child psychology, pediatric psychology, school psychology, and so on.

3. States should strengthen their laws for standards of practice, both licensed independent practice and practice in public service settings. States should contribute substantially to training for public service settings.

Public Service System Responsibilities for Adults and Children
With Serious Mental Illness*

Recently, adults with serious mental illness have been rediscovered primarily because of, first, the failure of a nationwide effort to deinstitutionalize the mentally ill by discharging them from state psychiatric hospitals and moving them into communities, and, second, the discovery of power by families of the mentally ill and patients themselves to influence legislative and executive agendas. Deinstitutionalization brought patients from inpatient hospital wards to the main streets of towns and cities and displayed the failure of that policy for all to see. Family/consumer advocacy is changing the allocation of state and federal resources to provide service programs for seriously mentally ill adults.

While these new policy directives and resource allocations are occurring for seriously mentally ill adults, children with mental disorders have usually not received increased resources. In fact, children's programs have sometimes suffered cuts. Also, it has become quite evident that the education of mental health professionals to serve both adults and children has not kept step with the latest and most effective service approaches for the public sector. University training programs often are continuing to produce graduates more suited to office practice and trained to serve clients who have less serious problems. What is needed are mechanisms to bridge the increasing gap between professional psychology training programs and the service system needs of seriously mentally ill adults and children.

Because of its duties regarding the health and safety of its citizens, the state is ultimately responsible for providing services to persons with serious mental illness. Within this context, the roles and responsibilities of state and local governments for the service needs of the seriously mentally ill are complex and changing. As states vary greatly from one to another in size and in style of operation, many important aspects of a state's role are unique. In spite of these differences, certain overarching issues are common to all state and local public mental health systems that arise directly from deinstitutionalization and the political involvement of family members and consumers, plus a third fact of life in the public sector--the need to contain costs.

Mental health services are very labor intensive. About 85 percent of the states' mental health service expenditures are for personnel (National Institute of Mental Health, 1987). Therefore, every service issue raises an additional issue: How can human resources be used most effectively?

To address this issue at the federal level, since the late 1970s NIMH has sponsored the state Human Resource Development (HRD) program in all 50 states to help states develop and manage their mental health personnel more effectively, through special grants exclusively to the states. Out of NIMH's 1989 clinical training budget of $12.8 million, the NIMH state HRD program's budget was $3.1 million, funding 29 grants to state-level HRD offices.

Also since the late 1970s, NIMH has sponsored a remarkably successful services demonstration program, the Community Support Program (CSP), for seriously mentally ill adults based on community-based psychosocial rehabilitation and case management approaches. In 1989 the CSP program for seriously mentally ill adults was operating in almost all 50 states and had 113 funded grants totaling $14.8 million.

---

*This section is based on the paper "The States' Role in Public-Academic Linkages for Clinical Training for Services to Persons with Serious Mental Illness" (Stratoudakis, Tomes, & Wohlford, 1990).

Based on the excellent record of CSP's addressing the comprehensive service needs of adults who are seriously mentally ill, in 1984 NIMH launched a parallel program for seriously emotionally disturbed (SED) children and adolescents, called the Child and Adolescent Service System Program (CASSP). In 1989, the CASSP program for SED children was also operating in almost all 50 states and had 51 funded grants totaling $9 million. A large part of CASSP's program is joint funding with other federal agencies. Many experts, including the authors of the Congress-sponsored report Children's Mental Health: Problems and Services (U. S. Congress, Office of Technology Assessment, 1986), have high expectations of the CASSP program's potential to address fragmentation and other complex problems in children's services. Friedman and Duchnowski (Chapter 3) and Hanley (Chapter 4) describe the CASSP program in more detail in the next two chapters.

In 1982, along with many other federal programs, the Community Mental Health Centers were shifted from a federally directed program to a block grant program to the states. The main effects of this shift were to reduce the total funding and to give states a freer rein in how they spent the federal mental health dollar. In FY 1990, the Alcohol, Drug Abuse, and Mental Health Block Grants to the states totaled $1,192,851,000.

Partly because of their greater autonomy, states were seen as uneven in adopting modern community-based psychosocial rehabilitation techniques, as seen in the CSP and CASSP programs, in the care of the seriously mentally ill. Therefore, Congress enacted the State Comprehensive Mental Health Services Plan Act of 1986, Public Law (PL) 99-660, requiring each state to have an acceptable State Mental Health Plan for the period 1990-1992 to provide services for the seriously mentally ill, with special emphasis on community-based psychosocial rehabilitation, case management, and systems approaches. All state plans must devote a special section to services for children and adolescents; also, all plans must include families, consumers, and other important stakeholders in the planning process. Consumers, family members, and labor unions were accorded special input into the planning process. But psychologists and other care providers should also have input--indeed, all citizens are entitled to have input--to their state's mental health plan. Unlike earlier state mental health plans, PL 99-660 has a severe penalty if the state is not in compliance: Up to 8 percent of the state's mental health block grant funding can be withheld.

Some feel that PL 99-660 presents an opportunity for states to integrate CSP, CASSP, and HRD programs in synergistic interaction to improve the entire service system. These joint planning efforts may enable states to identify and begin to communicate the knowledge, skills, and abilities required for the staff mix that is necessary to provide high quality care. It is hoped that the 1990-1992 state mental health plans also will project patient needs, describe services to meet patient needs, estimate the number and kind of staff need to provide these services, and estimate the costs for these services. However, others feel less optimistic about likely progress under PL 99-660, at least during 1990-1992, and consider it necessary to have to be extended beyond 1992.

In summary, regardless of the extent of the impact of PL 99-660, it is very clear that over the past decade, states, which always had primary responsibility for the mental health services of their citizens, have received increasing support to do their job better. Federal CMHCs were shifted to state block grants. New programs created infrastructures in state mental health departments to become more responsive to the service needs of the seriously mentally ill; especially notable is the Child and Adolescent Service System Program, establishing a child advocate presence at the state level.

NIMH's Support of Clinical Training for Children's Services

One of the original purposes of the National Institute of Mental Health when it was created in 1947 was to train professionals who would provide mental health services to this country. The mandate was to increase the supply of general mental health providers in the four core disciplines of psychiatric nursing, psychiatry, psychology, and social work, with no specification of priority service populations such as seriously emotionally disturbed children.

Funding of Clinical Training for Children's Services

The NIMH clinical training budget for the four disciplines rose steadily from about $1 million in 1948 to its high point of about $93 million in 1969, as Table 2 illustrates. Then, with the Vietnam War and other factors, it gradually declined until 1980, when it was a little under $70 million. Draconian budget cuts came in the next three years, 1981 to 1983, when the budget dropped to under $18 million, and general clinical training support was terminated. Several reasons were given for the cuts: First, federal aid to the clinical training program had accomplished its original purpose: namely, to supply a pool of trained professionals. It was argued that there was no longer a shortage. Second, many former trainees were not serving those who were in the most need, but only the middle and upper classes. Third, it was argued, students preparing for careers in the mental health professions should pay for their own education, just as lawyers and accountants do.

Although one may disagree with these arguments, the fact is that the clinical training budget was cut tremendously. There is no prospect of restoring the budget to what it was 10 years ago. Even the advocates for mental health training are much more modest--and realistic--in their requests. The Coalition for Mental Health recommended $26 million for FY 1990, up from $12.8 million in FY 1989, but less than half of the near $70 million in 1980. Each dollar that is restored to NIMH's clinical training support will have to be justified to a budget-minded Congress and administration by solid evidence from successful training programs that are turning out professionals who serve the public need.

Table 3 illustrates that as the amount of NIMH clinical training support steadily declined, the number of trainees nevertheless increased, with the exception of psychiatric nursing. From 1976 to 1986, the number of trainees supported by NIMH dropped from 3,974, or 22% of the field, to just 478, or 2%. At the same time, the total number of trainees has increased from 17,800 to 21,800.* To opponents of clinical training, this fact is the final nail in the coffin of federal support for clinical training.

Until now, we have considering general mental health service providers--not those specializing in work with children. In 1981-1983, while there was a phaseout of general clinical training, in 1983 Congress restored (over the administration's opposition) limited new clinical programs marked by three things:

1. Lower budget: The budget for the four disciplines was less than $18 million in 1983.

2. Priority populations: Clinical training programs had to produce mental health service providers for a recognized priority population of national need, namely, children and adolescents with serious emotional disorders, seriously mentally ill adults, elderly with mental disorders, and minority students.

3. Payback in service: Individual trainees receiving NIMH support are obligated, after completing their training, to work in a public service setting with a priority population for a time equal to the training support they received, or else they must pay back their support.

---

*These figures are critically important, for they are the basis of how the clinical training budget may be decided. For instance, the 1986 House Appropriations Committee noted that while federal support for clinical training was reduced by 70 percent since 1979, "graduate enrollment increased from 77,000 trainees to almost 81,000" (U.S. House of Representatives, Committee on Appropriations, 1986, p. 92). The committee's figures appear to be greatly inflated. More accurate figures would consider only the clinical psychology enrollment of 9,277, not the total psychology enrollment of 40,650, including experimental psychology, and so on, which may be what the committee did. Nevertheless, the Committee Report trend is correct: The total number of clinical trainees increased from about 18,000 in 1979 to about 21,800 in 1986.

From 1980 to 1989, the clinical training grant program for the four disciplines declined, but interestingly, the proportion of clinical training for children's services rose. For instance, in 1980 when the NIMH clinical training budget was about $70 million, relatively few grants were specifically for training for children's services. In 1986, when the total NIMH clinical training budget was $20 million and the clinical training grants totaled about $10 million, supporting about 220 clinical training programs in all disciplines, 77 of these programs concerned NIMH's priority on child mental health. They constituted more that one third of the supported programs, totaling $3,349,000. In 1987, Congress reduced the NIMH clinical training budget from its 1986 level of $20 million to $15 million. The House report noted, however, that "priority should be given to training systems which produce professionals to serve children and the aged" (U.S. House of Representatives, Committee on Appropriations, 1986, p. 92). Unfortunately, this congressional mandate was not followed. In 1987, while certain other NIMH clinical training programs made new awards, more than half of the 77 child clinical training grants terminated without a chance for continuation.

In 1988, the NIMH clinical training budget received its first increase in 7 years, from $15 million to $16.8 million. Only 21 new clinical training grants were funded, all of them for minority students, and totaled $1.4 million. These included 9 focusing on children's services.

In 1989, the budget was again reduced, from $16.8 million in 1988 to $12.8 million. Because of the 3-year grant cycle, 101 grants terminated, including 28 on children. However, 39 new grants were funded, including 22 on children, bringing the number of active grants in 1989 to 60, totaling $4.1 million, including 31 on children, totaling $2.1 million.

Also in 1988, a new clinical training program, the Individual Faculty Scholar Awards, was introduced. The purpose of this program is to facilitate the career development of promising young faculty. By 1989, 27 Faculty Scholar Awards were funded, totaling $2 million, including 12 in the child area, totaling $889,000.

In 1989, the grand total of Institutional Clinical Training Grants plus Faculty Scholar Awards was 87 grants and awards, totaling $6.1 million; of these half were in the area of children: 43 grants and awards, totaling $3 million. The distribution of these 43 awards across the discipline was: 21 in psychology (including 4 multidisciplinary programs in which the Training Program Directors are psychologists), 12 in psychiatry, 8 in social work, and 2 in psychiatric nursing. Psychology, with half of the children's clinical training grants, appears to be the lead discipline in this area.

In summary, over the last year 3 years, 1986-1989, while the overall NIMH clinical training budget was reduced from $20 million to $12.8 million, a decrease of 36%, the institutional training grants suffered a relatively larger cut, from $10 million to 4.1 million, a decrease of 59%. In this period, child training grants were cut in number from 77 to 31, a decrease of 60%, and were reduced in amount from $3.3 million to $2.1 million, a decrease of 37%. Considering both Faculty Scholar and clinical training grants for children, the reduction was much less, from $3.3 million to $3 million, a decrease of 9%. While the reductions in the overall program were occurring in this period, the proportion of training grants for children actually increased from one third of the 1986 awards (77 of 220) to one half of the 1989 awards (43 of 87).

In 1990, Congress again increased NIMH's total clinical training budget, from $12.8 million in 1989, to $13.7 million. As this chapter goes to press, it is too early to determine the exact impact on child training grants, though the trend is clear: Any increase in the institutional clinical training grant budget would probably have at least a proportional increase in grants for children's services.

<u>Children's Service Providers: Estimates of the Number of Present Providers and Future Needs</u>

The best available estimates of the current number of mental health service providers, including both adult and child, are shown in Table 4.

TABLE 2

NATIONAL INSTITUTE OF MENTAL HEALTH
SUPPORT FOR CLINICAL TRAINING 1948-1986
FOUR CORE DISCIPLINES
DIVISION OF MANPOWER AND TRAINING PROGRAMS (DMTP)*

Dollar amounts represent money available to programs each year and are expressed in thousands of dollars.

The figures in parentheses represent number of stipends. For psychiatry, beginning in 1957, the first stipend figure represents postdoctoral (e.g., residency) stipends and the second indicates undergraduate (medical student) stipends.

Year	DMTP Clinical Training $	Psychiatry	Psychology (Clinical)	Social Work	Nursing
1948	$ 1,140	$ 483(69)	$ 210(40)	$ 212(50)	$ 212(54)
1949	1,633	625(74)	359(51)	324(65)	280(74)
1950	3,098	1,425(109)	510(87)	543(109)	463(145)
1951	3,587	1,730(161)	595(103)	596(127)	544(160)
1952	4,199	2,000(205)	698(136)	701(145)	628(178)
1953	4,072	1,915(189)	698(124)	681(145)	627(187)
1954	4,398	1,965(208)	863(183)	686(165)	741(179)
1955	4,610	2,037(225)	749(153)	754(189)	639(172)
1956	6,206	3,012(300)	932(187)	961(194)	952(210)
1957	11,327	5,415(485-294)	1,687(368)	1,844(522)	1,755(360)
1958	13,827	6,139(571-424)	1,973(362)	2,133(576)	2,473(394)
1959	18,456	8,728(760-749)	2,880(551)	3,118(818)	2,195(283)
1960	21,137	10,289(908-749)	3,262(525)	3,709(800)	2,563(292)
1961	26,120	13,077(1109-797)	3,880(631)	4,495(952)	2,841(311)
1962	35,523	18,111(1547-832)	4,748(795)	5,959(1150)	4,289(487)
1963	44,609	22,626(1912-859)	5,747(956)	7,505(1394)	5,489(683)
1964	59,353	28,878(2188-939)	6,454(1,066)	8,996(1,668)	7,342(1,079)
1965	68,075	32,150(2307-1221)	7,202(1,144)	10,225(1,727)	8,443(1,338)
1966	77,314	35,670(2464-1290)	8,137(1,242)	11,712(1,799)	9,574(1,450)
1967	79,975	40,282(2795-1315)	9,095(1,382)	13,382(1,936)	11,196(1,827)
1968	83,577	39,989(2462-1362)	9,757(1,438)	14,628(1,901)	11,453(1,681)
1969	93,146	46,047(2540-1425)	11,932(1476)	15,220(1,770)	12,061(1,630)
1970	89,947	43,700(2364-1406)	12,071(1528)	14,068(1,596)	12,032(1,432)
1971	88,393	42,671(2194-1439)	11,790(1510)	12,784(1,492)	11,579(1,363)
1972	87,209	38,525(2050-1323)	12,633(1611)	13,053(1,476)	11,254(1,287)

Table 2 (Continued)

Year	DMTP Clinical Training $	Psychiatry	Psychology (Clinical)	Social Work	Nursing
1973	85,499	37,173(2096-755)	12,414(1640)	12,024(1400)	9,788(1190)
1974	79,630	32,417(1786-656)	12,183(1625)	13,992(1310)	10,584(1490)
1975	73,865	31,872(853-1349)	11,550(1662)	11,883(1073)	9,370(1169)
1976	68,558	26,630(402-1300)	10,614(1582)	10,356(767)	8,950(1268)
1977	66,158	24,376(273-1001)	10,276(1565)	10,596(843)	8,339(1092)
1978	67,225	22,826(230-930)	9,974(1619)	10,060(787)	7,931(907)
1979	72,375	24,267(223-885)	10,445(1497)	11,507(809)	8,459(874)
1980	69,706	23,147(155-739)	10,088(1134)	10,884(787)	8,163(797)
Totals	$1,513,947	$670,197(36214-24039)	$206,406(29,973)	$239,511(30542)	$193,209(26043)
1981	57,323	19,774 (105-?)[4]	8,302 (894)	9,500 (711)	7,070 (802)
1982	30,886	12,884 (36-?)	5,781 (706)	6,945 (574)	5,276 (610)
1983	17,981	5,447 (22-?)	2,536 (270)	2,497 (241)	2,079 (236)
1984[1]	16,238[2]	6,711 (45-?)	3,372 (371)	2,995 (304)	2,516 (176)
1985	14,148[3]	5,763(7-?)	3,028 (341)	2,957 (318)	2,279 (179)
1986	9,888	3,225 (28-?)	1,914 (172)	2,138 (194)	1,224 (97)

[1] Figures for stipends include those provided in the aging program.

[2] Does not include 11 multidisciplinary projects funded @ $643,000.

[3] Does not include 2 multidisciplinary projects funded @ $121,000.

[4] Figures for medical student support in psychiatry are unavailable 1981-1986. The figure provided is for stipends requiring payback.

* The author wishes to thank Dr. Stanley F. Schneider of NIMH for providing the 1948-1980 data. The 1981-1986 data were compiled by the author.

TABLE 3
NIMH Trainee Distribution, 1976-1986

Discipline/Funding Source	1976	1977	1978	1979	1980	1981	1982	1983	1984	1985	1986
Trainees supported with federal funds:[1]											
Psychiatry[2]	399	275	229	227	155	106	36	10	13	7	24
Psychology/Clinical[3]	1582	1565	1619	1553	1120	946	726	324	371	341	168
Psychiatric Nursing[4]	882	740	714	779	714	756	548	130	133	179	97
Soc. Work/Mental Health[5]	1111	1000	890	784	764	719	565	255	304	347	189
Subtotal	3974	3580	3452	3343	2753	2526	1875	719	821	874	478
Trainees supported with other funds:[6]											
Psychiatry[2]	4183	4226	4106	4249	4182	4731	4727	4976	5167	5382	5393
Psychology/Clinical[3]	4902	5349	5727	5935	7082	9187	8224	8755	8906	9674	10,202
Psychiatric Nursing[4]	266	323	345	306	521	224	314	645	537	401	405
Soc. Work/Mental Health[5]	3516	3738	4150	4141	4111	4059	3952	4020	5084	5153	5336
Subtotal	12,867	13,636	14,328	14,631	15,896	18,201	17,217	18,396	19,694	20,610	21,336
Total trainees:											
Psychiatry[2]	4582	4501	4335	4476	4337	4837	4763	4986	5180	5389	5417
Psychology/Clinical[3]	6484	6914	7346	7488	8209	10,133	8950	9079	9277	10,015	10,370
Psychiatric Nursing[4]	1148	1063	1059	1085	1235	980	862	775	670	580	502
Soc. Work/Mental Health[5]	4627	4738	5040	4925	4875	4778	4517	4275	5388	5500	5525
Total	17,841	17,216	17,780	17,974	18,649	20,727	19,092	19,115	20,519	21,484	21,814

22

*For Footnotes, please see next page.

Footnotes - Table 3

(1) Trainees Supported With Federal Funds: The figures in this section refer specifically and exclusively to support from NIMH (not other federal agencies). Within NIMH, up to 1980, the support came from the Division of Manpower and Training Programs; since 1980, it has come from the Education and Training Branch (not other divisions or branches). Caution should be used in the interpretation of these figures: Since one trainee may receive support in more than one year, one cannot simply add across years to determine the number of individual trainees who complete their training. Also, each discipline varies in the average length of time required, ranging from 2 years in social work for an MSW to 7 years in clinical psychology for a PhD.

(2) Psychiatry: (a) Although stipends are awarded to medical students, they are not included with the postdoctoral stipend counts since they are limited to only 8-week periods on an elective basis for experiences in a supervised project in psychiatry in one of the currently supported child mental health, chronically mentally ill, minority/disadvantaged student or public psychiatry programs, which may be receiving NIMH support intended primarily for postgraduate training.

(b) The figures for postgraduate stipends as shown in the table are total for child and basic psychiatry residents who may be enrolled in full-year programs or have stipends split and apportioned for short-term training programs. Included are: (1) before 1983, stipends in psychiatry comprehensive education in basic residency, medical student and consultation/liaison psychiatry, scientific methodology, public psychiatry, and geriatric psychiatry; (2) beginning in 1983, stipends for minority and disadvantaged students; child faculty development; and child mental health, public psychiatry, and chronically mentally ill programs. Enrollments in the child and basic psychiatric residency training programs were furnished by the AMA.

(3) Psychology: Estimates of the total number of clinical psychology trainees for years 1978-1985 were provided by the Office of Scientific Information of the American Psychological Association and the National Science Foundation (NSF). Figures for 1976, 1977, and 1986 were obtained by extrapolating from the 1978-85 figures.

The term "total trainees" refers only to clinical psychology students working toward a PhD or PsyD on a full-time or part-time basis, not to psychology students in master's programs or in other specialties (e.g., experimental, social, school, or counseling). However, the term "trainees supported with federal funds" may include a few students in counseling or school psychology (probably fewer than 5% of this number). The reason for restricting total trainees to clinical psychology students is that these figures are less ambiguous; e.g., many counseling and school psychology graduates receive an EdD degree, which are not included in the NSF figures from which these estimates were made. It is estimated that at least 95% of the psychology trainees who received NIMH support were in the field of clinical psychology.

(4) Psychiatric Nursing: The term "trainees" refers to full-time students in training at the master's or doctoral level, not at the undergraduate level. The figures for the total trainees for 1984-1986 are extrapolated on the basis of the actual 1981-1983 figures.

(5) Social Work: It has been estimated that 25% of social workers are engaged in mental health service delivery, and a similar percentage of currently enrolled social work students have a mental health service career as their goal. Thus, the figures for "total trainees" were calculated by taking 25% of the total number of social work students, estimated by the Council on Social Work Education.

(6) Trainees Supported With Other Funds: The figures in this section were calculated by subtracting NIMH-supported trainees (above) from total trainees (below). The assumption was made that all trainees received support from some source.

TABLE 4
Estimated Number of Mental Health Service Providers in the Four Core Disciplines, 1986-1987

Type of provider	Number of providers	
	Child Only	Total (adult and child combined)
Psychiatrists	3,000	31,000
Psychiatric nursing (at master's or doctoral level)	1,000	13,000
Clinical psychologists (doctoral level)	5,000	35,000
Social workers in mental health	7,000	26,000
Total	16,000	105,000

Notes . The child figures are from the OTA report (U.S. Congress, OTA, 1986). The total figures are from National Institute of Mental Health (in press).

The OTA report stated, "There are approximately 3,000 child psychiatrists, 5,000 clinical psychologists, 7,000 child and family-oriented social workers, and 1,000 child/family-oriented mental health nurses.... Estimates of the numbers of professionals needed have consistently been much higher" (U.S. Congress, OTA, 1986, p. 141). However, the OTA report does not specify exactly how many professionals are needed to work with children.

There is a great need for a careful data-based study to determine more exactly the number of child mental health professionals needed. Such a study in the field of health and aging was mandated by Congress and resulted in the report Personnel for Health Needs of the Elderly Through Year 2020 (National Institute on Aging, 1987).

In 1989, Congress expressed its concern

> about the projected shortages of mental health personnel, particularly psychiatric nurses, psychologists, and psychiatric social workers, and the impact of these shortages on the delivery of quality mental health services. The Committee urges NIMH to support creative strategies to address this critical issue, such as interdisciplinary training of mental health professionals. In addition, the Committee recommends that NIMH carry out a feasibility study to describe the current mental health service providers, both professional and nonprofessional, in both public and private sectors, as well as those presently receiving mental health training. (U.S. Senate, Committee on Appropriations, 1989, p. 173)

One would hope that such a careful data-based study as Congress recommends would take into account the special mental health needs of children, as discussed above, most of whom are not seen in traditional inpatient and outpatient mental health facilities. One potentially exciting source of data may be found in the 50 States Comprehensive Mental Health Plans under PL 99-660, which should include a separate section addressing children's and adolescents' mental health services. These state plans may serve as the foundation of a national data-based management system of child mental health services, which does not yet exist. Such a national data-based management system of child services should be created for management, fiscal, and program accountability. This system would provide a foundation for planning for children's services and, specifically, to estimate the number of personnel who are necessary to provide these services.

In the last Presidential Commission on Mental Health, all six recommendations for prevention concern children, youth, and families (President's Commission on Mental Health, 1978, pp. 51-54). Research on problems of childhood and adolescence was mentioned as one research priority (p. 49). There is now a lack of appropriately trained personnel to provide direct services, and even more personnel would be needed for prevention programs. At this time, it is not possible to project the exact levels of personnel or cost necessary to provide even direct services for adequate child mental health. A new initiative in prevention would require additional personnel and resources, at least in the short term. However, projections of personnel and costs would be based on the nature of the services and personnel strategy; for instance, in the long run, a preventive services approach to high-risk children would probably be more cost-effective than a casualty approach.

In summary, on the threshold of the last decade of the twentieth century, a study of future mental health personnel shortages should estimate the needed personnel for mental health services for the general population and also should estimate the needed specialized personnel for children's direct services and preventive services. Also, the impact of drug/alcohol abuse services and AIDS-related services must be included in the mental health personnel equation. The total number of available mental health professionals and paraprofessionals undoubtedly will be reduced by these new demands.

Evaluation of NIMH Support of Child Clinical Training Programs

There are many possible ways to evaluate the effects of NIMH support on the clinical training programs in child mental health. In the study reported by Levine in Appendix B at the end of this volume, he relied upon the self-reports of the training directors. While these self-reports have various limitations, including a positive bias toward their own programs, the training directors' views constitute one source of data that is essential to a comprehensive evaluation. Also, program directors are required to submit annual reports, and every 3 years, final reports. These reports are a gold mine of information, yet little systematic use is made of them, partly because of the form they are in, partly because they are not readily coded on a computer, partly because the administration may already have decided to cut the programs, and partly because of staff cutbacks. A comprehensive evaluation may be visualized as having at least three overlapping circles, or domains of inquiry, as shown in Figure 1.

The most important single piece of evaluation data for training programs is outcome. How many trainees in the last 5 or 10 years are now giving services to children with serious emotional disorders? Since the payback requirement was started in 1981, NIMH has started to amass data that will be useful to address this issue in the future.

Finally, when the clinical training programs were restored by Congress in 1983, the administration had already dissolved the standing review committees for the review of new clinical training grant applications. New applications have been reviewed by ad hoc committees, with all the perils associated, and no site visits have been made. Obviously, in a comprehensive evaluation, an important source of data must come from outside observers, ideally those who have actually site-visited the program.

Conclusions and Recommendations to Improve Public-Academic Linkages for Clinical Training

As with improving services and provider training for the seriously mentally ill adult (see Stratoudakis, Tomes, & Wohlford, in press), a systems approach should be used to improve services for seriously emotionally disturbed children, and, simultaneously, to improve clinical training to providers. Just as constructive innovation should occur at each level, stage, or setting to improve services to the seriously mentally ill, so too public-academic collaboration should occur at each level, stage, or setting to improve the clinical training of the next generation of psychologists providing services for the seriously mentally ill. This includes, but is not limited to:

• Faculty development and curriculum development.
• Clinical research, as well as clinical competencies and administrative skills.

FIGURE 1

A CONCEPTUAL MODEL FOR EVALUATING TRAINING PROGRAMS

**PROGRAM DIRECTOR
AND FACULTY**   **TRAINEES**

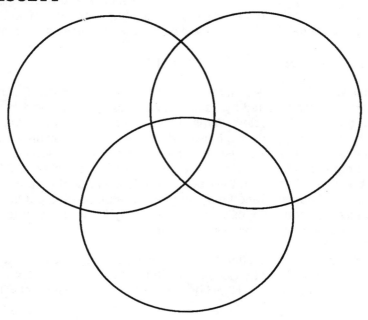

OUTSIDE OBSERVERS (SITE VISITORS)

- Academic training at all levels from the undergraduate (where interest in helping seriously emotionally disturbed children may first arise) to graduate school: master's and doctoral coursework and research.
- Practica, predoctoral internships, and postdoctoral fellowships.
- Retraining and continuing education.

States and the federal government, in collaboration with universities, should develop incentives (i.e., financial support) for faculty and students to become involved in working and training in these settings. Faculty would be offered opportunities either to practice or to conduct research, or both, in public settings with emphasis on the needs of seriously mentally ill persons.

Additionally, predoctoral psychology internships and practicum sites should be developed to involve publicly supported psychology staff members in training partnerships with university faculty members to develop meaningful internships in public settings that prepare students for work with seriously emotionally disturbed children. An obstacle to such development in the field of psychology is the uneven level of, and sometimes poor communication between, doctoral training programs and internship programs. It would be particularly helpful if NIMH started a new clinical training grant program that would require both state mental health authorities and psychology training programs (including both doctoral and internship programs) to be cosponsors, with incentives for states to gradually assume some level of financial responsibility, over a 3- to 6-year period.

Education and Training of Professional Child Psychologists for Services to Children, Youth, and Families

Overview

The overarching issue of this book is how we should train for services that are comprehensive, multidimensional, multidisciplinary, and so on, as discussed earlier in this chapter. Shore concludes Chapter 5 in this volume by organizing and articulating the training issues as follows:

1. What generic training is needed?
2. What are the boundary issues among clinical psychology, school psychology, and applied developmental psychology, all of which are delivering psychological services?
3. What different roles are there, and do they require different kinds of training at different levels?
4. What different models are there? For example, should a multidimensional comprehensive set of services be administered by one individual, or should a person be primarily a facilitator coordinating a multiple number of services?
5. What different standards are there for the different tasks?
6. How do we train for new types of research in service delivery, which is so broad and highly complex?
7. Considering the vast expanse of this model of service delivery, how can we avoid becoming dilettantes who dabble and have merely superficial knowledge of the wealth of information and choices? Indeed, one of the questions is whether there is so much to learn that there is a danger that we may not know anything well.

This is our challenge if we are to deal with the seriously emotionally disturbed child. Are we willing to take the risks? (Shore, Chapter 5, this volume)

The scope of this book is limited to psychology and its subfields. However, by expanding the boundary issue question from fields within psychology (clinical, school, and so on) to all disciplines, a comprehensive national agenda is created, to be addressed in the future: What are the boundary issues among child psychiatry, clinical child psychology, pediatric psychology, school psychology, child and family-oriented social work, marriage and family therapy, special education, and so on?

Shore's last question on the vast expanse of services included under this model may be reframed from the perspective of a new student who wishes to enter the field: How much can be learned in the finite period of graduate school? The median length of doctoral graduate training in psychology is 7.4 years (Thurgood & Weinman, 1989, p. 63); in clinical psychology this includes a full year of predoctoral internship. Thus, either all necessary training and experience to assure competence must be compressed into this period, or the period of formal training must be expanded, for instance, to include a postdoctoral, prelicensure year, as recommended at the 1987 Gainesville Conference on Internships in Psychology (Belar et al.,1989). Therefore, the question to be asked of each subspecialty within professional child psychology is: What didactic and experiential training components should be included within the training period to assure the attainment of clinical competencies for service to children in that subspecialty? Not all the answers will be provided in this volume, but a start will be made, to be completed, we hope, in the not-too-distant future.

Historical Developments in Training Clinical Child Psychologists

The historical development of clinical psychology serving children and the first recognition of clinical child psychology, per se, was traced by Ross (1959) and updated in a volume edited by Williams and Gordon (1974). In a very important contribution in the latter volume, Cass (1974) traced training issues in clinical child psychology as a specialty. Tuma (1975) reviewed training for clinical child psychologists. Routh (1977) surveyed the background and interests of members of the APA Section on Clinical Child Psychology. Tuma (1977) and Fischer (1978) compiled lists of training facilities in pediatric psychology and graduate programs in clinical psychology, respectively. In Chapter 6, Tuma traces the development of particular psychology training programs for children's services over the last decade and a half.

In 1985, the Hilton Head Conference on Training Clinical Child Psychologists (Tuma, 1985) made substantial progress in articulating the complex issues in training clinical child psychologists. While the mechanisms to implement the conference's recommendations were somewhat unclear, the conference was the kickoff of other meetings that resulted in publication of "Guidelines for Clinical Child Psychology Internship Training" (predoctoral) (Elbert, Abidin, Finch, Sigman, & Walker, 1988) and "Guidelines for Postdoctoral Training in Clinical Child Psychology" (Ollendick, Drotar, Friedman, & Hodges, 1988). If one uses the 1983 APA Division 37 (Child, Youth, and Family Services) guidelines, "Guidelines for Training Psychologists to Work with Children, Youth, and Families" (Roberts, Erickson, & Tuma, 1985), for the academic component of training, which the Hilton Head Conference apparently did, then a set of guidelines is complete: academic training, predoctoral internship, and postdoctoral training. The present volume brings these suggested guidelines together in one place: a) for academic training guidelines, see Chapter 8, by Erickson; b) for predoctoral internship guidelines, see Appendix 1 following Chapter 6, by Tuma; and c) for postdoctoral guidelines, see Appendix 2 following Chapter 6. Using the clinical neuropsychology training guidelines as a model (Division of Clinical Neuropsychology, 1987), the clinical child guidelines are being refined to make them more concise and usable to communicate clearly to: (a) other psychologists about what professional or clinical child psychologists do and how they are trained to do it; (b) those in other disciplines for building inter- or multidisciplinary teams; (c) the public for general consumer information; and, perhaps most importantly, (d) prospective students who may wish to enter the field.

Future Directions: Assuring Breadth and Depth of Training of Future Clinicians

Clinical child psychology and pediatric psychology are on the threshold of gaining recognition as specialties in professional psychology, aided by structures and processes recommended by the recent APA Task Force on Accreditation Criteria (Reich, 1988). After many years of discussion and debate, culminating in the 1987 Salt Lake Conference on Graduate Education in Psychology (Bickman, 1987), the 1987 Gainesville Conference on Internship Training in Psychology (Belar et al., 1989) and the 1990 Gainesville National Conference on Scientist-Practitioner Education and Training for the Professional Practice of Psychology (Belar & Perry, 1990), it is clear that graduate training in clinical psychology wishes to:

1. Proceed sequentially from broadly based didactic/experiential courses that make up a scientific core and a professional core in the first years of education/training,
2. Focus increasingly on area/field proficiencies in the middle years of education/training,
3. Retain the predoctoral internship as a period of general professional role acquisition, and
4. Relegate specialty training primarily to a postdoctoral year (or years).

These processes are represented in Figure 2, from the Report of the APA Task Force on Accreditation Criteria (Reich, 1988). While the whole field is slowly rumbling to consensus on the above points, a glaring exception exists with regard to the need for the predoctoral internship to be general: A sizable number of APA-accredited predoctoral internships specialize in children and adolescents, developing the proficiency of many clinical child psychologists and pediatric psychologists. This historical fact may be a leading argument in the formal recognition of these areas as specialties.

While the process of articulating standards for education and training in professional psychology has made some progress recently, it is not complete. For example, the Joint Council on Professional Education in Psychology began in 1988 and plans to make a formal report in 1990 (T. Stigall, personal communication, 1990). NIMH plans to sponsor a National Conference on Public-Academic Linkages for Clinical Training in Psychology in December 1990 to help to implement the recommendations of the three 1988 national conferences (Johnson, in press; Magrab & Wohlford, 1990 (this volume); Myers, Wohlford, Echemendia, & Guzman, in press) in a single coherent plan and to make the training of psychologists optimally relevant to the public mental health services system.

The framework provided by the Task Force on Accreditation Criteria (see Figure 2) should be utilized by clinical child psychology and pediatric psychology (preferably a joint statement from the two subspecialties), to articulate what training experiences constitute the minimal requirements for entry into the field, and when and in what sequence these training experiences should occur. This framework is immensely useful because it is pluralistic; multiple paths can lead to the same goal. The opportunity for the specialties now is there: It is just necessary, as Shore observes, to take the risk of articulating a position to move the field forward for the welfare of seriously emotionally disturbed children.

I have two recommendations for the architects of the new specialty criteria, both of which underscore the plurality of pathways to a specialty in professional child psychology. First, students planning to enter graduate school in a professional child specialty have at least four options, in a 2 X 2 matrix: they may be in a PhD program or in a PsyD program, and this program may offer a clinical child specialty track within general clinical psychology or not. Which of the four types of programs the student enters will influence later choices on the pathway to the goal of attaining the specialty recognition.

Second, the architects of the new specialty criteria in clinical child psychology and pediatric psychology should propose academic and practicum/internship guidelines that are flexible, pluralistic, and yet specific regarding required hours in key settings to assure that a trainee is competent to comprehensively evaluate and recommend interventions for a wide spectrum of seriously emotionally disturbed children and adolescents. On the assumptions that proficiency with children requires a postdoctoral year of training of 2,000 hours, and that an intensive clinical program requires 2,000-hours of practicum and other clinical training, in addition to the 2,000 hour predoctoral internship, a total of 6,000 hours is available for an individual trainee's practicum/internship program. For purposes of breadth and depth in training both clinical child psychologists and pediatric psychologists, Table 5 proposes a distribution of hours across child age-span, across types of disorders, and across settings, so that all trainees have at least minimum clinical competencies in primary health, school, and social service agencies, as well as mental health agencies. Also, all trainees have some proficiency with adults; this experience, like the prepracticum experiences of interviewing techniques and testing techniques, may come early in graduate school, as part of the generic clinical training sequence. Mandatory experience with families in family interviewing and family therapy should be included as a specialized and highly demanding set of skills. This training

FIGURE 2

Specialization in Professional Psychology

Recognized Specialties
(e.g., Clinical, Counseling.
School, Forensic,
Neuropsychology,
Mental Retardation,
Applied Developmental,
etc.)

Postdoctoral training

Predoctoral education &
training
 Internship and
 area/field proficiency

 Professional core

 Scientific core

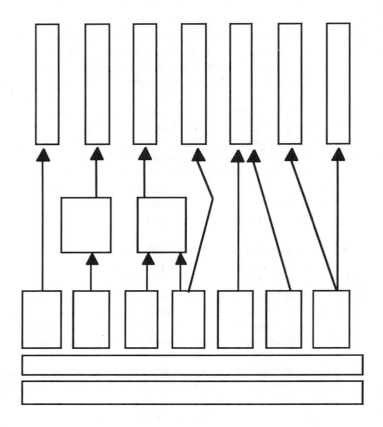

Each professional "specialty" will be defined by its members. Publicly stated criteria and procedures will govern the process by which a group of psychologists will seek national recognition of their professional specialty. Accredited doctoral programs may or may not have the label of a recognized specialty. Doctoral programs will be accredited in professional psychology with a title selected by the program (e.g., clinical, applied developmental, family, etc.). Specialties, once recognized, may specify the types of professional psychology education and training programs through which persons may enter the specialty (i.e., specify the content of the area/field portion of predoctoral preparation, and if necessary, postdoctoral programs). In some specialties, for example, there may be more than one field of emphasis appropriate at the predoctoral level through which to qualify for postdoctoral training or practice in those specialty areas, whereas in another specialty, there may be fewer options. All professional training at the predoctoral level, however, will have a foundation based upon the scientific discipline core of psychology and a general professional core, regardless of the applied field of emphasis in preparation for professional practice entry level.

From <u>Proposed Scope of Accreditation for Education and Training in Professional Psychology</u> by J. Reich, 1988, Report Number 4, Section B, APA Task Force on Review of the Scope and Criteria of Accreditation. Washington, DC: American Psychological Association.

TABLE 5

Possible Guidelines for Breadth/Depth Training in Clinical Child Psychology and Pediatric Psychology: Recommended Distribution of Training by Age, Disorder, and Setting

Age of at-risk population	Frequent mental disorders	Setting	Recommended hours for clinical child psychology	Recommended hours for pediatric psychology
New mothers, fathers, infants (0-3)	Bonding, child abuse, etc.	Primary health, social welfare	—	500
Infants, older children (0-3, 3-18)	Developmental, neuropsychological disorders; comorbidity with physical health problems	Primary health and mental retardation facilities	250	1,000
Preschool children (3-6)	Hyperactive behavior disorders	Day care, nursery schools, kindergartens, Head Start	500	500
Young and older children (3-18)	Neurotic and psychotic disorders	Child guidance clinics; mental health clinics and hospitals	750	500
School-age children (6-12)	Learning disabilities, psychoeducational problems	Schools	750	500
Adolescents (12-18)	Juvenile delinquents, school dropouts, runaways, substance abuse, etc.	Juvenile justice, schools, welfare agencies, etc.	750	500
Parents, children of all ages	Marital and family problems	Mental health clinics, homes, etc.	750	750
General adult population	Neurotic and psychotic disorders	Outpatient and inpatient mental health facilities	750	250
		Total required:	4,500	4,500
		Prepracticum:	500	500
		Electives:	1,000	1,000
		Grand totals	6,000	6,000

31

probably should occur in the later stages of training after trainees have demonstrated their abilities with individual children, with adolescents and adults, and with group therapy or counseling.

For purposes of depth of training, individual trainees probably should concentrate most of their 1,000 elective hours in one or two age-problem-setting groups. For instance, a pediatric psychology trainee may be expected to--and want to--concentrate most elective hours in a primary health setting working with children with developmental disabilities, neuropsychological disorders, psychosomatic disorders, and comorbidity problems of mental disorders with physical health problems. Hence, the foregoing trainees may have 2,000 hours of the 6,000-hour total in a primary health setting.

In conclusion, the draft training guidelines (see Table 5) were offered as a means of facilitating discussion and resolving the ambiguities that still exist in this area, despite decades of attention. It is clear that although APA has not yet officially recognized them, clinical child psychology and pediatric psychology are in fact specialties. Graduate students who wish to attain one of these specialties should have the opportunity to learn what the requirements and the options are in their pursuits.

Some time in the future, it is hoped, Pion and Sechrest's recommendations for empirical assessment of clinical competencies will be achieved. Some time after that, perhaps, one could make an empirically based study across all disciplines to determine which approaches to clinical training are most effective.

References

American Psychological Association. (1990). Ethical principles of psychologists. American Psychologist, 45, 390-395.

Belar, C.D., Bieliauskas, L.A., Larsen, K.G., Mensh, I.N., Poey, K., & Roelke, H.J. (1989). The National Conference on Internship Training in Psychology. American Psychologist, 44, 60-65.

Belar, C.D., & Perry, N.W. (1990, January). Resolutions of the National Conference on Scientist-Practioner Education and Training for the Professional Practice of Psychology. Gainesville, FL: University of Florida, Department of Clinical and Health Psychology.

Bickman, L. (Ed.) (1987). Proceedings of the National Conference on Graduate Education in Psychology, University of Utah, Salt Lake City, June 13-19, 1987 [special issue]. American Psychologist, 42, 1041-1085.

Cass, L.K. (1974). The training of clinical child psychologists. In G.J. Williams and S. Gordon (Eds.), Clinical child psychology: Current practices and future perspectives (pp. 463-484). New York: Behavioral Publications.

Division of Clinical Neuropsychology, American Psychological Association. (1987). Guidelines for doctoral training programs in clinical neuropsychology. Clinical Neuropsychologist, 1, 29-34.

Elbert, J.C., Abidin, R.R., Finch, A.J., Jr., Sigman, M.D., & Walker, C.E. (1988). Guidelines for clinical child psychology internship training. Journal of Clinical Child Psychology, 17, 280-287.

Fischer, C.T. (1978). Graduate programs in clinical child psychology and related fields. Journal of Clinical Child Psychology, 7, 87-88.

Garmezy, N. (1978). DSM III: Never mind the psychologists: Is it good for children? The Clinical Psychologist, 31, 1-6.

Institute of Medicine. (1989). Research on children and adolescents with mental, behavioral and developmental disorders: Mobilizing a national initiative. Washington, DC: National Academy Press.

Johnson, D.L. (Ed.) (in press). Training psychologists to work with the seriously mentally ill. Washington, DC: American Psychological Association.

Magrab, P., & Wohlford, P. (Eds.). (1990). Improving services for children and adolescents with severe mental disorders: Clinical training in psychology. Washington, DC: American Psychological Association.

Myers, H., Wohlford, P., Echemendia, R., & Guzman, L.P. (Eds.) (in press). Improving training and psychological services for ethnic minorities. Washington, DC: American Psychological Association.

National Institute of Mental Health. (1987). Mental health, United States, 1987. R.W. Manderschied & S.A. Barrett (Eds.) (DHHS Pub. No. ADM 87-1518). Washington, DC: U.S. Government Printing Office.

National Institute of Mental Health. (in press). Mental health, United States, 1990. R.W. Manderschied, (Ed.). Washington, DC: U.S. Government Printing Office.

National Institute on Aging. (1987). Personnel for health needs of the elderly through the year 2020. Bethesda, MD: National Institutes of Health.

Ollendick, T.H., Drotar, D., Friedman, M., & Hodges, K. (1988). Guidelines for postdoctoral training in clinical child psychology. Journal of Clinical Child Psychology, 17, 288-289.

President's Commission on Mental Health. (1978). Report to the President from the President's Commission on Mental Health. (Vol. I). Washington, DC: U.S. Government Printing Office.

Reich, J. (1988). Proposed scope of accreditation for education and training in professional psychology (Report No. 4, Section B). APA Task Force on Review of the Scope and Criteria of Accreditation. Washington, DC: American Psychological Association.

Roberts, M.C., Erickson, M.T., & Tuma, J.M. (1985). Guidelines for training psychologists to work with children, youth, & families. Journal of Clinical Child Psychology, 14, 70-79.

Ross, A.O. (1959). The practice of clinical child psychology. New York: Grune & Stratton.

Routh, D.K. (1977). What is a clinical child psychologist? The Clinical Psychologist, 30, 23-25.

Stratoudakis, J., Tomes, H., & Wohlford, P. (1990, December 10-12). The states' role in public-academic linkages for clinical training for services to persons with serious mental illness. Paper presented at the National Conference on Public-Academic Linkages for Clinical Training in Psychology, Georgetown University, Washington, DC.

Thurgood, D.H., & Weinman, J.M. (1989). Summary report 1988: Doctorate recipients of United States universities. Washington, DC: National Academy Press.

Tuma, J.M. (1975). Pediatric psychologist: Do you mean clinical child psychologist? Journal of Clinical Child Psychology, 4, 9-12.

Tuma, J.M. (1977). Practicum, internship, and postdoctoral training in pediatric psychology: A survey. Journal of Pediatric Psychology, 2, 9-12.

Tuma, J.M. (Ed.). (1985). Proceedings: Conference on training clinical child psychologists. Washington, DC: American Psychological Association, Section on Clinical Child Psychology, Division of Clinical Psychology.

U.S. Congress, Office of Technology Assessment. (1986). Children's mental health: Problems and services--A background paper (OTA-BP-H-33). Washington, DC: U.S. Government Printing Office.

U.S. House of Representatives, Committee on Appropriations. (1986). Report on Departments of Labor, Health and Human Services, and Education, and Related Agencies Appropriation Bill, 1987. Washington, DC: U.S. House of Representatives.

U.S. Senate, Committee on Appropriations. (1989). Report on Departments of Labor, Health and Human Services, and Education, and Related Agencies Appropriation Bill, 1990. Washington, DC: U.S. Senate.

Williams, G.J., & Gordon, S. (Eds.). (1974). Clinical child psychology: Current practices and future perspectives. New York: Behavioral Publications.

Wohlford, P. (1975). Potentials and problems in achieving quality psychological services in Head Start and day care programs. In E.M. Neumann & E.H. Williams (Eds.), Twelfth annual distinguished lecture series in special education and rehabilitation (pp. 89-124). Los Angeles: University of Southern California Press.

Chapter 3
Service Trends in the Children's Mental Health System:
Implications for the Training of Psychologists

Robert M. Friedman
Albert J. Duchnowski
Florida Mental Health Institute
University of South Florida

The purpose of this paper is to present some of the trends in the public mental health sector with regard to services for children with serious emotional problems and to discuss the relevance of these trends for the training of psychologists.

Within the public mental health sector, the 1980s have clearly been a time in which the primary focus in children's services has been on children with the most serious emotional problems (Friedman, 1986). At a Federal level, this can be seen in the Child and Adolescent Service System Program (CASSP), an initiative of the National Institute of Mental Health (NIMH) designed to help states improve their capacity to serve seriously emotionally disturbed (SED) children and their families. It can also be seen in the funding, for the first time, of two research and training centers specifically focused on SED children and their families. These centers, located at the Florida Mental Health Institute of the University of South Florida and the Regional Research Institute of Portland State University, are jointly funded by NIMH and the Department of Education.

More recently, in 1986 the Mental Health Planning Act was passed by the U.S. Congress (PL 99-660) and specifically focuses on the development of plans for comprehensive, community-based services for adults and children with the most serious problems.

This emphasis at the federal level, on the one hand, was partly stimulated by interest at a state level, and, on the other hand, has clearly increased the focus on SED children in states. The State Mental Health Representatives for Children and Youth (SMHRCY), the national organization composed of those individuals in each state with primary responsibility for children's mental health services, advocated with NIMH the development of a program such as CASSP and was a partner in the development of the program. During the first year that grants were available through CASSP, 44 states or territories applied, attesting to the great interest in the program. When the most recent grant recipients are announced in fall 1988, the total number of states with CASSP grants will be approximately 40.

The emphasis on SED children is partly in response to a national study by Knitzer (1982) on behalf of the Children's Defense Fund, one of the most influential child advocacy organization that exists today. Since that time, the National Mental Health Association (NMHA) devoted its national conference to children's issues in 1986, and has launched a national project called the "Invisible Children's Project," which is focused on children in residential placements far away from their home communities. The National Alliance for the Mentally Ill (NAMI), a rapidly growing advocacy organization formed primarily by parents of adult children with major mental illnesses, has clearly emphasized as a priority population those individuals with the most serious mental illnesses. In July, 1988, the nation's largest foundation devoted specifically to health care issues, the Robert Wood Johnson Foundation, announced a multisite grant program also focused on children with the most serious problems.

From a variety of directions, therefore, there has been a consistent emphasis in the children's field on the need to improve services for SED children and their families. This is not very different from, in fact, and perhaps can be said to follow upon by a few years, a parallel emphasis in the adult mental health field. NIMH's Community Support Program, for example, has just celebrated its tenth anniversary, and the Robert Wood Johnson Foundation program for chronically mentally ill adults preceded the children's program by several years.

Still, this focus on the most seriously disturbed children has not been without the concern that unless a parallel focus on prevention and early intervention efforts is initiated, short-term gains achieved with SED children are not likely to be translated into long-term benefits for children overall, and for the field. Indeed, one of the major dilemmas that policymakers have been struggling with is, given the limited resources at their disposal, how can they strike a balance between a clear responsibility in the public sector to serve those with the most serious problems and the recognition of the need to plan for the future through prevention and early intervention efforts.

This dilemma notwithstanding, however, with the support of advocacy groups and the Federal government, most states have clearly chosen to make service for SED children their top priority in the children's area. This is reflected, for example, in a study looking at the priorities of state mental health commissioners (Ahr & Holcomb, 1985) in which the highest ranked children's item is "Develop/maintain a continuum of services for children and adolescents," which is ranked number 6 out of 62 in the whole list.

Status of Services

Further, this attention seems justified by the state of services for SED children around the country, In her study, Knitzer (1982) found that only seven states were even in the early stages of developing a continuum of care in the children's mental health field. While that situation has unquestionably improved, the "Invisible Children" project of the NMHA has issued preliminary findings showing that approximately 23,000 individuals under 18 were in state hospitals since 1987, and approximately 5,000 children were in out-of-state residential placements (Update, 1988a). Testimony presented before the U.S. House of Representatives Select Committee on Children, Youth, and Families in 1987 clearly emphasizes that while significant progress has been made in the development of more effective services around the country, there is a major gap between knowledge and the implementation of that knowledge (Fine, 1987; Friedman, 1987; Knitzer, 1987; Saxe, 1987). This gap, which contributes to youngsters' being served in less effective and more restrictive settings than they need, was also emphasized in a report done on behalf of Congress in 1986 (U.S. Office of Technology Assessment, 1986).

Part of the problem is obviously the amount of money available for services. From a financial policy standpoint, however, the more important issues may be the fiscal incentive system that exists and often encourages more restrictive placements than are needed and the manner in which existing funds are used. Recently published data indicate that there are eight states or territories in which the per capita expenditures under the direct control of state mental health agencies (SMHA) in fiscal year 1985 were less than $20 (Lutterman, Mazade, Wurster, & Glover, 1988). In contrast there are nine states where the per capita expenditure is over $40, ranging as high as $90 in New York.

Perhaps even more important, while the percentage of expenditures for community-based services has risen in recent years, it still represents only 32% (Lutterman et al., 1988) of SMHA expenditures. In contrast the expenditures on state hospitals constitute 64% of SMHA expenditures.

Analyses of expenditures for children's mental health suggest that in 1983 the percentage of total mental health expenditures going for children was about 15%, despite the fact that children represent about 26% of the population (Update, 1985). It is further noteworthy that in many states data are not broken down in a way that permits a determination of expenditures for children.

Given the state of services for SED children, particularly at the beginning of the 1980s, and the manner in which expenditures have been distributed, the emphasis on the specific target population of SED children certainly seems warranted and needed. The recent emphasis within NIMH clinical training programs on preparation of mental health professionals to work with the populations with the most serious mental health needs is a logical and reasonable extension of this type of policy focus.

36

Definition and Prevalence

One of the first questions that is often asked about this emphasis has to do with definition of the population of SED children. It is clear that there are a variety of definitions and that they often differ from system to system (Behar, 1985; Stroul & Friedman, 1986). In its CASSP program, NIMH dealt with this issue by providing a general definition that emphasized not only that SED children have a DSM-III diagnosis but also that their problems are of at least one year's duration, require services from multiple systems, and have a significant disabling effect on the child's functioning (Stroul & Friedman, 1986). Some state or communities have chosen to focus more specifically on populations of youngsters in out-of-state placements (for example, Alaska, as described in Update, 1987) or at risk of out-of-home placements (Ventura County, California, 1987), for example.

Within the educational system, under the Education for Handicapped Act passed by Congress in 1975 and also known as PL 94-142, despite the fact that a consistent (although general) definition is offered of SED, there is tremendous variability in the percentage of children identified by states as being SED (U.S. Department of Education, 1987). This ranges from about one-tenth of one percent to close to three percent. Further, there is variability between states in whether they call these children emotionally disturbed or behaviorally disordered; this in an issue that elicits strong feeling (SRA Technologies, 1985).

Without question, there is more work that needs to be done around the complex definitional issues and the related aspect of measurement. There is a strong need for partnerships between university faculty and public system officials in tackling these questions. Hopefully the problems around definitional issues will not prevent partnerships from developing because the service needs and challenges are strong and present and will always be so, regardless of the status of the definitional issues. Further, the definitional ambiguity has not prevented progress from being made in many communities and states.

It does seem clear, however, that while the definitional problems are important ones, the actual children being served present varied and multiple problems. Our Research and Training Center is currently conducting a four-year longitudinal study of a sample of 812 youngsters from four states. It is obvious from our early results (Friedman, Duchnowski, Kutash, Prange, & Silver, 1988; Friedman, Brandenburg, Duchnowski, Kutash, Prange, & Silver, 1987; Silver, Friedman, Kutash, Duchnowski, Brandenburg, & Prange, 1987) and the results of other studies (Florida--Friedman & Kutash 1986; Ohio--Urban Systems Research and Engineering, 1987; Washington--Low, 1988) that the children served vary greatly from those with low prevalence psychiatric disorders to those who are aggressive and potentially dangerous to those who are anxious and withdrawn. They frequently display both behavioral and emotional disturbances, have deficiencies in social and adaptive skills, tend to cluster towards the lower end of the normal intelligence range, come from families that in some cases are very supportive and well-functioning but are often very troubled themselves, and have difficulties functioning in school and the community, bringing them into contact with multiple special services.

Given the difficulty in defining SED children, and the obvious complexities of the measurement process, the task of determining the prevalence of serious disturbances in children is extremely difficult. A recent review of the literature conducted at our Center identifies a variety of other issues that further complicate epidemiological research and concludes with an estimate that at any point in time there are probably two to five percent of children who have emotional disturbances that are long-lasting, have a significant effect on their functioning, and are agreed upon by several sources (Brandenburg, Friedman, & Silver, 1987). This is a broad range, and clearly there is a need for further research in this area as well.

Developments in the Field

The primary service development in recent years has been the emphasis on the need for comprehensive, community-based systems of care (Behar, 1985; Stroul & Friedman, 1986; U.S. Office of Technology Assessment, 1986). This has been based on a set of values that emphasizes an individualized set of service, a strong focus on families and on community-based services, and treatment in the least restrictive setting that is appropriate to a child's needs. A part of the emphasis on a system of care is a recognition that in order to appropriately meet the needs of youngsters and families with varied problems, strengths, and interests, a wide range of services is necessary. In particular, there has been much attention on intensive in-home services, day treatment, therapeutic foster care, and intensive case management.

In addition, there is recognition of the fact that the youngsters in the public system typically have a variety of problems and require services from several different agencies. Further, these youngsters are typically not good candidates for traditional types of therapies, and oftentimes they and their families require more intensive services than have typically been provided in office-based outpatient settings. In fact, one of the most significant developments in the field has been the recognition that intensive services can be provided outside of a traditional residential treatment center. For example, in the Homebuilders approach, a family may receive as many as 20 hours of service per week in their own home on a time-limited basis (Kinney, Madsen, Fleming, & Haapala, 1977). Day treatment approaches provide at least five hours a day of service and often combine that with family service (Baenan, Stephens, & Glenwick, 1986; Friedman, Quick, Palmer, & Mayo, 1982; Tolmach, 1985). Therapeutic foster care programs provide active treatment programs in the least restrictive of the out-of-home alternatives that are often more intensive than services provided in more restrictive residential settings (Hawkins, Meadowcroft, Trout, & Luster, 1985). Intensive case management services, particularly with low caseloads and when combined with flexible funding to facilitate individualized services, are also extremely intensive (Roberts, Mayo, Alberts, & Broskowski, 1986; Update, 1986). Systems approaches, such as the Alaska Youth Initiative, that emphasize individualized programming also provide very intensive service (Update, 1987, 1988b).

To a considerable extent, psychologists have played a leading role in many of the new developments. As the head of children's mental health in North Carolina, Behar played a leadership role in converting a class action lawsuit (Willis M. vs. the State of North Carolina) into a demonstration of the potential power of a well-developed system of care (Behar, 1985, 1986). Knitzer was instrumental in identifying the problems in the system (1982) while several psychologists helped develop key components of the service system (Kinney et al., 1977, with the Homebuilders model of intensive home-based services, and Hawkins, Meadowcroft et al., 1985, with PRYDE, a therapeutic foster care model, for example). Project Wraparound, designed by Burchard (1988) and presented here, is another example of an innovative approach with strong leadership by psychologists.

Despite this, however, as the public system evolves to emphasize a wide range of services, intensive non-residential alternatives, outreach approaches and in-home services, multi-agency approaches, and intensive case management, the gap between the public sector approaches and needs and the emphasis within university training programs seems to be widening. For example, within the Ventura County system, a system that has demonstrated success with SED youngsters, less than 25% of the service is provided in an office (R. Feltman, personal communication, 1988). Such a heavy emphasis on outreach services is characteristic rather than exceptional within the community systems that have incorporated the new developments.

This is similar in the area of assessment. In the Alaska Youth Initiative, for example, a three-day environmental assessment is conducted by which a team of individuals visits the home community of a youngster, observes the youngster in a variety of settings, interviews key people in the child's network, identifies strengths, interests, and resources, and then uses all of the information to help develop a genuinely individualized approach (J. VanDenberg & T. Risley, personal communication, 1988). While other systems and programs do not use such an intensive environmental assessment approach, there is clearly a growing trend toward more ecologically oriented assessment and therapy. However, for a psychologist to be able to effectively serve the types of SED youngsters seen in the public system, there is a need for his/her preparation to be broader and to include exposure to, and experience with, the newer approaches with their emphasis on intense service, timely service, outreach, family support and involvement, and more ecologically oriented assessments. There is also a need to understand systems issues, including the role of various agencies and strategies for working effectively in a collaborative way with staff from other agencies.

From a research perspective, training in applied methodologies along with approaches to program and systems evaluation is very important for involvement in the public sector. There are many critical issues calling for research investigation that would greatly benefit from the involvement of university-based psychologists.

The exposure to the public sector can and should be provided in classes, practicum experience, and internships. At the Florida Mental Health Institute we have a newly approved clinical internship that has a strong public system focus, including an opportunity for a split rotation within our Department of Epidemiology and Policy Analysis. This provides interns with an opportunity to learn about system functioning as well as learning strategies for analyzing and influencing policy.

Overall, however, beyond specific classes and practical experiences, there is a important need to bridge the gap between university-based psychologists and the public sector. Both the public sector and the university-based psychologists stand to benefit from partnerships around a range of service delivery, research, and training issues. Unless psychology departments have a core of faculty members who are very familiar with the functioning of the public system, it is not possible to provide the types of experiences for students that will help prepare them to work effectively with SED youngsters.

The mechanisms for forging these partnerships can include opportunities for university-based psychologists to get experience in the public system through consultation, seminars, and research activities. The public system would greatly benefit from the perspective and skills of the university-based psychologist. The psychologist would find that the public sector is very receptive to such partnerships, provided they are based on a commitment to work together over time rather than just a one-time occurrence and on mutual respect and understanding.

The emphasis within the public sector on services to SED children is not likely to diminish. Given the growth of the private sector in the mental health field, and its potential to serve individuals who will come to office settings and may benefit from more traditional treatment and assessment approaches, the responsibility of the public sector is more clearly being directed toward those youngsters with the most serious problems for whom private sector services are either not appropriate or accessible (often for financial reasons). Further, the emphasis within NIMH on individuals with the most serious problems is not likely to diminish, nor is the emphasis within the mental health advocacy community.

There is a need within the public mental health sector and an opportunity within psychology training programs that are complementary. This is a situation that is not likely to change but rather can be expected to continue if not actually grow. It is hoped that these two important components of the mental health community will be able to come together to forge partnerships that will result in psychologists who are better prepared to make important contributions to the public sector.

References

Ahr, P.R., & Holcomb, W.R. (1985). State mental health directors' priorities for mental health care. Hospital and Community Psychiatry, 36, 39-45.

Baenan, R., Stephens, M.A.P., & Glenwick, D. (1986). Outcome in psychoeducational day school programs: A review. American Journal of Orthopsychiatry, 56, 263-271.

Behar, L. (1985). Changing patterns of state responsibility: A case study of North Carolina. Journal of Clinical Child Psychology, 14, 188-195.

Behar, L. (1986). A model for child mental health services: The North Carolina experience. Children Today, 15(3), 16-21.

Brandenburg, N.A., Friedman, R.M., & Silver, S. (1987). The epidemiology of childhood psychiatric disorders: Recent prevalence findings and methodologic issues. Unpublished manuscript, Florida Mental Health Institutes, Tampa.

Burchard, J.D. (1988, May). Project Wraparound: Training clinical psychologists through a revised service delivery system for severely emotionally disturbed children and adolescents. Paper presented at National Conference on Clinical Training in Psychology: Improving Psychological Services for Children and Adolescents with Severe Mental Disorders, Washington, DC.

Fine, G. (1987). Prepared statement to the U.S. House of Representatives Select Committee on Children, Youth, and Families, Hearings on "Children's Mental Health: Promising Responses to Neglected Problems." U.S. Government Printing Office, Washington, DC.

Friedman, R.M. (1987). Prepared statement to the U.S. House of Representatives Select Committee on Children, Youth, and Families, Hearings on "Children's Mental Health: Promising Responses to Neglected Problems." U.S. Government Printing Office, Washington, DC.

Friedman, R.M., Brandenburg, N.A., Duchnowski, A., Kutash, K., Prange, M., & Silver, S. (1987, May). Characteristics of emotionally disturbed adolescents. Paper presented at National Institute of Mental Health research meeting on "Treatment/Assessment of Violent and Emotionally Disturbed Youth," Raleigh, NC.

Friedman, R.M., Duchnowski, A., Kutash, K., Prange, M., & Silver, S. (1988, August). Children's mental health services: Who gets what and why. Paper presented at annual meeting of the American Psychological Association, Atlanta.

Friedman, R.M., & Kutash, K. (1986). Mad, bad, sad, can't add? Florida Adolescent and Child Treatment Study (FACTS): Executive Summary. Unpublished manuscript, Florida Mental Health Institute, Tampa.

Friedman, R.M., Quick, J., Palmer, J., & Mayo, J. (1982). Social skills training in a day treatment program for adolescents. Child and Youth Services, 5, 139-152.

Hawkins, R.P., Meadowcroft, P., Trout, B.A., & Luster, W.C. (1985). Foster family-based treatment. Journal of Clinical Child Psychology, 14, 220-228.

Kinney, J.W., Madsen, B., Fleming, T., & Haapala, D.A. (1977). Homebuilders: Keeping families together. Journal of Consulting and Clinical Psychology, 39, 905-911.

Knitzer, J. (1982). Unclaimed children. Washington, DC: Children's Defense Fund.

Knitzer, J. (1987). Prepared statement before U.S. House of Representatives Select Committee on Children, Youth, and Families, Hearings on "Children's Mental Health: Promising Responses to Neglected Problems." U.S. Government Printing Office, Washington, DC.

Low, B.P. (1988, February). Washington State CASSP systems analysis project. Poster presented at conference on "Children's Mental Health Services and Policy: Building a Research Base." Tampa, FL.

Lutterman, T.C., Mazade, N.A., Wurster, C.R., & Glover, R.W. (1988). Expenditures and revenues of state mental health agencies, 1981-1985. Hospital and Community Psychiatry, 39, 758-762.

Roberts, C., Mayo, J., Alberts, F., & Broskowski, H. (1986). Child case management for severely disturbed children and adolescents. Unpublished manuscript, Northside Centers, Inc., Tampa, FL.

SRA Technologies (1985). Special study on terminology. Washington, DC: U.S. Department of Education.

Saxe, L.S. (1987). Prepared statement before U.S. House of Representatives Select Committee on Children, Youth, and Families, Hearings on "Children's Mental Health: Promising Responses to Neglected Problems." Washington, DC: U.S. Government Printing Office.

Silver, S., Friedman, R.M., Kutash, K., Duchnowski, A., Brandenburg, N.A., & Prange, M.E. (1987, August). Emotionally disturbed children: Who are they? What do they need? Paper presented at the annual meeting of the American Psychological Association, New York City.

Stroul, B.A., & Friedman, R.M. (1986). A system of care for severely emotionally disturbed children and youth. Washington, DC: Georgetown University Child Development Center.

Tolmach, J. (1985). "There ain't nobody on my side." A new day treatment program for black urban youth. Journal of Clinical Child psychology, 14, 214-219.

United States Office of Technology Assessment (1986). Children's mental health: Problems and services--A background paper. Washington, DC: U.S. Government Printing Office.

Update (1985). Study reports state mental health expenditure by age group. 1(2), 1, 16.

Update (1986). Case management. 2(2), 10-12.

Update (1987). Flexible funds key to Alaska Youth Initiative. 3(1), 13.

Update (1988a). Invisible children. 3(2), 15.

Update (1988b). Individualizing services. 3(2), 10-12.

Urban Systems Research & Engineering, Inc. (1987). Children in out-of-home care. Columbus, OH: Ohio Department of Human Services.

U.S. Department of Education. (1987). Ninth Annual Report to Congress on the Implementation of the Education of the Handicapped Act. Washington, DC: Office of Special Education.

Ventura County Children's Mental Health Services Demonstration Project. (1986). First annual report. Unpublished manuscript, Ventura, California.

Chapter 4
State Mental Health Needs and Adequacy of Personnel to Meet These Needs

Jerome H. Hanley
Director, Division of Child and Adolescent Services
South Carolina Department of Mental Health

Given the increasing interest in children's mental health issues, the state mental health authorities are or will soon be one of the primary employers of mental health professionals trained to work with children. To assume the responsibilities inherent in carrying out a broad state mission, current training will have to be altered to meet our clinical and system needs.

From the state mental health perspective, there are a number of issues directly or indirectly associated with the production of clinical child psychologists that we feel need to be considered by those responsible for developing young professionals. Some of these issues are: (1) what constitutes, by training, a clinical child psychologist, (2) the numbers of these specialists currently being produced and the need for more, (3) the need for M.A. as well as Ph.D.-level clinical child psychologists, (4) the types of clients being served, (5) the skill repertoire of clinical child psychologists, (6) their familiarity with, and competence in, various service modes, (7) the extreme need for minority professionals, (8) limited financial and clinical resources.

I will briefly address each of these issues. The supply and distribution of mental health practitioners trained to work with children (psychologists-Ph.D., M.A.; social workers, counselors, psychiatrists) is a national problem. Jeff Koshel, in a 1985 National Governor's Association issues brief, reported that "the commission on mental health for children, the national consortium on mental health services for children, and the President's commission on mental health have each identified a chronic and severe shortage of trained professionals to provide mental health services for children and youth."

If the situation is bad nationally, it is even worse in the more rural regions of the country, where "it is difficult to obtain ongoing treatment services beyond diagnosis for emotionally disturbed children" (Southern Regional Education Board, 1982). Money is an important missing resource, but even more important is the limited supply of mental health practitioners trained to work with children. The state of South Carolina is representative of other semirural states and, in this case, has much in common with states in other regions of the country as well. Data on current staff were collected from fourteen of the seventeen community mental health centers in South Carolina. The questions posed were how many of their clinical staff work with children at least fifty percent of the time, and how many are psychologists, social workers, counselors, and psychiatrists. Of the 198 professionals listed, 9 (or 5%) were M.A. psychologists and 10 (or 5%) were Ph.D. psychologists. Psychologists working with children represent 10% of the total number of professionals providing mental health services to children in fourteen centers in South Carolina. There was no reasonable way to determine the nature of the training that psychologists or the other professionals received to prepare them for their duties. Informal conversations lead one to believe that much of the training was on the job.

Another survey of the community mental health centers revealed a clear unmet need for clinical child psychologists. Interestingly, however, the centers expressed twice the need for M.A. trained clinical child psychologists, as opposed to Ph.D. psychologists, to staff programs and carry out the hands-on, less glamorous clinical responsibilities central to working with children and their families.

Oftentimes the children and their families who seek or are referred to the state's mental health system do not fit nicely into a DSM III-R category. In fact many are nontraditional clients (poor and/or minority) with a justifiable distrust of the mental health system because of its historical lack of sensitivity and responsiveness to their issues. Oftentimes the referral is made not because the child and/or family are troubled, but because they are troubling to others. These children and their families have frequently touched many of the health and human services agencies with minimal results. Far too frequently their problems stem from cultural, social, political, economic, educational, historical, language, and racial issues, not to mention psychological or psychiatric ones.

Our state mental health systems are confronted with developing and providing services that are appropriate to the client's clinical needs and culturally sensitive. Clearly, no program is any better than the professionals staffing it. Unfortunately few of those staff psychologists are African-American, Hispanic, Native American, or Asian-American. Dr. Wade Nobles recently reported at a conference on mental health services and minority youth that of all psychologists nationally, only 4% are Black. Given the multitude of needs many clients bring with them to the state systems, it is rare to be able to think in terms of the fifty-minute hour or weekly sessions of individual, family, or group therapy with severely disturbed or dysfunctional families. With the encouragement and support of the federal Child and Adolescent Services System Program (CASSP), states are moving toward integrated systems of service delivery. At the same time states are moving toward developing flexible arrays of services, which can be altered to meet the needs of any given child and family.

Beth A. Stroul of the Georgetown CASSP Technical Assistance Center and Robert M. Friedman of the Florida Mental Health Institute coauthored a book entitled <u>A System of Care for Severely Emotionally Disturbed Children and Youth</u>. This book has served as the basis of many state child and adolescent mental health planning documents. This effort highlights where mental health systems are going and how training must prepare clinical child psychologists to practice their art and science. The optimal full array of clinical services is composed of both nonresidential and residential services, as follows:

<u>Nonresidential Services</u>	<u>Residential Services</u>
Prevention	Therapeutic foster care
Early identification and intervention	Therapeutic group care
Assessment	Therapeutic camp services
Outpatient treatment	Independent living services
Home-based services	Crisis residential services
Day treatment	inpatient hospitalization
Emergency services	

The trained clinical child psychologist should have had some exposure to these various treatment options and understand their strengths, weaknesses, and clinical indications during training. The clinical child psychologists who choose to work in a noninstitutional public setting (i.e., community mental health center) become responsible for the delivery of all clinical, and oftentimes, nonclinical services related to the needs of their young clients. Our professionals are unable to refuse to serve a child based upon diagnosis or personal preference.

Within any given week, the clinical child psychologist can expect to be called upon to impart information on any behavioral or developmental concern raised about a person between the ages of 0 and 17. The psychologist must also have the skills to provide assessment, treatment, consultation and education, case management, child advocacy, training and supervision, public relations, and fund raising, as well as engage in administration and program development.

States appear on the verge of making a significant financial commitment to children as reflected in the National Governor's Association policy resolution, which states, in part, that "states should support the development of a federal and state health policy that provides equal access to mental and physical health services for children regardless of income or residence."

It is clearer than ever that the institutions of training and the institutions of service provision (employment) can no longer simply coexist; they must actively cooperate. Children's mental health technology is changing rapidly, and the states are struggling to keep up. We need a steady stream of ethnically diverse, competent clinical child psychologists to assist and lead us in this new adventure. There are young people who are willing to accept the challenge of the public sector and who understand the vast rewards, both personal and professional. We need badly for these young professionals to be well trained to meet the challenges of the public sector, especially in community mental health. We call for a renewed partnership between academia and the public mental health sector that will jointly provide both the formal training and practical experience necessary to serve the severely disturbed youth of the nation.

Reference

Southern Regional Education Board. (1982). Staffing patterns and state mental health manpower development. Atlanta, GA: Author.

SECTION III

PSYCHOLOGY'S ROLE IN PROVIDING TRAINED PERSONNEL TO MEET THESE NEEDS

Chapter 5
Background and Recent History of Psychology's Role in Improving Psychological Services for Children

Milton F. Shore
Psychologist in Independent Practice, Silver Spring, MD
Adjunct Professor, American University, Catholic University of America

Psychology's involvement in the delivery of psychological services for children can be said to have mirrored society's neglect of children and youth. The history of much of psychology's involvement with children and youth has been summarized by Don Routh in his chapter in the Hilton Head Proceedings of the Conference on Training Clinical Child Psychologists. I will supplement some of his thoughts and do a rapid review.

In 1945 when the current structure of the American Psychological Association was set up, there were two divisions that dealt with children: the Division of School Psychology and the Division of Developmental Psychology. Division 12, the Division of Clinical Psychology, arose from the establishment of clinical psychology as a profession in the Veteran's Administration. In 1961 Alan Ross, recognizing that there was no entity that fostered clinical services for children within APA, established Section 1, the section on clinical child psychology in Division 12. In 1978, the Division of Child, Youth, and Family Services (Division 37) was established. It currently has 1500 members. Originally the thought was to transform Section 1 into a division of clinical child psychology, but it was believed that the delivery of psychological services to children was much broader than just clinical services. Therefore, Division 37 became an umbrella for all those in other divisions related to children who were interested and/or involved in the delivery of psychological services to children and families. Meanwhile the American Psychological Association established a task force on children, youth, and families, which later became a committee. About 8 years ago a person was specifically designated in the APA Central Office to be responsible for child, youth, and family policy. Currently Brian Wilcox is the designee and is under the Public Interest Directorate. Meanwhile psychologists who were Congressional Fellows for the Society for Research in Child Development made many contributions on a national level, with individuals such as Judith Meyers helping develop the CASSP programs when she was a Congressional Fellow.

Out of all of this we see that greater visibility has been given to child, youth, and family issues among psychology, which has paralleled a greater visibility within government, including the establishment of the Select House Committee on Children, Youth, and Families. The broad area of services for children, youth, and families has been legitimized by not only an interest in practice and the delivery of services, but by a body of knowledge that has been developed through research and evaluation unique to service delivery (we now talk of "services research").

But above all, psychology's greatest contribution to improving services for children has lain in its reconceptualization from a child-centered approach, which brought in the family as ancillary, to a broader ecological model of the child's functioning within the total context of family and the family's functioning within the total context of the community. This has been brilliantly elaborated by Urie Bronfenbrenner in his ecological system, which was derived from his experiences with Head Start.

It is clear now that there are certain principles of service delivery to children, especially severely emotionally disturbed children, which psychology has played a major role in developing and facilitating on the basis of this ecological conceptualization. My early work with lower class delinquent youth, the work in North Carolina by Lenore Behar (the Willie M program), and the national study by Jane Knitzer, all psychologists, have fostered certain principles of service delivery. These are:

1. Comprehensiveness. In order to meet the multiple needs in these multiproblem children and families, services across many areas are needed; that is, education, medical, recreational, social, and vocational-all have to be addressed. Even within mental health itself, one needs a comprehensive set of services along a continuum based on least restrictive principles.

2. Multidimensional. The services will include self-help, individual work, group work, family therapy, in a number of different combinations, within a verbal and nonverbal framework.

3. Different settings. The services need to be delivered not only in hospitals and offices, but in courts, streets, homes, clubs, and so on.

4. Different roles. The service deliverer will play the role of advocate, teacher, case manager, therapist, parent, and so on, at different times.

5. There will be multidisciplinary activities. Interactions will be necessary with teachers, social workers, doctors, day care workers, employers, lawyers.

6. All of the service elements need to be interconnected, integrated, organized, and funded in a flexible fashion. Time constraints cannot be present, and ways of collecting statistics will need to be different from the frequency count of the number of people seen in a given period of time.

The big issue is how we train for services based on these principles. That is,

1. What generic training is needed?

2. What are the boundary issues between clinical psychology, school psychology, and applied developmental psychology, all of which are delivering psychological services?

3. What different roles are there, and do they require different kinds of training at different levels?

4. What different models are there? For example, should a multidimensional comprehensive set of services be administered by one individual, or should a person be primarily a facilitator coordinating a multiple number of services?

5. What different standards are there for the different tasks?

6. How do we train for new types of research in service delivery, which is so broad and highly complex?

7. Considering the vast expanse of this model of service delivery, how can we avoid becoming dilettantes who dabble and have merely superficial knowledge of the wealth of information and choices? Indeed, one of the questions is whether there is so much to learn that there is a danger that we may not know anything well.

This is our challenge if we are to deal with the seriously emotionally disturbed child. Are we willing to take the risks?

Chapter 6
Standards for Training Psychologists to Provide Mental Health
Services to Children and Adolescents

June M. Tuma
Department of Psychology
Louisiana State University

Children and adolescents are in need of mental health services. Children are underserved by psychologists and other mental health service providers. Both statements are as true today as they were a decade ago.

Have we made any progress? I should like to address the qustion, What is the current status of training psychologists to provide services to these children and adolescents in need?

Almost a decade ago, we heard that there existed a shortage of fully trained psychologists providing services and that by 1989 we would need approximately 10,000 more psychologists to provide services to children in need (VandenBos et al., 1979). Because of the manpower shortage, many inadequately trained psychologists were placed in service delivery roles for children and youth. Clearly, attention to psychology's ability to train the needed psychologists for this important population in need was and is mandatory. However, there was not much known at that time about training psychologists to work with children. There were no standards for practice or training. Those serving children had to borrow from standards and guidelines that existed for psychologists serving adults.

Being concerned about this state of affairs, Sections 1 and 5 of Division 12 of the American Psychological Association put together training committees to gather information about the status of training in the area. Thus, more than a decade ago, we were trying to put together a training conference to address the need for standards for training clinical child psychologists (Tuma, 1977). The conference seemed crucial because there were no agreed upon guidelines for training. Because of this, existing training programs developed their own training philosophies and requirements.

Availability of Specialty Training

There have always been only a few doctoral programs training clinical child psychologists. Table 1 shows that in 1972, Ross could locate only a few clinical child psychology programs; in 1978 (Fischer) there were 12 and in 1979 (Roberts, 1982) there were 15. After NIMH priorities targeted child mental health training, it was possible to identify 34 (Mannarino & Fischer). However, several years later, about the same number can be located in Clinical Child Psychology Ph.D. Programs (Tuma, 1988).

TABLE 1
Number of Academic Programs in Clinical Child Psychology

Year	Source	Number
1972	Ross	Few
1978	Fisher	12
1979	Roberts	15
1982	Mannarino & Fisher	34*
1988	Tuma	38

*52 informal programs were also identified. Production rates of trained clinical psychologists = 88/year (formal programs) and 93/year (informal programs). From "Crisis in Training Pediatric Psychologists" by J.M. Tuma, 1981, Professional Psycholgogy, 12. Copyright 1981 by the American Psychological Association. Reprinted by permission.

A similar picture emerges with internship and postdoctoral training in clinical child and pediatric psychology. First of all, those programs offering concentrations in working with children are difficult to identify because of the listing procedures of the Association of Psychology Internship Centers (APIC). In 1976, the Society of Pediatric Psychology sponsored the publication of a directory of programs that offered internship and postdoctoral training in that area. Since 1980, the directory has been updated yearly. Table 2 provides some interesting data concerning the number of programs concentrating in clinical child and/or pediatric psychology training. The number of internships rose slightly from 1976 to 1979 and, although not shown in the table, remained stable at about 60 predoctoral internship and about 25 postdoctoral fellowship programs until 1987. In 1987, a great increase in the number of listings, especially at the predoctoral level, occurred (Tuma, 1987). In 1981, I attempted to compare the number of trainees the doctoral and internship levels handled. It is apparent from these tables that more trainees are receiving specialty training at the internship levels than at the doctoral levels.

TABLE 2
Number of Predoctoral Internships, Postdoctoral Internships, and
Postdoctoral Fellowships in Clinical Child and Pediatric Psychology

Year	Source	Predoc Internship	Postdoc Internship	Postdoc Fellowship	Total
1976	PP	-	-	-	63
1980	CCP/PP*	57	14	23	94
1988	CCP/PP	118	20	33	171

PP = Directory of Internship and Postdoctoral Resources in Pediatric Psychology.
CCP/PP = Directory of Internship Programs in Clinical Child and Pediatric Psychology.
*These positions in combination with APIC listings for the same year were calculated to offer 379 positions.
From "Crisis in Training Pediatric Psychologists" by J.M. Tuma, 1981, Professional Psychology, 12.
Copyright 1981 by the American Psychological Association. Reprinted by permission.

The Practice of Psychologist Health Care Providers

A decade ago, we had minimal information about the psychologists who offered services to children and youth. Several things occurred during the past decade that put us in a much more advanced position. First, we have obtained some data concerning what clinical child psychologists do in practice (Tuma, 1983). Survey data of members of Section 1, the Society of Pediatric Psychology, and Division 37 show that psychologists working with children utilize assessment techniques appropriate uniquely for children (e.g., WISC, WISC-R, achievement tests, Stanford-Binet, Kinetic Family Drawing, various objective child rating forms) and intervention techniques (e.g., play therapy, parental counseling, family therapy) geared for humans with immature verbal development and who are dependent upon their parents. Practice data thus support the need for academic training in techniques that are discriminably different from those appropriate for psychologists who work with adults.

Secondly, some data on the training of these clinical child psychologists (Tuma, 1983) have been collected. Table 3 shows that course work and supervision specifically related to clinical child psychology was obtained by respondents at all levels of education to some degree. However, while it is understandable why child training was not obtained at all doctoral programs, at all practicum sites, and that not all clinical child psychology practitioners obtained postdoctoral training, it is not at all understandable why they did not all receive field training to work with children at the internship level of training.

TABLE 3
Clinical Child Psychology Training Received by Surveyed Members
of the Section on Clinical Child Psychology, the Society of
Pediatric Psychology, and the Division of Children, Youth, and Families*

Type of Training	Percentage
Academic program	40%
Child practicum	33
Child internship	27
Child postdoctoral fellowship	22
On-the-job training	54

*Answers to "Where did you receive child training?" Adapted from "Specialty training for psychologist service providers to children?" by J.M. Tuma, 1983, American Psychologist, 38. Copyright 1983 by the American Psychological Association. Adapted by permission.

The survey (Tuma, 1983) also addressed the degree to which clinical child psychology course work was available in the doctoral programs of respondents. Table 4 shows that specialty training programs were attended by 25% of the respondents, 47% of programs offered an optional concentration in child courses, and 29% offered clinical child psychology training combined with another area of psychology.

TABLE 4
Percentage of Respondents Indicating Specialty Training
Received in Doctoral Programs

Category	Percentage
Specialty program	25%
Optional concentration in child courses	47
Clinical child psychology program combined with another area of psychology	29

Adapted from "Specialty training for psychologist service providers to children?" by J.M. Tuma, 1983, American Psychologist, 38. Copyright 1983 by the American Psychological Association. Adapted by permission.

Models of Training

The existing models of training clinical child psychologists have been described more fully by Roberts (1982). Although specialty training in its purest sense was relatively rare, Roberts identified the extremely common model of obtaining clinical child psychology training within a general clinical psychology program and two other models, also not very common (e.g., clinical child psychology offered in combination with either school or developmental psychology). This analysis suggests that the only viable clinical child psychology doctoral training offered throughout the country was a track concentration of training embedded within a general clinical psychology program, with few exceptions.

<u>Training Standards and Guidelines</u>

During the past decade, some exciting developments have occurred that put us today in a much more favorable position when we attempt to address training issues. Several guidelines and recommendations have been formulated by the APA divisions and sections concerned with serving children and youth (see Table 5). Minimal guidelines for training psychologists to serve children, youth, and families were developed by Division 37 (Erickson, Roberts, & Tuma, 1985; see Appendix E of Hilton Head Proceedings). In 1985, a training conference sponsored by Section 1 and held at Hilton Head yielded 17 recommendations for training clinical child psychologists (Tuma, 1985). The Hilton Head Conference developed detailed recommendations for doctoral programs, in particular. Because conference participants felt that internship and postdoctoral and continuing education were not considered in as much detail as was desirable, the Section 1 training committee immediately appointed task forces to produce reports on guidelines for internship training, postdoctoral training, and continuing education. Appendix 1 is the guidelines for internship training; Appendix 2 is the postdoctoral guidelines. The guidelines were sent to participants for study in preparation for this conference (Elbert et al., 1988; Ollendick et al., 1988). The 1988 conference on training helped us to put all of these things together to further the development of guidelines for quality training of psychologists who deliver services to children.

TABLE 5
Sources of Information on Training in Clinical Child Psychology

Year	Source
1983	Division 37 Task Force Report: Guidelines for Training Psychologists to Work with Children, Youth, and Families
1985	Section 1 Hilton Head Conference: Conference on Training Clinical Child Psychologists
1988	Section 1 (Section on Clinical Child Psychology) Task Force Report: Guidelines for Clinical Child Psychology Internship Training
1988	Section 1 (Section on Clinical Child Psychology) Task Force Report: Guidelines for Postdoctoral Training in Clinical Child Psychology
1988	NIMH National Conference on Clinical Training in Psychology

In addition to developments concerning training of clinical child psychologists, other developments have broad impact on all training in psychology and particularly areas in professional psychology. Several other conferences have been held: (1) the 1987 National Conference on Graduate Education in Psychology, (2) the 1986 Conference on Doctoral Education and Training in Professional Schools of Psychology, and (3) the 1987 Conference on Internship Training in Professional Psychology. What these conferences appear to have in common is to be more creative in looking at the options we have for quality training in psychology. All conferences appear to agree that a longer period of training, including another year of internship or postdoctoral fellowship, would be desirable for professional training; they are more accepting of additional specialty areas; and all insist that these changes be incorporated into APA accreditation procedures. Thus, a number of roadblocks to alternative conceptualizations of training have been removed. We have more freedom to choose. This additional freedom, coupled with earlier work accomplished on guidelines for training psychologist health service providers to children, bodes well for significant accomplishments in our endeavor.

References

Elbert, J.C., Abidin, R.R., Finch, A.J., Jr., Sigman, M.D., & Walker, C.E. (1988). Guidelines for clinical child psychology internship training: Section 1 task force report. Journal of Clinical Child Psychology, 17, 280-287.

Erickson, M.T., Roberts, M.C., & Tuma, J.M. (1985). Guidelines for training psychologists to work with children, youth, and families. In J.M. Tuma (Ed.), Proceedings: Conference on the training of clinical child psychologists (pp. 164-167). Baton Rouge, LA: Section on Clinical Child Psychology.

Fischer, C.T. (1978). Graduate programs in clinical child psychology and related fields. Journal of Clinical Child Psychology, 7, 87-88.

Mannarino, A.P., & Fischer, C.T. (1982). Survey of graduate training in clinical child psychology. Journal of Clinical Child Psychology, 11, 22-26.

Ollendick, T., Drotar, D., Friedman, M., & Hodges, K. (1988). Guidelines for postdoctoral training in clinical child psychology. Section 1 task force report. Journal of Clinical Child Psychology, 17, 288-289.

Roberts, M.C. (1982). Clinical child psychology programs: Where and what are they? Journal of Clinical Child Psychology, 11, 13-21.

Ross, A.O. (1972). The clinical child psychologist. In B.B. Wolman (Ed.), Manual of child psychopathology. New York: McGraw-Hill.

Tuma, J.M. (1977). National conference on training clinical child psychologists. Unpublished manuscript.

Tuma, J.M. (1981). Crisis in training pediatric psychologists. Professional Psychology, 12, 516-522.

Tuma, J.M. (1983). Specialty training for psychologist service providers to children? American Psychologist, 38, 340-342.

Tuma, J.M. (Ed.). (1985). Proceedings: Conference on training clinical child psychologists. Baton Rouge, LA: Section on Clinical Child Psychology.

Tuma, J.M. (Ed.). (1987). Directory of internship programs in clinical child and pediatric psychology (7th ed., 1987-1988). Baton Rouge, LA: Author.

Tuma, J.M. (1988). Clinical child psychology Ph.D. programs. Manuscript in preparation.

VandenBos, G.R., Nelson, S., Stapp, J., Olmedo, E., Coates, D., & Batchelor, W. (1979). APA input to NIMH regarding planning for mental health personnel development. Washington D.C.: American Psychological Association.

GUIDELINES FOR CLINICAL CHILD PSYCHOLOGY INTERNSHIP TRAINING

by Jean C. Elbert, Richard R. Abidin, A. J. Finch, Jr., Marian D. Sigman, and C. Eugene Walker

Section 1 (Section on Clinical Child Psychology) of Division 12 (Division of Clinical Psychology) of the American Psychological Association (APA) has long been concerned with the absence of comprehensive standards for training clinical child psychologists. The formation of the Training Committee in 1983 was an effort to gather data from professional clinical psychologists and to develop training guidelines for clinical psychologists who work with children. The culmination of this committee's efforts was the National Conference on Training Clinical Child Psychologists, Hilton Head, South Carolina, May 1985 (Elbert, 1985; Johnson, 1985; Tuma, 1985). Out of this conference, recommendations for training included the three levels of predoctoral graduate training, internship training, and postdoctoral training/ continuing education. The scientist-practitioner model was endorsed for training at all three levels. Conference participants agreed that insufficient attention had been addressed to clinical child psychology training at the internship level; consequently, Section 1 created the Task Force on Internship Training of Clinical Child Psychologists with the goal of expanding the Hilton Head Conference recommendations.

General standards for internship training have been promulgated by the National Register, the Association of Psychology Internship Centers (APIC), the Veteran's Administration (VA), and the American Association of State Psychology Boards. Basic standards for internsip training are the requirements (a) that the internship be directed by a psychologist who is licensed or certified in the state(s) in which he or she is practicing, (b) that a minimal number of interns (i.e., two) is necessary, (c) that

This document is the official report of the Section 1 Task Force on Internship Training, of APA, members of which were the authors.

These guidelines were approved by the Section 1 Executive Committee on January 13, 1988.

We acknowledge the contributions made to the report by the Executive Committee and by Joseph Weaver and Steven Pfeiffer.

Reprinted from the Journal of Clinical Psychology, 17, pp. 280-287. Copyright 1988 by Lawrence Erlbaum Associates, Inc., Publishers. Reprinted by permission.

an appropriate title (i.e., intern, resident, or fellow) be used, and (d) that there be a written brochure describing the expectations and responsibilities involved in the internship program available to the prospective interns prior to selection.

In addition, recommendations from the Hilton Head Conference (Tuma, 1985) had specified that for internships that identified themselves as child-oriented, a minimum of two thirds of the 1-year internship experience should be devoted to child related activities. Subsequent to the Hilton Head Conference, the APIC-sponsored National Conference on Internship Training in Psychology was held in February 1987 in Gainseville, Florida. The recommendation was made for a 2-year internship, and a task force was to be developed to determine the content of the second year (Belar et al., 1987). The following report summarizes the additional recommendations of the Section 1 Task Force on Internsip Training of Clinical Child Psychologists.

Child Assessment Issues

General Goals of Child Assessment Training

It is recognized that clinical populations of children and youth who are available for diagnostic assessment during the internship year necessarily depend on the type of facility, special interests and expertise of the faculty, availability of types and ages of child clients/patients, and frequently, funding contingencies. Therefore, the recommendations for providing minimal training experiences must necessarily be flexible and are to be regarded as guidelines for program development. Supervised clinical experience, as well as didactic training in child-assessment techniques and interpretation, is regarded as basic to internship training in this area. A seminar that includes topics devoted to various aspects of child assessment is recommended (see Appendix).

Case conceptualization. Training in psychological evaluation of children should be viewed in the context of case conceptualization, formulation of hypotheses regarding behavior and diagnoses, and subsequent selection of appropriate assessment methods. The intent is not to train narrow test specialization but rather broad clinical problem-solving approaches.

Diversity of clinical population. A general goal of assessment training is to expose the intern to a broad range of child psychopathology and to types of cognitive and behavioral disorders, varying degrees of behavioral and emotional disturbance (including psychosis), chronic illness, children with sensory, motor, learning, and language handicaps, and abused children. A related goal is for the intern to be exposed to children referred from diverse settings (inpatient and outpatient) and from diverse ethnic and socioeconomic backgrounds. Selection of child assessment cases during internship should build on the intern's previous level of training and experience so that breadth and depth may be emphasized.

Diversity in developmental level. An intern who wishes to pursue specialized training in clinical child psychology should ideally have some minimal experience in assessment with infants, preschool age children, elementary school age children, and middle school age children and adolescents. Although type of setting will necessarily dictate the availability of some age levels of children, the intent is to provide at least minimal exposure to specialized types of assessment that infants and preschool children require. In addition, some interns may wish to develop more depth and specialized skills in the assessment of a particular type of child or developmental level.

In those settings with more restricted populations, it is suggested that use be made of volunteer or clinical faculty in private practice or through affiliations with other institutions/agencies in order to provide a broader range of child assessment experiences for interns.

Competency in general areas of assessment. The area of child assessment has become more specialized, and for populations of exceptional children, there is considerable overlap in the areas assessed by the subspecialties of child psychology (clinical child, pediatric, school, and applied developmental) as well as child neuropsychology and allied disciplines (speech and language pathology, special education, physical and occupational therapy). Although detailed knowledge of and experience with the vast array of children's assessment instruments is not possible in the predoctoral internship year, it is recommended that the intern have a general knowledge of assessment methods specific to clinical child psychology. These would include the following:

1. *Intellectual assessment.* Internship training should ideally prepare the clinical child psychologist for competence in the assessment of intellectual functioning in a broad age range of children. In addition, an intern should have sufficient awareness of the response capabilities of children to know when specialized test instruments are appropriate. This would presume familiarity with measures appropriate for children with visual, hearing, motor, and speech/language impairments.

2. *Other specialized ability assessment.* Although some clinical child interns will choose specialized training in child neuropsychological assessment, all clinical child interns should ideally have some exposure to the specialized

assessment of such areas as perception, memory, language, and motor skills. Observations of or consultation experiences with professionals from other disciplines who assess children (e.g., communication disorders, special education, occupational and physical therapy) is recommended.

3. *Observation and interviewing.* Supervised experience in the use of behavioral observations, parent and child interviewing, and the use of objective rating scales, behavior checklists, and self-report techniques should be available during the internship year.

4. *Personality assessment.* Ideally, the clinical child psychology intern should be familiar with a wide variety of assessment techniques appropriate for children and youth, and should be able to integrate such data into a meaningful diagnostic description of the child.

Use of child assessment in planning for intervention. In the effort to make psychological assessment most relevant to an individual child's needs, training in child assessment should ultimately result in the intern's being able to communicate test results and their interpretation clearly to parents and professionals. This presumes a minimal level of competence in both oral and written communication, as well as in the ability to generate specific goals for intervention that are grounded in the assessed strengths and weaknesses of an individual child.

Treatment and Intervention Issues

General Goals of Child Treatment and Intervention Training

In recommending treatment and intervention guidelines for clinical child psychology internships, it is recognized that each internship program will have various areas of strength and weakness. Those guidelines are designed to be goals for which programs should be striving rather than absolute criteria. The main intent of these recommendations is to ensure that interns in clinical child psychology receive as specialized training in treatment and intervention as is possible to prepare them to deal with a wide variety of child clients/patients. It is the responsibility of the internship program to insure that it is providing as diversified a training experience as is possible. Again it is recognized that the populations available to each facility will vary somewhat as will the types of interventions and treatment competences of the internship faculty. In some cases, additional experience outside of the primary internship site might be utilized to supplement the populations and treatment approaches available within the facility. Both supervised clinical experience and didactic training are recommended, with a minimum of one seminar devoted to child treatment techniques regarded as optimal (see Appendix).

Diversity in developmental level. Treatment and intervention during internship should provide experiences with a wide range of age groups. The internship should not be considered a clinical child internship if it offers training in intervention and treatment with only one developmental level, such as adolescents. Rather, internship programs should strive to provide treatment/intervention experience and supervision with a broad range of developmental levels including preschool, elementary school age, middle school age, as well as high school age children.

Second, interns in clinical child psychology should receive some training and supervision in treatment of adults who present as patients themselves in addition to those adults seen primarily as the parents of children having difficulty.

To achieve this goal, some clinical child internship programs might form cooperative relationships with child development clinics or pediatricians for infant experiences and with VA hospitals or other psychiatric hospitals, mental health clinics, and the like for adult experiences.

Diversity in severity of presenting problems. It is important that interns be provided with training in treatment/intervention with children and adolescents who present with varying levels of severity of clinical problems. It is desirable that interns receive supervised treatment/intervention experience with both inpatient and outpatient populations of children and adolescents. In addition, it is desirable that clinical child psychologists in training receive some exposure to normal functioning children who represent the broad range of individual differences.

Diversity in ethnic origins, socioeconomic status, and intervention setting. It is necessary for all internships to provide treatment/intervention experience and training with patients/clients from diverse ethnic origins and socioeconomic levels. Clinical child psychology internships have the responsibility to help train individuals to meet the service needs of all segments of the population regardless of race, creed, color, or economic status. It will be necessary for internships to have faculty who are especially sensitive to the needs of these patients/clients. It is recognized that internship sites will vary as to the populations whom they serve and that not all sites will serve all populations. However, each site should strive to provide as broad a population base as is possible.

In this regard, each site should provide breadth with regard to treatment settings and systems and provide intervention training and experience with children in the context of both public and private systems.

Diversity in treatment/intervention approaches. Internship programs have the responsibility to provide treatment/intervention training and experiences in a variety of methods and theoretical approaches. The diversity of children's problems requires that the clinical child psychologist be knowledgeable in a wide variety of approaches to treatment/intervention. The clinical child psychology internship program must prepare the future psychologist to recognize which treatment approach seems most appropriate for which client/patient. Strict adherence to narrow theoretical interpretations of problems and proposed interventions/treatments to the exclusion of consideration of alternative approaches should be avoided.

Diversity of supervisors and methods of supervision. Because it is important that the clinical child psychology intern receive as diversified training as possible, interns should have more than one supervisor for intervention/treatment. Supervisors should be carefully chosen to provide superior role models for interns. In addition, it is highly desirable that the clinical child intern gain supervised experience with professionals from such allied mental health disciplines as psychiatry and social work.

Internships should provide a variety of formats for supervision such as videotape review of sessions with the supervisor, live supervision, co-therapy supervision, and so on. Each format of supervision has some unique aspects that can be drawn on to ensure maximum gain in intervention/treatment skills during internship. It is recommended that supervision be developmental in nature with more intense supervision being provided during the early stages of the internship and the interns given more responsibility as they demonstrate and gain skills.

Consultation Issues

Clinical child psychologists are frequently involved with other professionals in order to (a) obtain information about the child and family, (b) provide information requested by a member of a different discipline, and (c) cooperate in collaborative interventions in several areas of the child's life. Interns should have some experience in consultation and collaboration with individuals from a variety of different institutions and disciplines.

Educational Institutions/Teachers

Because the professional psychologist often relies on information from colleagues in schools about a child who is being assessed or treated, the intern should be aware of the kinds of assessments carried out by school psychologists and teachers. Teachers may provide information about the child's functioning in cognitive and social domains that is not available from any other source, and interns should have some experience in obtaining this kind of information.

To provide information requested by schools, interns need to have some familiarity with the kinds of programs offered by the school for children of all age levels. The legal requirements faced by schools and the criteria for placement in different programs are often relevant to choosing how to communicate information to schools. In addition, some awareness of the kinds of problems faced by teachers and the knowledge that teachers are likely to possess is important for the trainee in tailoring communication to be most informative and effective.

Medical Services/Medical Personnel

Information about illnesses, complications of certain medical conditions, and the consequences of medical treatment is often critical for assessment and treatment of children. The trainee must develop some awareness of the knowledge possessed by medical personnel and how to formulate questions most appropriately. Furthermore, an appreciation for the problems that must be referred to medical personnel is necessary for good clinical treatment.

Often, medical personnel from such disciplines as pediatrics, psychiatry, neurology, and nursing refer patients to clinical child psychologists for assessment and treatment. Sophistication about the training and skills of individuals in these fields often is helpful for providing information to them.

Collaboration with medical professionals is frequent in the treatment of children. Some appreciation for the kinds of psychological processes that occur in institutions is important to the professional psychologist. Although all internships may not be able to offer both inpatient and outpatient collaborations, some experience working with medical personnel should be included in all training programs.

Community Agencies/Social Service Personnel

In addition to educational and medical institutions, trainees should have some familiarity with the kinds of information, responsibilities, and requirements that are common to social service agencies.

Community agencies often turn to clinical child psychologists for recommendations regarding family and school placement, as well as for treatment, for the children whose care they manage. Interns should have some experience with the programs offered and the skills possessed by personnel employed by these agencies in order to select appropriate assessment techniques and communication approaches.

Collaborations may involve arranging family, educational, or treatment placements. Frequently, the family may be treated by one individual while the child is treated by another, and these individuals may come from such varied disciplines as social work, nursing, speech therapy, and psychiatry. In some cases, the trainee may need to arrange specific services with a community agency, such as services for mentally retarded or physically handicapped children, Big Brothers, Girl Scouts, or religious groups. The broader the range of agencies contacted, the more comfortable the trainee will be in using community resources.

Legal Agencies/Legal Personnel

Legal agencies may have responsibility for placement decisions that have an impact on the treatments used by clinical psychologists, and trainees need to have some awareness of the implications of judicial decisions. In most situations, the psychologist, rather than the legal agency, is providing information. Trainees need to know about the use of records in courts and the kinds of issues that may be important in judicial proceedings to determine custody, for example, or in child abuse cases.

Ethical/Legal Issues

Clinical child psychology interns should be trained in the ethical responsibilities and professional "etiquette" expected of individuals who are engaged in service delivery to children and their families. There is a wide range of issues having to do with confidentiality for children who are in psychotherapy, the circumstances under which reports regarding children can be made available to various parties, the rights of parents (particularly in cases where a divorce has occurred and a parent does not have legal custody of the child), children's rights, protection of the child (e.g., in cases of child abuse), and similar issues.

In addition, there are numerous areas of professional etiquette, notably the question of who is in charge of a case when professionals from different disciplines are involved in a case, and appropriate use of referral/consultation with other professionals.

Training for interns in these areas can be accomplished by a seminar or series of guest lectures on relevant topics, by ongoing discussion of such issues in relation to each case seen by the intern under supervision, and by assigned readings from such APA sources as the *Ethical Standards for Psychologists, Standards of Professional Practice in Psychology,* as well as other prescribed readings in ethics in psychology.

To complete the process of understanding of the legal and ethical issues related to professionals involved in child care, it is necessary for interns to be exposed to the legal system because it has an impact on the child and the family. All trainees need to have some awareness of the juvenile justice system. Care should be taken to make clear to the clinical child psychology intern the role that the professional plays in this process and the legal responsibilities of practicing clinicians.

These goals can be accomplished by assigning to interns cases that involve forensic issues. In the context of these cases, the intern can read relevant literature, discuss the case with a supervisor, as well as make use of legal consultants on the staff of the internship site. When possible, the intern should be encouraged to spend a day or more observing proceedings in the juvenile court in which expert testimony is involved. Role playing and mock trials can provide interns with valuable experience in place of actual court appearances or serve as preparation for such an appearance. Selected readings on the legal rights of children, the role of the psychologist as a child advocate, divorce/custody issues, principles of expert testimony, and general issues in forensic psychology should be assigned at the appropriate times to facilitate the aforementioned experience.

Prevention

Although the balance of the internship will of necessity be devoted to the development and refinement of skills with clinically referred patients/clients, the well-rounded clinical child psychologist should also have some exposure to techniques and methods of prevention. Such exposure may be provided through pediatric well-child clinics, experience with anticipatory guidance for parents of at-risk infants and children, parent education methods, as well as preschool screening programs.

Research

It has been recommended that internships embody the scientist-practitioner model, and that research is a vital part of this training. Although it is clear that the focus of the internship is on the development and enhancement of the clinical skills of the intern and that the major research training and experience is provided by the universities, there still remains a significant role for research during the internship year. At a minimum, interns should be assisted in becoming intelligent research consumers. This can be accomplished by supervisors' encouraging the intern to critically evaluate articles relevant to treatment cases and to look carefully at the empirical evidence for various assessment and research procedures that may be employed in the course of clinical activity. In so doing, the supervisor should be careful to provide the student with a model of the kind of balance that is needed to function effectively as a clinician.

Interns should also be encouraged to participate in research or scholarly activity during the year. Library research and literature reviews relevant to cases in treatment, together with a case study might be selected for write-up and publication. It is also possible to do single subject design research with patients during the course of treatment. Research projects of a modest nature may be done in which new data are collected or existing data from the files of the internship facility are made available. In addition, interns may be involved in ongoing research by the faculty of the internship facility. These efforts might well result in presentations at professional meetings, as well as publications solely by the intern, or in collaboration with a supervising faculty member. It should be emphasized that research involvement should complement the main mission of the internship, which is the development and refinement of clinical skills. In this regard, it is highly questionable whether the intern should be permitted to pursue doctoral dissertation research during the internship, because this research generally tends to be very demanding and is likely to interfere with clinical training experiences.

Clinical Training Program/Internship-Setting Liaison

Clinical psychology training programs and internship settings share the responsibility for the education and preparation of clinical child psychologists. Each organization has a unique set of context constraints and purposes. Nevertheless, both settings are responsible to the public, the profession, and the intern , and both settings need to function as collaborative partners.

Expectations and Responsibilities of the Internship Setting

The internship setting needs to represent clearly the core clinical experiences to which all interns will be exposed. Although diversity of experience is to be expected and encouraged, all clinical child psychology interns in a given setting should be able to count on a common core of experience and training.

Internship settings should specify the expected and required experiential and knowledge-base background of interns. This specification will allow the interns and the training program to know if the intern is prepared for a given setting. If special knowledge or skills are desired, they too should be specified (e.g., basic knowledge in preschool/infant assessment, group therapy, behavioral medicine). Such information could aid prospective interns in curriculum planning, thus enabling them to ensure that coursework and practica prepare them adequately for the internship of their choice.

Expectations and Responsibilities of the Training Program

Each training program should prepare for review by the internship setting a statement that describes the minimal core of scientific and clinical knowledge that each predoctoral candidate from that program possesses. The director of clinical training should clarify the basic clinical skills that the student has developed and the level of supervision required. In addition to information regarding the areas of psychological knowledge and clinical skills, the director of clinical training should also provide internship settings with an accurate description of the prospective intern's professional development. Among the professional issues that must be commented on are knowledge of and adherence to ethical principles, work habits, and interpersonal relationships. This type of information will allow the internship setting to tailor the training program to individual students and their competencies and will allow for more efficient use of supervision resources.

Liaison Mechanisms

Effective liaisons between universities and internship sites are necessary to match students with appropriate settings and to ensure their success. Specification of the core elements of their training programs by both university training programs and internship settings would contribute to the establishment of effective liaisons. The three most common liaison mechanisms are written reports, phone conferences, and site visits.

Written communication. Written reports should include an exchange of expectations and performance evaluation criteria before the internship begins. It is recommended that regular evaluations be conducted of the intern to ensure that the internship is meeting the students' needs and that interns are aware of their progress. A written report of these evaluations should be sent to the intern's university program director.

In addition to having the internship personnel evaluated the intern, the intern should complete an evaluation of the internship setting. These evaluations should be shared with the director of training of the internship and the student's program director.

Phone conferences. Phone conferences with clinical supervisors and internship directors have been found to be helpful in defining more clearly the needs of the intern and the intern's skill development. Additional phone contact with the intern can provide the student with support and guidance. At least one phone conference should be conducted early on in the internship sequence to insure that lines of communication are open.

Site visits. Site visits are encouraged as a means of sharing information and building working relationships. Although frequently impractical because of the distance involved, site visits should be considered in situations in which either the intern or the internship setting is displeased with the performance of the other.

Summary of Recommendations

1. The internship is a training experience, and the intern's clinical experiences should reflect this.

2. One or more didactic seminars should be part of the clinical child internship program. These should include the topic of child assessment, child intervention/treatment, and professional issues.

3. It is recommended that clinical child psychology internships provide both didactic sessions and supervised clinical experience in child assessment. Training should include assessment experience with a broad clinical population of expectional children, diverse with respect to age, sex, presenting problem, source of referral, ethnic origin, and socioeconomic status.

4. A clinical child psychology intern should be provided with experience leading to the development of basic skills in behavioral observations, intellectual assessment, the assessment of other specialized abilities, and personality assessment. Familiarity with assessment techniques appropriate for the various age levels (infancy through adolescence) as well as the response capabilities/limitations of the child is recommended. Emphasis should be placed on the interpretation and integration of test results, as well as on training competence in oral and written communication of the results to parents and professionals.

5. Both didactic sessions and supervised clinical experience in child treatment/intervention techniques would be expected in a clinical child psychology internship. Training sites should strive to provide intervention experience with a broad range of children, diverse with respect to sex, developmental level, type and severity of presenting problems, ethnic origin, and socioeconomic status.

6. Clinical child psychology interns should be supervised in the use of a variety of intervention methods, should be exposed to multiple supervisors employing varying theoretical orientations to treatment, and should be trained in the selection and application of therapeutic techniques appropriate for an individual child.

7. Supervised training in treatment/intervention with adults who present as patients/clients is recommended, in addition to training in the treatment of the adult as parent or family member of the referred child.

8. Experience and training in consultation is essential in the clinical child psychology internship. Training in consultation with teachers and school personnel, physicians and medical personnel, community and social agencies, and legal/judicial agencies is recommended during the internship.

9. Clinical child psychology interns should receive training in the ethical and legal responsibilities of professionals involved in clinical service delivery. Training or experience with the juvenile court system, child advocacy, and divorce/custody issues is recommended.

10. The primary focus of the internship is on the development and refinement of clinical skills. However, in keeping with the scientist-practitioner model of training, we recommend that research experience be provided during the internship, either by modest data collection or literature reviews relevant to ongoing clinical experience.

11. Exposure to normal children with a range of individual differences and responses to stress, as well as to training and experience in methods of prevention (including anticipatory guidance, parent education, and preschool screening), is highly desirable during the internship year.

12. It is recommended that improved liaison mechanisms between graduate programs and internship sites be formed to improve the collaborative effort toward training clinical child psychologists. Clear communication from the internship site regarding expectations for preinternship preparation, realistic appraisal from the graduate program of the trainee's level of knowledge, clinical skills, and professional development, and regular evaluation of the intern's progress are recommended.

References

Belar, C. D., Bieliauskas, L. A., Larsen, K. G., Mensch, I. N., Poey, K., & Roehlke, H. J. (Eds.). (1987). *Proceedings: National Conference on Internship Training in Psychology.* Washington, DC: Association of Psychology Internship Centers.

Elbert, J. C. (1985). Current trends and future needs in the training of child diagnostic assessment. In J. M. Tuma (Ed.), *Proceedings: Conference on Training Clinical Child Psychology* (pp. 82-87). Washington, DC: Section on Clinical Child Psychology.

Johnson, J. H. (1985). Providing clinical training experiences in child treatment: Recommendations for the clinical child psychology specialty curriculum. In J. M. Tuma (Ed.), *Proceedings: Conference on Training Clinical Child Psychologists* (pp. 88-90). Washington, DC: Section on Clinical Child Psychology.

Tuma, J. M. (Ed.). (1985). *Proceedings; Conference on Training Clinical Child Psychologists.* Washington, DC: Section on Clinical Child Psychology.

Appendix

In preparation for the Hilton Head Conference (Tuma, 1985), a survey of training attitudes was conducted by the Section 1 Training Committee. Section 1 membership and professionals known to be actively involved in clinical child psychology training were surveyed regarding their views of what should be required training at the internship level (Elbert, 1985; Johnson, 1985). Respondents to this survey reported mean percentages of 31%, 43%, and 23% as the proportion of an intern's time that should be devoted to child assessment, child treatment/intervention, and consultation experiences, respectively. Responses from the sample surveyed (N=69) summarize opinions relative to required child assessment and treatment/intervention experiences (Table 3).

More than half of all respondents agreed that clinical assessment experiences in all of the areas listed should be required of clinical child psychology interns, with developmental assessment, child intellectual assessment, child behavioral assessment, and parent/child interviewing given primary endorsement (by at least 75% of the sample). Didactic seminar training in several areas of child assessment was likewise viewed as favorable. From such data, a seminar devoted to various aspects of child assessment would therefore appear to be indicated.

Data in Table 4 help to demonstrate the wide range of treatment and intervention activities engaged in by clinical child psychologists and represent how these approaches were felt to be taught best by clinical child psychologists during internship. With regard to seminars, there would seem to be indications that one or two seminars on child treatment and intervention may be needed during internship. One would be a general child treatment seminar including lectures and case management presentations/discussions by faculty and trainees. The second seminar might be designed to provide exposure to new and innovative approaches as they develop in the field (e.g., family therapy, cognitive behavior therapy, etc.).

Table 3.   *Internship Training in Child Assessment*

Child Assessment Topic Area	Percentage of Respondents		
	Separate Seminar	Seminar Topic	Clinical Experience
Developmental Assessment	20.0	21.5	75.4
Child Intellectual Assessment	20.0	21.5	84.6
Achievement Testing	1.5	35.4	60.0
Visual-Motor Assessment	1.5	35.4	60.0
Child Personality Assessment	15.4	23.1	67.7
Child Neuropsychological Assessment	10.8	30.8	55.4
Child Behavioral Assessment	7.7	36.9	75.4
Parent/Child Interviewing	7.7	27.7	83.1
Assessment of Handicapped Child	7.7	33.8	66.2

Table 4.   *Internship Training in Child Intervention and Treatment*

Child Assessment Topic Area	Percentage of Respondents		
	Separate Seminar	Seminar Topic	Clinical Experience
Methods of Child Treatment	44.6	29.2	43.1
Play Therapy	6.2	40.2	63.1
Child Behavior Therapy	13.8	36.9	72.3
Adolescent Psychotherapy	7.7	40.0	66.2
Pharmacological Treatment	10.8	67.7	29.2
Treatment of the Physically Ill	10.8	58.5	44.6
Family Therapy	30.8	33.8	66.2
Parent Training	12.3	41.5	63.1
Residential Treatment	1.5	44.6	52.3
School Intervention	4.6	40.0	56.9

GUIDELINES FOR POSTDOCTORAL TRAINING IN CLINICAL CHILD PSYCHOLOGY

by Thomas Ollendick, Dennis Drotar, Margaret Friedman, and Kay Hodges

Section 1 (Section of Clinical Child Psychology) of Division 12 (Division of Clinical Psychology) of the American Psychological Association (APA) has long been concerned about the absence of clear guidelines for training clinical child psychologists at the predoctoral, internship, and postdoctoral level. In response to this concern, the National Training Committee, consisting of Jean Elbert, James H. Johnson, Annette La Greca, Thomas H. Ollendick, Carolyn Schroeder, and June M. Tuma (chair) was appointed in 1983 by the person who was then president of Section 1, Diane Willis, to determine the feasibility of sponsoring a national training conference to examine these issues in more depth. This conference was held in 1985 at Hilton Head, South Carolina.

Many issues were raised at the conference and, as a result, task forces were established to prepare specific internship training guidelines at the predoctoral and postdoctoral level. The current guidelines address issues at the postdoctoral level; they are intended to be consistent with the recommendations of the National Training Conference (see Tuma, 1985).

To obtain data about current practices, a survey of existing postdoctoral training programs (N = 40) was undertaken. Results of this survey, conducted during the 1986-1987 year by the Task Force on Postdoctoral Training in Clinical Child Psychology, revealed much diversity in current orientations, required experiences, and practices. To wit, approximately 40% of the sites indicated that they were behavioral or cognitive-behavioral in orientation, whereas 24% espoused a psychodynamic allegiance. The remainder of the programs endorsed an eclectic point of view, with family systems and cognitive-developmental perspectives being represented minimally. Further, the amount of time spent in the delivery of direct clinical services ranged from 15% to 80%, with an average of 40%. Conversely, the amount of time spent in direct research activities ranged from 0% to 50%, with an average of 13%. The remainder of the time was spent, on the average, in attending didactic seminars (10%), providing consultative services (15%), receiving supervision (13%), providing supervision (3%), and other (6%). Finally, the postdoctoral training settings varied considerably in their goals (e.g., from highly specialized training with very specific populations to more generic training with "children and families").

Early on, the task force recognized the many faces of training in clinical child psychology and the different needs and goals for which these programs were developed. Further, several of the respondents indicated that they felt that postdoctoral training should continue to meet these diverse needs and goals. That is, they recommended that highly rigid guidelines not be developed and that the intrinsic value as well as the continued vitality of postdoctoral training resided clearly in the realm of specialty training. Thus, unlike training at the predoctoral internship level, in postdoctoral programs specialty training was deemed to be highly desirable. Such a conclusion was not inconsistent with the APA's notion of postdoctoral training as organized, supervised study beyond the doctoral level in a specialty area.

Postdoctoral training, as described herein, is designed to provide clinical training to produce an advanced level of competence in clinical child psychology. It is recognized that, consistent with the directives of the National Training Conference, postdoctoral training should embrace the scientist-practitioner model of training. Therefore, we have viewed clinical child psychology as a scientifically based discipline that is continually evolving as new findings emerge. Further, we have endorsed a research component to training. Thus, the current guidelines are concerned with postdoctoral training that is specifically geared toward producing professionals who are adept at both clinical practice and research. The guidelines do not specifically address research training in clinical child psychology, however.

Entry Criteria

Entry into a clinical child psychology postdoctoral training program should be based on completion of a regionally accredited doctoral program in psychology (clinical, counseling, or school) or completion of a "respecialization" program in one of these areas of study. In all cases, admission into postdoctoral training in clinical child psychology should be based on demonstration of training and *experience* commensurate with the scientist-practitioner model of training. An APA-approved predoctoral internship must also have been completed prior to candidacy.

This document is the official report of the Section 1 Task Force on Postdoctoral training, members of which were the authors.

These guidelines were approved by the Section 1 Executive Committee on January 13, 1988.

Reprinted from the Journal of Clinical Child Psychology, 17, pp. 288-289. Copyright 1988 by Lawrence Erlbaum Associates, Inc., Publishers. Reprinted by permission.

General Considerations

All individuals receiving postdoctoral training should be called "fellows" in order to differentiate them from predoctoral interns or residents and to acknowledge their advanced status. In general, postdoctoral training in clinical child psychology should occur in an organized program that is institutionally recognized. Basic standards for postdoctoral training include (a) that the postdoctoral training program be directed by a psychologist who is licensed or certified in the state(s) in which he or she is practicing and who has specialty training in clinical child psychology, (b) that a minimal number of postdoctoral fellows (at least two) be involved in the training program, and (c) that there be a written brochure describing the expectations and responsibilities of the training program. Moreover, the program should specify the amount and nature of the supervision provided. Although guidelines regarding the size and diversity of the training faculty are difficult to specify, a goal of all postdoctoral training programs should be to expose the postdoctoral fellow to multiple supervisors from diverse backgrounds, including, but not limited to, psychology, psychiatry, and pediatrics. Further, although it is desirable to expose the fellow as much as possible to diverse client populations, service settings, and psychological practices, it is recognized that such may not be possible in all postdoctoral training programs.

In most cases, the postdoctoral training program should extend over a 2-year period. The only exceptions would be for individuals who have completed a predoctoral internship in clinical child psychology or who have completed a predoctoral graduate training program with a specialization in clinical child psychology. If prior specialization has occurred at either of these levels, the postdoctoral program may be completed in 1 year. In all cases, however, the individual must meet the exit criteria (see later). As a general guideline, the postdoctoral training program should provide approximately 50% time in clinical service delivery (to include both consultative and preventive activities), approximately 25% time in clinical research, and approximately 25% time in supervision (direct supervision, co-therapy, collaborative clinical or research work with supervisors). Variance within these guidelines should be tailored to the needs of the individual.

Specific Considerations

Postdoctoral training should be provided in both a didactic and experiential format, and should address the following areas: (a) developmental theory and, in particular, developmental psychopathology; (b) interview, diagnostic, and assessment practice; (c) methods of intervention specific to clinical child psychology; (d) consultation to auxiliary services and settings; (e) principles and practices of prevention; (f) ethical and legal principles as they relate to the practice of clinical child psychology; and (g) research methods specific to the populations, problems, and settings served.

In all cases, it should be recognized that such didactic and experiential training may be achieved in several ways including, but not limited to, lectures, seminars, workshops, readings, direct clinical practices, and research presentations and publications. In no case should rigid guidelines be applied, other than to ensure that these substantive areas be addressed.

Exit Criteria

At the conclusion of the postdoctoral training program, the individual should be able to undertake the practice of clinical child psychology on an independent basis. Evidence of such mastery should include an awareness of (a) the diversity and complexity of developmental psychopathology, (b) psychometrically sound assessment instruments, (c) empirically based intervention practices, and (d) sound consultation strategies and prevention practices. Finally, the fellow should (e) embody the scientist-practitioner model of training and (f) be cognizant of sound professional and ethical practices. Overall, the program should be designed to produce competent practitioners of clinical child psychology. Moreover, it should be designed to produce individuals who would qualify for certification by the American Board of Professional Psychology, with clinical child being the area of specialization.

Reference

Tuma, J. M. (Ed.). (1985). *Proceedings: Conference on Training Clinical Child Psychologists*. Washington, DC: Section on Clinical Child Psychology.

Chapter 7
Assessing Competencies for Delivering Services to Seriously Emotionally Disturbed Children: The First Step in the Process

Georgine Pion, Vanderbilt University
Lee Sechrest, University of Arizona

The 1980s have been a time of increased federal concern over the mental health problems of severely emotionally disturbed (SED) children and adolescents and the lack of appropriate services for this population. For example, special studies (e.g., U.S. Office of Technology Assessment, 1986) have been commissioned to examine the problem, and monies have been targeted for developing more comprehensive and coordinated service delivery systems capable of addressing the multiple needs of these individuals (e.g., Child and Adolescent Service System Program).

Given that "we currently know more about how to prevent and treat children's mental health problems than is reflected in the care available" (U.S. Office of Technology Assessment, 1986), attention also has been directed at the pool of actual care-providers themselves--both in terms of supply and quality. At present, available data suggest that there may be insufficient numbers of well-trained professionals to meet current and future demands for services. As a result, the mental health professions have been urged to include as one of their major training priorities the development of practitioners who can provide services to SED children and adolescents.

Improving Psychology's Capacity to Provide Trained Personnel

What does this mean for psychology? What must we do to respond most effectively to this important national need? To answer these questions well, we first need to know much more about supply-and-demand issues. On the demand side, information is needed on the total number of qualified psychologists currently working with this population and, within this total, the numbers providing services to various client subpopulations as defined by diagnosis, age, sex, ethnic or minority status, and geographic distribution. We then need to know how many psychologists are needed to work with SED children and adolescents now and over the course of the next 10-20 years. Answers to these questions would then allow us to determine the magnitude of any discrepancies between demand and supply.

Unfortunately, there are no definitive answers to any of these questions at the present time. Epidemiological estimates that address the current need for mental health services for children and adolescents on a national level vary widely, depending on the definitions used and the sources of the data. Moreover, we do not even have a clear idea of the current supply of psychological personnel providing services to this population in terms of numbers, qualifications, and other characteristics. The prevailing view, however, is that the pool is reasonably small. For example, it has been reported that only about 1% of all psychologists treat primarily children (Children's Defense Fund, 1985), and previous APA survey data suggest that even when children are part of psychologists' caseloads, the majority of problems handled are not those associated with serious mental disorders.

Assuming there is a sufficient supply of qualified professionals to work with this population, psychology needs to consider training more psychologists. The question then becomes "How should we do this?" Once again, we need more information to answer this question. For example, we need to know which types of training (e.g., specific coursework or practica) produce qualified practitioners, how many graduate programs actually incorporate these training components, and how "productive" these programs are in supplying individuals who successfully work with SED children and adolescents. Armed with this type of information, the psychology training system would be better equipped to modify existing programs and launch new training initiatives aimed at improving practitioner competencies.

Unfortunately, we do not know the answers to these questions either. In fact, no systematic data exist: about the training process as a whole for programs that train students for practice (American Psychological

Association, Task Force on the Evaluation of Education, Training, and Service, 1982); about what is actually happening in programs designed to train students for services delivery (e.g., number of minutes per case per week of individual supervision or hours of experience with children under the age of ten); about what practitioners do (e.g., data on what services are provided to which patients); about the specific skills and competencies that are required for competent practice; and about how these skills are most successfully instilled (e.g., through coursework, preinternship practica, predoctoral internship, and/or postdoctoral training). All that is available to us at present are the findings of isolated, episodic, and often haphazard surveys; individual case-studies; personal anecdotes; and individual experience. Although informative, this type of material is insufficient to successfully mount broad-scale training initiatives.

The major point of this paper is that we must begin to answer these questions -- at least those that pertain to the supply of well-trained psychologists -- in terms of the SED child and adolescent population. We need to know how we can best train psychologists to work with these clients so that successful strategies can be disseminated to and adopted by graduate programs.

A reasonable first step in this process is to identify the skills and competencies needed to deliver services to this population and then to work toward developing measures that can evaluate these skills and competencies. Once developed, adequately tested, and refined, these measures can then be used by training programs themselves to evaluate students and ultimately to compare specific training strategies and components. Over time, the end result will be a body of knowledge about how to effectively train psychologists to provide services to SED children and adolescents.

Identifying Skills and Competencies Needed to Deliver Services

To understand what type of training is needed to produce competent professionals to deal with the SED population first requires a knowledge of the services needed by this group and the resulting skills and competencies necessary to effectively deliver these services. The research to date, although limited, does lend some insight into these questions. For example, certain specific treatment strategies have been shown to be effective for certain disorders (e.g., behavioral and family therapies). It appears that successful interventions may share some common characteristics such as parental involvement in treatment as much as possible, the use of multiple interventions, including behavioral therapy and skills building, and case management and advocacy (Knitzer, 1984; U.S. Office of Technology Assessment, 1986).

Further, we do know something about the skills and competencies required to deliver mental health services to children and adolescents. The various sets of guidelines for training in clinical child psychology (e.g., Drotar et al., 1988; Elbert et al., 1988; Tuma, 1985) have all identified broad, generic skill areas such as developmental theory and psychopathology, assessment procedures, and consultation. Cochrane and McPheeters (1987) have developed a quite specific list of informational, intellectual, interpersonal, intrapersonal, and interventional competencies necessary for any staff member (e.g., psychologists and social workers) who delivers services to emotionally disturbed children and adolescents. In addition, requisite competencies for all professionals who provide mental health services to children and for those who deal with special subgroups (e.g., juvenile justice youth) are discussed in several papers in this volume.

These individual efforts need to be integrated into a comprehensive set of competencies necessary for delivering mental health services to the SED population -- a list that can eventually be used as the basis for developing measures to assess competence. To do this requires incorporation of the following strategies:

Include skills and competencies needed for mental health services delivery in general, for providing services to children and adolescents, and for working with SED children and adolescents. Undoubtedly, competence in a wide range of knowledge and skill domains is a prerequisite for functioning as an effective mental health services provider. Further, as the guidelines for clinical child psychology training have stated, certain competencies may be required to provide services to children and adolescents (e.g., the use of specific types of assessment strategies and special ethical principles). However, we also need to know whether any subset of knowledge or skills is required to work with seriously emotionally disturbed children and adolescents, given the types of problems characteristic of this population (e.g., autism, multiple handicaps, and sexual abuse). Knowing whether there are unique skill configurations needed for dealing with SED clients has important implications for how graduate training programs should be structured.

Incorporate the major competency domains that influence quality of care, including knowledge, attitudes, and skills. Adequate coverage of three broad content areas has been shown to be important in enumerating essential clinical competencies: (1) knowledge; (2) personal qualities, values, and attitudes; and (3) fundamental skills. There are several relevant examples that may be illustrative of the competencies needed for mental health services delivery to SED clients. For example, knowledge of the indications and contraindications for particular drugs, along with their side effects, appears important, given that pharmacotherapy is often used to treat children who are severely disturbed. Skills in appropriate assessment techniques for children also are necessary. Certain attitudes held by practitioners (e.g., an overconfidence in one's ability to predict "dangerousness") may work against effectively delivering services to this population.

Focus on skills and competencies that are "trainable." Graduate training programs operate on the crucial assumption that they can instill certain types of competencies in their students. These competencies, however, are those that have their basis in possessing a specific body of knowledge, in acquiring proficiency in particular types of therapeutic modalities, and in adopting a set of core attitudes and values.

There also may be certain personality characteristics that are helpful in working with clients and SED children and adolescents in particular. Although it would be helpful to know what these are, however, training programs could do little about these save at the time of selecting students (assuming that the existence of these characteristics in individuals can be accurately identified in the admissions process). Thus, any set of competencies must focus on trainable characteristics in order to be most useful to training programs.

Address the fact that several types of mental health professionals deliver services to SED children and adolescents. A variety of providers work with SED children and clients, and presumably certain core competencies are necessary for each discipline and for each level of training. For example, one would suppose that all professionals should have an understanding of developmental psychopathology and a knowledge of the symptoms indicative of drug side effects. At the same time, however, other competencies may stem from the particular roles that are appropriate for the different disciplines, based on the type and level of training. So, for example, in the case of psychology, it may be appropriate for individuals trained at the master's level to be especially proficient at skills building techniques; doctorally prepared psychologists, on the other hand, may play especially important roles in patient assessment, treatment planning, staff supervision and training, and program evaluation. Such differences need to be identified so that master's and doctoral psychology programs incorporate the key instructional and experiential components in their curricula, so that graduates are not working roles that extend beyond their limits of competence, and so that underutilization of highly specialized advanced training does not occur.

Use both detailed task analysis and expert validation in the development of the final list of competencies. A tentative list of competencies can be developed, using the results of past efforts to identify skills, findings from relevant treatment effectiveness research, and guidelines and standards for training previously developed by national conferences and "blue-ribbon" panels. However, we need to go two steps further. The first step involves collecting data on what psychologists are actually doing in terms of providing services to SED children and adolescents, their assessments about whether these service delivery activities are indeed appropriate, their views concerning possible activities they should be doing but are not for a variety of reasons, and their judgments as to the adequacy of their own training for preparing them to carry out these responsibilities. (See Schippmann et al., 1988, and Rosenfeld et al., 1984, for examples of previous efforts to identify generic clinical competencies.) Only then can we get a firm grasp on the types of competencies needed to deliver appropriate psychological service to the SED population.

Further, expert validation is needed to develop a final list of competencies -- one that can then be used to identify the domains for which assessment measures should be developed. In identifying a group of experts for this validation process, care must be given to obtaining a broad range of expertise -- in training professionals who work with SED children and adolescents, in conducting relevant research on child and adolescent disorders and effective treatment strategies, and in actually working with this client population. This validation process should be systematic and solicit judgments as to unique competencies, the types of professionals that should be proficient in these areas (e.g., psychologists or psychiatrists), and the levels of training that are required (e.g., master's vs. doctoral vs. postdoctoral).

Only in this way can the stage be adequately set for developing measures that can assess service delivery competencies needed to treat SED children and adolescents and for ultimately understanding how to best prepare psychologists to work with this population. During this process, a significant amount of additional information will be uncovered -- data that will allow us to better understand the roles and contributions of psychologists in addressing this unmet mental health need, the relationship of psychologists to other service providers, and the areas training programs should attend to in preparing qualified service deliverers. With this information, such specialties as clinical child psychology, pediatric psychology, and school psychology will have a head start in ensuring that their training programs are functioning well, and the discipline as a whole will have a better notion of what at least some psychologists do and how their training has prepared them for these careers.

References

American Psychological Association, Task Force on the Evaluation of Education, Training, and Service. (1982). Summary report. Washington, DC: Author.

Children's Defense Fund. (1985). A children's defense budget. Washington, DC: Author.

Cochrane, J.L.J., & McPheeters, H.L. (1987). Improving performance of staff who serve emotionally disturbed children and adolescents. Atlanta, GA: Southern Regional Educational Board.

Drotar, D., Friedman, M., Hodges, K., & Ollendick, T. (1988). Guidelines for postdoctoral training in clinical child psychology. Unpublished manuscript, Division of Clinical Psychology, Section 1, American Psychological Association.

Elbert, J.C., Abidin, R.R., Finch, A.J., Sigman, M.D., & Walker, C.E. (1988). Guidelines for clinical child psychology internship training. Unpublished manuscript, Division of Clinical Psychology, Section 1, American Psychological Association.

Knitzer, J. (1984). Mental health services to children and adolescents: A national view of public policies. American Psychologist, 39, 905-911.

Rosenfeld, M., Shimberg, B., & Thornton, R.F. (1984). Job analysis of licensed psychologists in the United States and Canada. Princeton, NJ: Educational Testing Service.

Schippmann, J.S., Smalley, M.D., Vinchur, A.J., & Prien, E.P. (1988). Using structured multidomain job analysis to develop training and evaluation specifications for clinical psychologists. Professional Psychology, 19, 141-147.

Tuma, J. (Ed.). (1985). Proceedings of the conference on training clinical child psychologists. Baton Rouge, LA: Land and Land Printers.

U.S. Office of Technology Assessment. (1986). Children's mental health: Problems and services -- A background paper (OTA-BP-H-33). Washington, DC: U.S. Government Printing Office.

SECTION IV

CLINICAL RESEARCH FOUNDATIONS OF TRAINING IN CLINICAL CHILD PSYCHOLOGY

Chapter 8
Standards for Training Clinical Child Psychologists in University Doctoral Programs

Marilyn T. Erickson
Virginia Commonwealth University

Achieving our goal of increasing the number of well-trained psychologists who are capable of delivering clinical services to children with severe mental disorders depends on at least four factors: (1) translation of relevant knowledge into the curriculum, (2) the faculty entrusted to transmit that knowledge, (3) the characteristics and motivations of the students expected to assimilate that knowledge and its clinical application, and (4) society's needs.

Let me say a few words about each of these factors in reverse order. First, society's needs have been well known for some time (National Institute of Mental Health, 1983), but there remains a significant discrepancy between society's needs for clinical child psychologists and both society's and the clinical programs' willingness to produce them. Even though many of the available psychology positions call for child/adolescent/family services, the clinical training programs have not been optimally responsive to these social needs. About half of the current APA-accredited doctoral programs have no requirements that involve children. Although APA accreditation criteria presume at least an introduction to life-span clinical psychology, many programs continue to produce clinicians with virtually no didactic training in child psychology. More than a few of these psychologists have taken positions in which they deliver or supervise clinical services to children. This situation needs to be identified by APA accreditation teams and remedied by the training programs!

In summary, it seems clear that there is currently a social need for clinical psychologists who have been trained to deliver services to children and adolescents. It is also clear that both the APA accreditation process and the clinical programs themselves are not attending to this social need.

Second, the students who wish to become clinical child psychologists continue to be extremely well qualified. More than ever, our graduate students have multicultural backgrounds, and more attention to their special needs as well as to the special needs of the clients that many of them wish to serve needs to be given in our training programs.

We faculty members need to be more responsive to the motivation of our students to become service deliverers. Some programs are clearly negative about their students' wishes to become service deliverers and reward only the scientific aspects of students' activities. Students in some programs are still being led to believe that becoming a clinician is a second-rate choice. Our role models for the scientist-practitioner to be less than optimal. Not very many faculty members are viewed by themselves or by their students as competent researchers, competent teachers, _and_ competent clinicians.

Given that most entering students are strongly motivated in the service delivery direction, training programs might be advised to introduce them to the full breadth of behavior disorders during their predoctoral years so that they may discover their personal areas of interest. If a student is not exposed to a particular type of psychopathology or developmental disability, there is little likelihood that a long-standing interest can develop. Sometimes, a little exposure can go a long way. Some years back, we invited a deaf master's level psychologist to present at a staffing. One of my first-year students became interested enough in the deaf to add signing courses to her already heavy curriculum; we tailored several practicum and research activities to her interest area, and today she is a staff member at Gallaudet's Counseling Center.

The third factor, faculty, seems to be improving gradually. Some departments have added more clinical child faculty to their programs. However, there are still many clinical programs that maintain a single "token" child-oriented faculty member. These single representatives (often female) have tremendous responsibilities placed on them, and turnover appears to be high. In my opinion, a clinical program cannot maintain a viable track in clinical child psychology with only a single faculty member. The minimum number must be two or three in order to cover the necessary didactic, practicum, and research breadth (Erickson, 1985).

I believe that we currently have the resources to train the future academic child clinicians. Historically, training people to be like ourselves has been psychology's traditional training approach in academics. Unfortunately, there seem to be a substantial number of excellent students and young faculty members with genuine interest in teaching and research who have become "turned off" to academic careers. Some of their problems appear to be related to an uncaring and exploitive faculty attitude as well as to enormous pressures being placed on younger faculty members to secure grant funding. The academic life style is no longer as psychologically attractive as it used to be, and it certainly has been losing out to private practice when economic factors (time devoted to career and salary) are considered.

The fourth factor, curriculum, is one that requires considerable attention (Roberts, Erickson, & Tuma, 1985). Because professional psychology training programs already have many requirements, specialty training can be given relatively little attention at the predoctoral level. However, predoctoral didactic courses and practicum experience can introduce students to the material they will have to know in order to provide services to children and families. Internships and postdoctoral programs must then be designed to expand upon predoctoral programs' offerings.

My recommendations are that this conference accept the APA criteria that define psychology doctoral training programs, the Hilton Head Conference (Tuma, 1985) recommendation that predoctoral training remain in the context of general clinical psychology training programs, and the Utah Conference (1987) recommendation that professional doctoral training programs reaffirm the Boulder scientist-practitioner model.

I would like to present a sample curriculum to demonstrate how such training might be provided (Table 1). Courses with one star reflect general psychology content areas, including Statistics and Research Design, Learning, Biological, Social, History, and Ethics. Courses with two stars might be described as generic (or adult) clinical psychology; they include Introduction to Clinical Psychology, Assessment of Intelligence, Interviewing, Adult Psychopathology, Introduction to Therapy and Counseling, Assessment of Personality, Personality Theory, and Multicultural Issues.

Courses with three stars focus on children and adolescents and are therefore of particular interest to this Conference. Didactic topics include Child and Adolescent Assessment, Psychopathology, and Child, Family, and Community (including School) interventions. Within this curriculum, students would have both adult and child practicum activities with at least a full year of supervised practicum with children and adolescents, and families. About half of this curriculum is concerned with didactics, practicum, or research with children, adolescents, and families.

I would advise this conference to support a three-tiered training model such as this one at the predoctoral level and to recommend training grant support for one or two years at the predoctoral level for advanced students who are completing a curriculum that focuses on children and youth and who will work in agencies serving children one year for each year that support is given.

TABLE 1
A Sample Curriculum That Provides Basic
Training in Clinical Child Psychology

FALL	SPRING	SUMMER
YEAR 1		
* Statistics/Design	*Statistics/Design	
** Intro Clinical	** Assessment/Interviewing	
** Assessment/Intelligence	*** Assessment/Child & Adolescent	*Learning/Cognition
** Adult Psychopathology	*** Child Psychopathology	
	*Ethics	
YEAR 2		
** Intro Therapy & Counseling Adults	** Assessment/Personality Adult	
*** Child Intervention	** Personality Theory	* Biological
*** Practicum	*** Practicum	*** Practicum
*** Thesis	*** Thesis	*** Thesis
YEAR 3		
*** Child/Family Intervention	** Multicultural Issues	
* Social Psychology	* History of Psychology	
*** Life Span Development	*** Life Span Development	
*** Practicum	*** Practicum	*** Practicum
YEAR 4		
*** Child/Family/Community Intervention	Elective	
*** Practicum/Elective	*** Practicum/Elective	
*** Dissertation	*** Dissertation	

* General Psychology content areas
** Generic (or adult) clinical content areas
*** Child track content area

References

National Institute of Mental Health. (1983). Announcement: Mental health clinical training in child mental health, geriatric mental health, and support for minority and disadvantage students for the fiscal year 1983. Washington, DC: Author.

Roberts, M., Erickson, M.T., & Tuma, J. (1985). Addressing the needs: Guidelines for training psychologists to work with children, youth, and families. Journal of Clinical Child Psychology, 14, 70-79.

Erickson, M.T. (1985, May). Clinical child psychology training in the context of a general clinical psychology program. Proceedings: Conference on Training Clinical Child Psychologists, Hilton Head Island, SC. Baton Rouge, LA: Land and Land, Printers.

Tuma, J. (Ed.). (1985, May). Proceedings: Conference on Training Clinical Child Psychologists. Hilton Head Island, SC. Baton Rouge, LA: Land and Land, Printers.

Chapter 9
Developmental Psychopathology as a Conceptual Framework for Training in Multiple Settings

Thomas M. Achenbach
Department of Psychiatry, University of Vermont

The term "developmental psychopathology" highlights the value of viewing psychopathology in relation to the major changes that typically occur across the life cycle. It does not dictate any particular theoretical explanation for the nature of particular disorders, their causes, or their outcomes. Instead, it suggests a conceptual framework for organizing the study of psychopathology around milestones and sequences in areas such as physical, cognitive, social-emotional, and educational development. Its heuristic value is analogous to that of terms such as "learning," "cognition," "genetic," and "biological." The utility of such terms does not stem from definitions of a field, but from their potential for stimulating awareness of connections among phenomena that otherwise seem haphazard and unrelated.

Developmental Psychopathology as a Macroparadigm

To capitalize on developmental psychopathology's potential for expanding rather than restricting our thinking, it is better viewed as a guide to important problems and relationships than as a source of ready-made answers. Accordingly, it can be thought of as a "macroparadigm" to distinguish it from paradigms and theories pertaining to more limited sets of variables, methods, or explanations. Figure 1 illustrates relations between developmental psychopathology viewed in this way and several more specific paradigms and theories relevant to development and psychopathology. The biomedical, behavioral, psychodynamic, and other paradigms are designated as "microparadigms" only in the sense of dealing with one facet of phenomena whose linkages are not apt to be adequately dealt with by any one of them alone. Most of them cover large domains, but each can be viewed as a subset of methods, constructs, and theories that may contribute to the developmental study of psychopathology.

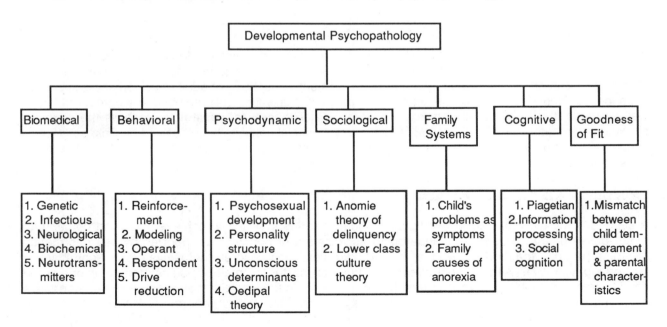

Figure I
Schematic overview of Developmental Psychopathology as a
macroparadigm in relation to other conceptual levels.
Copyright 1990 by T.M. Achenbach. Reprinted by permission.

The location of the developmental psychopathology box above the others in Figure 1 does not mean that they are subordinate to developmental psychopathology. On the contrary, each microparadigm and theory has a life of its own, apart from its relation to the macroparadigm of developmental psychopathology. In fact, several of the microparadigms would serve as a macroparadigm in other hierarchical schemes. For purposes of studying psychopathology in relation to development, however, it is helpful to organize the many potentially relevant paradigms and theories around a central conceptual structure. This structure should provide a framework for integrating diverse ideas and findings that would otherwise appear unrelated. By highlighting interconnections and providing an overarching conceptual map, it should also stimulate awareness of common issues. Even though individuals tend to specialize within particular microparadigms and theories of the sort listed in Figure 1, reference to the macroparadigm of developmental psychopathology can enhance the value of the more specialized contributions.

Applications to Training

Because multiple research and clinical specialties are involved in the study and treatment of psychopathology, no single core training curriculum is shared be all the relevant professionals. To apply the developmental view of psychopathology, it would by desirable to have a common core of concepts and goals to guide the training of professionals concerned with troubled children. Such a core need not consist of utopian requirements for all trainees. However, by specifying a model set of training components for the highest level trainees, such as child psychiatrists and Ph.D. clinical child psychologists, we could reduce the fragmentation that now hinders communication and limits the supply of broadly trained professionals. If these training components set standards for the highest levels of training, trainees and programs could be evaluated in terms of their deviation from the standards. For child psychiatrists and psychologists, omissions of key training components would be considered deficiencies to be remedied. For workers not expected to have such comprehensive training, the omissions would be indicative of the differences between their qualifications and those of the people expected to be most broadly qualified in child clinical work. Some key components of training suggested by developmental psychopathology include normal development, standardized assessment procedures, specific disorders of childhood and adolescence, organic development and its deviations, and a variety of interventions.

Normal Development

All professionals working with children should have a basic grounding in life span development. This would include important milestones in physical development, language, cognition, skills, behavior problems, social-emotional issues, and adult development. The study of adult development is important even for child specialists, in order to highlight the adaptive challenges children need to be prepared for, as well as those that their parents are experiencing. Major theoretical constructs--such as the cognitive changes hypothesized by Piaget (1983) and the psychosocial conflicts hypothesized by Erikson (1980)-- should be central components of training, without necessarily assuming acceptance of these theoretical explanations for development.

Standardized Assessment Procedures

A second component of training would be standardized tests of ability, achievement, and perceptual-motor development, as well as standardized assessment of behavior as reported by key informants, including parents, teachers, clinicians, trained observers, and children themselves (see Achenbach & McConaughy, 1987). Although not all trainees need to master the methodological underpinnings or the details of administering such procedures, trainees should be familiar with their theoretical and normative basis, their content, relations to various aspects of development, and general predictive power. They should also know where to obtain details about reliability and validity when needed. Depending on their specialties, some trainees will need specific skills in administering infant development tests such as the Bayley Scales, ability tests such as the WISC-R, or neurological exams such as the PANESS (Mikkelsen, Brown, Minichiello, Millican, & Rapoport, 1982).

Disorders of Childhood and Adolescence

A third component of training concerns the disorders typical of childhood and adolescence. This would involve not only the prevailing nosology, but alternative conceptions of disorders, since official nosologies are rather arbitrary and changeable. By considering alternative conceptions, as well as data on age of onset and typical course, trainees should acquire a sophisticated perspective on the relations between development and psychopathology. This would entail recognition that most child and adolescent disorders involve quantitative variations on the normal course of development, rather than qualitatively distinct disease entities. It would also highlight the need to set therapeutic goals in terms of promoting further development rather than restoring children to their premorbid status.

Organic Development and Abnormalities

Although organic treatments would be the responsibility of physicians, all trainees should learn about major organic determinants and changes, such as physical maturation, changes in hormone levels, the course of puberty, and developmental aspects of pharmacokinetics. Genetic factors in organic development and developmental behavior genetics (Plomin, 1986) are likely to become increasingly important in the study of relations between development and psychopathology. Trainees should also learn enough about symptoms of organic abnormalities and the psychological concomitants of disease to facilitate appropriate medical referrals and collaboration with medical personnel.

Interventions

Unlike adults, children seldom seek treatment for themselves. Nor are they the primary informants about their problems or history. Instead, help is sought by adults, such as parents and teachers, for problems reported mainly by the adults. Furthermore, the child's dependence on adults means that interventions usually focus as much on the adults as the child. Multiple interventions are therefore needed in many cases, and the trainee must be prepared to use a greater variety of techniques than when treating only adults, who often seek a practitioner specializing in one treatment approach.

Although practitioners cannot be experts in all techniques, trainees should receive didactic instruction and experience in behavioral, family, psychodynamic, cognitive, psychoeducational, and social skills techniques, as well as techniques for helping parents change their behavior toward their child group and milieu approaches are also desirable for work with certain populations. Pharmacologic training would be needed by child psychiatrists, but nonmedical trainees should learn about indications and contraindications for particular drugs, side effects, and ways of meshing other interventions with pharmacotherapy.

Clinical and Research Tracks

As a discipline becomes more differentiated, it is increasingly difficult for a single individual to master all its aspects. In earlier days, leaders of a field were idealized as simultaneously being great teachers, clinicians, researchers, and theoreticians. Although some people may, in fact, display exceptional talent in all these areas at some point in their career, it is unrealistic to expect people to make significant contributions in all of them at once. Instead, training and career ladders need to help people maximize their contributions in the one or two areas where they are strongest. This argues for a differentiation between the advanced training of those who will be primarily clinicians and those who will be primarily researchers.

The small size and heterogeneity of most programs in clinical child psychology (Tuma, 1985) would make it difficult for them to create a viable research track in addition to basic clinical training. It would certainly be desirable, however, for all such programs to teach trainees to evaluate current research literature in their field, including research design, standard measures, statistics, and the logic of drawing conclusions from data. The trainees would not necessarily be expected to generate their own research but should become skilled consumers who can evaluate and communicate about the research reported in the literature of their field.

For more differentiated clinical and research training in developmental psychopathology, it is probably necessary to look to the postdoctoral level for psychologists and the postfellow level for child psychiatrists. Training at this level is, of course, common in many fields today. It is at this level that clinical and research specialization becomes more feasible. Those oriented toward clinical careers would learn more specialized skills and would be given greater supervised responsibility with a wider range of more difficult cases than feasible at the psychological intern or psychiatric residency level. Those oriented toward research careers would work closely with research mentors, collaborating on research, obtaining instruction in methodology, learning how to obtain grants, and initiating and reporting their own research. Considering the lagging supply of rigorously trained child clinicians and the gaps between the available research training and the field's potential for advancement, it may be worth investing in a few flagship programs to provide both clinical and research leadership.

Implications of Training Across Multiple Settings

Services for troubled children date back to the beginning of the twentieth century. Improvements are needed, however, in the distribution, accessibility, coordination, and evaluation of services. Few communities offer a clear-cut continuum of care, whereby the initial identification of problems leads directly to the most appropriate type and level of help. Instead, a child manifesting problems may be seen at one point by a practitioner who favors one kind of assessment and intervention, but later by practitioners of other persuasions. Although extensive records may be compiled at each step, the differences in approach often preclude integrating data from one step to the next. This duplicates costly efforts and makes it hard to track changes in the child's functioning from one point to another.

To make better use of existing services and to provide training that will promote a clear focus for developing new services, it is necessary to have a common core of procedures and concepts. Because no single treatment model is appropriate for all facets of all disorders, it would be desirable for the common core to comprise assessment procedures and concepts that are widely applicable, unrestricted by the philosophies of individual practitioners. This is already done to a large extent in the assessment of cognitive ability and school achievement, where certain standardized tests are widely used for assessment of learning problems. The assessment of behavioral and emotional problems, however, has been subject to much more variation, based largely on differences in practitioners' personal philosophies. Psychodynamically oriented workers, for example, tend to use projective tests to infer underlying conflicts and personality structures. Analogously, psychometricians use personality tests to tap traits; behaviorists use direct observations to identify target behaviors and environmental contingencies; and medically oriented workers use interviews and test data to make nosological diagnoses.

The developmental psychopathology macroparadigm implies a normative-developmental approach that assesses the problems and competencies of individual children in relation to those of normative samples of agemates. Standardized assessment should be linked to taxonomic procedures that reflect syndromes or patterns of problems, population-based epidemiological data, and data on developmental differences in problems and competencies. Assessment should also take account of differences between a child's functioning in different contexts, as reported by different informants. To illustrate this approach, Table 1 lists five major axes relevant to assessment of most child and adolescent disorders. Axis I (parent reports), Axis II (teacher reports), and Axis V (direct assessment of the child) reflect the type of normative-developmental assessment of problems and competencies implied by developmental psychopathology. Two other important facets of child assessment are represented by Axis III (standardized cognitive assessment) and Axis IV (biomedical assessment).

TABLE 1
EXAMPLES OF MULTIAXIAL ASSESSMENT

PARENT DATA	TEACHER DATA	COGNITIVE TEST DATA	MEDICAL DATA	DIRECT ASSESSMENT DATA

1. Child behavior profile
2. Interview
  a. Developmental history
  b. Details of present problems
  c. Relevant background
  d. Workability for interventions
	1. Teacher's report form
	2. Interview
	  a. Detail of present
	  b. Relevant background
	  c. Workability for interventions
		1. Ability
		2. Achievement
		3. Perceptual-motor functioning
		4. Speech and language
			1. Neurological exam
			2. Relevant illnesses
			3. Handicaps
			4. Medications
				1. Direct observation form
				2. Youth Self-report
				3. Interview
				  a. Child's view of problems
				  b. Interpersonal competencies
				  c. Workability for interventions

If all child services drew on a common set of assessment procedures such as those listed in Table 1, this could link training more effectively to the diverse service settings in which clinicians work. For example, if the same standardized instruments were used for case finding via screening, needs assessment, and referral procedures, they would provide common reference points for all the child training and services in a community. The same standardized data would thus be available, whatever the route by which a child was initially identified as needing help. If a child were seen by one practitioner and then referred to another, the assessment process would not have to be repeated each time. Instead, the standardized aspects of the initial assessment would be useful to subsequent practitioners, although they would also be free to add other components as they saw fit. Furthermore, even if a child is seen by only one practitioner, the use of standardized assessment procedures to obtain baseline data makes it easy to evaluate outcomes by repeating the procedures at later points, such as after an intervention has time to take effect, and again at longer follow-up periods, such as 6,12, or 24 months. This enables the practitioner or agency to document outcomes for children having particular presenting problems and receiving particular interventions. If outcomes are consistently poor for particular kinds of problems, this would argue for changing the services offered for these problems or referring children to services specializing in such problems.

Conclusions

In conclusion, a developmental approach to psychopathology can bring conceptual order out of a welter of contrasting concepts and activities. Its most compelling applications are in the period from birth to maturity, but it is potentially applicable to later periods as well.

As knowledge advances, training and services are likely to become more specialized rather than more general. A macroparadigm of developmental psychopathology is therefore needed to provide integrative concepts and common reference points in the face of inevitable specialization.

The centrality of developmental concepts stems from the massive biological, cognitive, and social-emotional changes that occur from birth to maturity. If we look at the dramatic differences between an infant, preschooler, fourth grader, early adolescent, and college student, it is obvious that developmental changes have a tremendous impact on the challenges faced by the individual, the individual's self-concept, and other people's expectations. The extent to which the environment and people's expectations are geared to the typical capabilities of each age level gives normative-developmental assessment a key role in identifying deviance and evaluating subsequent change. Training and service can be improved by reference to the common denominator of developmental norms and by viewing specific forms of deviance in relation to the developmental sequences in which they are embedded. It is by integrating concepts of psychopathology around normative sequences and highlighting maladaptive deviations from such sequences that a macroparadigm of developmental psychopathology can make a major contribution.

References

Achenbach, T.M., & McConaughy, S.H. (1987). Empirically based assessment of child and adolescent psychopathology: Practical applications. Newbury Park, CA: Sage.

Erikson, E.H. (1980). Elements of a psychoanalytic theory of psychosocial development. In S.I. Greenspan & G.H. Pollock (Eds.), The course of life: Psychoanalytic contributions toward understanding personality development. Vol. 1. Infancy and early childhood. Adelphi, MD: NIMH Mental Health Study Center.

Mikkelsen, E.J., Brown, G.L., Minichiello, M.D., Millican, F.K., & Rapoport, J.L. (1982). Neurologic status in hyperactive, enuretic, encopretic, and normal boys. Journal of the American Academy of Child Psychiatry, 21, 75-81.

Piaget, J. (1983). Piaget's theory. In P.H. Mussen (Ed.), Handbook of child psychology (4th ed.): Vol. 1. History, theory, and methods. New York: Wiley.

Plomin, R. (1986). Development, genetics, and psychology. Hillsdale, NJ: Erlbaum.

Tuma, J.M. (1985). Proceedings: Conference on training clinical child psychologists. Washington, DC: American Psychological Association.

Chapter 10
Developmental Psychopathology and Prevention

David F. Ricks
Department of Psychology, University of Cincinnati

Developmental psychopathology is a research discipline that studies the origins and outcomes of disturbed behavior. Its models and methods come from developmental psychology; typical concerns are the stages through which disorders develop and types of continuity or predictability that may be found between different life periods. The problems that developmental psychopathologists address come from pediatric, school, clinical, and counseling psychology as well as psychiatry and social work. A long-term goal, now partially realized in the study of schizophrenia (Marcus & Hans, 1984; Ricks, 1983), heroin addiction (Runyan, 1982), and school failure (Ramey, 1978) is the construction of developmental models to replace the overly static typologies of traditional psychology and psychiatry.

Developmental psychopathology began with clinical inquiries into the etiology of adult syndromes. A group of patients with a common diagnosis was assembled, and common features in their self-recalled histories described (Cohen et al. 1954). Concern with distortions in long-term memory then led to a search for data recorded in childhood, primarily in child guidance clinic and school records. To differentiate this method from retrospective research relying on adult memory for childhood, using data recorded in childhood was termed follow-back research. The major advantages of this research are the objectivity of the data and the size of the samples that can be assembled. In the Judge Baker Guidance Center studies of the origins of schizophrenia, we were able to identify about 200 people who had the adult diagnosis of schizophrenia and fairly substantial child guidance clinic files, composed of several hours of recorded observations by skilled, perceptive, and caring clinicians.

Follow-back research, however, has no control over the data originally gathered. Most research currently under way has used longitudinal designs, in which children with a specific risk factor, most frequently a disturbed parent, are tested, interviewed, and observed in childhood, then followed up to adult life (Mednick & Schulsinger, 1970). Current research is likely to focus on several risk factors, as they influence the child's development, over time. Marcus and Hans (1984) have shown that a combination of having a schizophrenic parent, symptoms suggestive of neurological damage, poor parenting, and unpopularity with peers raises the probability of a schizophrenic outcome to about 60%.

An unexpected dividend of risk research has been discovery of children who show unusual resilience, surviving and doing well in spite of multiple risk factors (Garmezy, 1987; Rutter, 1987). Study of these children has suggested effective ways to reduce the impact of risk factors, pull children out of escalating destructive chain reactions, support self-esteem and feelings of efficacy, and open up opportunities for social participation.

Such research also discovers protective factors in the home and community. Wilson (1985) found that low birth weight twins, a group at high risk for handicapped mental development, showed initial deficits. However, if the mother was moderately educated and not living in poverty, so that she knew something about nutrition and had enough money to feed the twins adequately, the effects of low birth weight essentially disappeared by about 3 years of age.

Developmental psychopathology is a descriptive science, a natural history approach to the varied adult psychopathologies and successful struggles against adversity. It also has powerful implications for prevention. "Primary prevention refers to those interventions which seek to alter precursors to disorder" (Felner & Lorin, 1985). The risk factor that overrides all others, in study after study, is poverty, with its attendant stress, physical illness, and malnutrition. Any change that decreases the amount of poverty, or that minimizes its impact on children, can be expected to decrease the frequency of psychopathology (Brooks-Gunn et al., 1988).

A set of risk factors that is usually not studied by developmental psychopathologists, but that should be is the concern of a newborn field called behavioral teratology (Adams, 1986). Toxins that cause deficits in growth and in motor function and that are also being demonstrated to have powerful behavioral effects include lead, mercury, PCBs, ethanol, methadone, and phenytoin. These negative effects include impaired sensory/perceptual and cognitive functioning. Much of the behavior currently classified as attention deficit disorder, with or without hyperactivity, may be the result of exposure to these toxins, either in utero or in early childhood (Jacobsen et al., 1984; Shaheen, 1984; Streissguth et al., 1984). Prevention, through removal of the toxins from the environment, education of parents and potential parents, and punishment of environmental contaminators, is likely to be far more effective than attempts to treat already damaged children.

A second set of risk factors has to do with the health, nutritional status, and age of the mother. Rates of pregnancy in older teenagers have been decreasing for some time. If we can also get younger adolescents to decrease their rates of pregnancy, we will decrease the frequency of low birth weight and other vulnerable infants (Brooks-Gunn et al., 1988). A particularly interesting finding comes from a long-term follow-up of one early childhood intervention program (Gray & Ramsey, 1986). Eight of Gray's experimental subjects and 6 of her controls became pregnant in adolescence. There is no difference in the rate of pregnancy, but there is a striking difference in the competence with which better prepared girls handle this real life stress. Seven of the 8 experimental subjects (87%) stayed on and finished high school, and only 2 had a second child while still adolescent. Five of the 6 controls (83%) dropped out of high school, and 4 were soon pregnant again.

The goals of preventive interventions have been well reviewed (Kendall et al., 1984; Peterson & Roberts, 1986). Prevention is so often cost-effective and practical that it is hard to see why only about 5% of the resources of most community mental health centers, hospitals, and so on, are devoted to prevention and community work. The main reason for this lack of focused effort may be that preventive goals are often hard to define. Here developmental psychopathology provides a knowledge base secure enough, even now, to allow clear intervention strategies and specific evaluations (Kendall et al., 1984).

In general, the goals of prevention are to reduce illness, to promote coping skills and competence, to improve physical and emotional well-being, and to change behavior related to known risk factors for future disorder. Developmental psychopathology provides guidelines for all of these goals (Kohlberg, Ricks, & Snarey, 1984). If our goal is to prevent schizophrenia, for instance, three decades of research have indicated about 25 different methods are likely to be effective, beginning before birth with genetic counseling and adequate prenatal care and concluding in early adulthood with vocational guidance into low stress areas and jobs.

Each method of intervention can be related to the age of the child, the developmental tasks of that age, the sources of vulnerability in the child, and the relationships and experiences the child describes at that time (see Table1).

If we wish to prevent delinquency and crime, a combination of a weak genetic influence, powerful family and neighborhood influences, and early antisocial behavior leading to rejection by the "straight" segment of the school and community points to the child most at risk. The community rightly regards crime as too important to leave to clinicians. Our roles are mainly research and clinical intervention in issues such as school achievement, vocational guidance, and family conflict, in which we have some specific training and skills.

New methods in neuropsychology are likely to lead to improved predictors of both schizophrenia and delinquency. These neurological deficits, in childhood, are likely to be traced back to fetal and infancy exposure to environmental toxins, and to malnutrition.

Developmental psychopathology research suggests an admittedly visionary possibility for implementing intervention with high-risk children. Building on exemplary work with parents of autistic and retarded

TABLE 1
Possible Sources of Vulnerability and Potentially Helpful Methods of Intervention in Preschizophrenia

Age and life phase	Possible sources of vulnerability	Relationships, experiences, symptoms	Potentially helpful methods of intervention
Before birth	genetic factors, poor maternal health, poor maternal nutrition, attempts to abort		genetic counseling; adequate prenatal care
0-2, infancy	birth damage, postpartum depression, early illness leaving permanent damage, restriction and under-stimulation	overly dependent; slow in developing speech; poor coordination; shy	adequate obstetrical care; adequate pediatric care; treatment for mother's depression; early stimulation & training
3-6, early childhood. . . .	low IQ, low social competence, hyperreactive nervous system, influence of disturbed family	shy, sensitive, irritable; poor peer relationships; speech problems; awkward and rigid; hyperactive	speech therapy; physical training; nursery school training in socialization
7-12, late childhood. . . .	low IQ, low social competence, poor school achievement, disturbed family	shy; poor peer relationships; teachers report: indifferent, unlikable, stubborn, unhappy, lazy, scatterbrained	tutoring in speech, reading; play therapy; therapeutic camps & schools; family therapy; foster home or residential school placement
13-18, adolescent	sexual maturation in self and peers, failures in adolescent developmental tasks, life stress	poor peer relationships; withdrawal, tantrums, defiance; feelings reported: vulnerability, anxiety, alienation, unreality; some psychotic-like symptoms begin	reality-oriented psychotherapy; tutoring in school subjects; vocational guidance into low-pressure jobs and areas; foster home or residential school placement
19-25, early adulthood . .	failure in young adult social and vocational development, life stress	withdrawal; despair; apathy; psychotic syndromes apparent but often not stabilized	drug treatment to minimize anxiety; psychotherapy; vocational guidance into low-stress areas & jobs; institutional care; vocational and social rehabilitation

children (Schopler et al., 1982), could we form an organization of the adults interested in high-risk children, including their parents but not restricted to relatives? Call if CARHOP (Children at Risk: Help, Outreach, Prevention). Could such a group enlist community support for long-term efforts to strengthen these children and prevent disorder?

Using as a model the successful diversion programs that have kept many delinquent children out of jail and aided their rehabilitation with vocational training, we might design programs that would divert the child heading toward schizophrenia and hospitalization away from both. Small scale models for such programs already exist in special schools like Bob and Mary Belenky's "Neighbors' School."

It is a good idea to confront directly the various kinds of opposition to using what we already know for prevention efforts, thereby increasing our knowledge base. First, many people underestimate how much we know. They do not believe that Ramey (1978) and his team can predict failure in first grade from information present at birth, or that Kellam et al. (1980) or Block et al. (1988) can predict adolescent drug use from information present by age five or six. But there is a strong developmental psychopathology research base, and knowledge does not have to be complete to guide us in making a helpful difference in the lives of children. Rutter, in fact, has cautioned us against the other extreme, being too confident of what we know and can do, a tendency encouraged by the robust findings of much developmental psychopathology research.

A second obstacle to using our knowledge is ambiguity of boundaries. The Cincinnati Social Skills Development Program helped many children, did exemplary research, and won support from parents and many teachers and principals. It lost funding because it could not be clearly defined as either a school program, supportable by school funds, or a health program, supported by public health money

A third obstacle, now being overcome in many settings, is traditional thinking and funding patterns that support treatment but do not provide for prevention.

The fourth obstacle is by far the most difficult. Powerful people have a stake in keeping conditions, including poverty, just as they are. Children are homeless because rich, politically sophisticated landlords have a stake in keeping housing scarce and rents high. Children need access to mainstream institutions-- schools, jobs, recreation--but these are closed off to many young people. If we can honestly provide young people with consistent messages about adult role expectations, with opportunities to succeed, we can divert many who are now headed for trouble (Gideonse, 1988). We know what we have to provide to children in order to help them make a go of life. Whether we will use that knowledge is questionable.

References

Adams, J. (1986). Clinical relevance of experimental behavioral teratology. Neurotoxicology, 7(2): 19-34.

Block, J., Block, J.H., & Keyes, S. (1988). Longitudinally foretelling drug usage in adolescence: Early childhood and environmental precursors. Child Development, 59, 336-355.

Brooks-Gunn, J., McCormick, M.C., & Heagarty, M.C. (1988). Preventing infant mortality and morbidity: Developmental perspectives. American Journal of Orthopsychiatry, 58 (2), 288-296.

Cohen, M.B., Baker, G., Cohen, R.A., Fromm-Reichmann, F., & Weigert, E.V. (1954). An intensive study of twelve cases of manic-depressive psychosis. Psychiatry, 17, 103-137.

Felner, R.D., & Lorion, R.P. (1985). Clinical child psychology and prevention: Toward a workable and satisfying marriage. In Tuma, J.M. (Ed.), Proceedings: Conference on Training Clinical Child Psychologists. Washington, DC: American Psychological Association.

Garmezy, N. (1987). Stress, competence, and development: Continuities in the study of schizophrenic adults, children vulnerable to psychopathology, and the search for stress-resistanant children. American Journal of Orthopsychiatry, 57, (2), 159-174.

Gideonse, S. (1988). Determinants of youth's successful entry into adulthood. Washington, DC: William T. Grant Foundation Commission on Youth and America's Future.

Gray, S.W., & Ramsay, B.K. (1986). Adolescent childbearing and high school completion. Journal of Applied Developmental Psychology, 7, 167-179.

Jacobsen, J.L., Jacobsen, S.W., Fein, G.G., Schwartz, P.M., & Dowler, J.K. (1984). Prenatal exposure to an environmental toxin: A test of the multiple effects model. Developmental Psychology, 20(4), 523-542.

Kellam, S.G., Ensminger, M.E., & Simon, M.B. (1980). Mental health in first grade and teenage drug, alcohol, and cigarette use. Drug and Alcohol Dependence, 5, 273-304.

Kendall, P.C., Lerner, R.M., & Craighead, W.E. (1984). Human development and intervention in childhood psychopathology. Child Development, 55, 71-82.

Kohlberg, L., Ricks, D., & Snarey J. (1984). Childhood development as a predictor of adaptation in adulthood. Genetic Psychology Monographs, 110(1), 91-172.

Marcus, J., & Hans, S. (1984). Offspring of schizophrenic patents: Vulnerable and invulnerable children 15 years later. Paper presented at American Academy of Child Psychiatry, Ontario, Canada.

Mednick, S.A., & Schulsinger, F. (1970). Factors related to breakdown in children at high risk for schizophrenia. In M. Roff & D.F. Ricks (Eds.), Life history research in psychopathology (Vol. I). Minneapolis, MN: University of Minnesota Press.

Peterson, L., & Roberts, M.C. (1986). Community intervention and prevention. In H. Quay and C. Werry (Eds.), Psychopathological disorders of childhood, 3rd. ed. (pp. 622-660). New York: Wiley.

Ramey, C.T., Stedman, D.J., Borders-Patterson, A., & Mengel, W. (1978). Predicting school failure from information available at birth. American Journal of Mental Deficiency, 82(6), 525-534.

Ricks, D.F. (1983). Conclusions: Life history research in the public arena. In D. F. Ricks & B. S. Dohrenwend (Eds.), Origins of psychopathology. New York: Cambridge University Press.

Runyan, W. Mc. (1982). Life histories and psychobiography. New York: Oxford University Press.

Rutter, M. (1987). Psychosocial resilience and protective mechanisms. American Journal of Orthopsychiatry, 57(3), 316-331.

Schopler, E., Mesibov, G., & Baker, A. (1982). Evaluation of treatment for autistic children and their parents. Journal of the American Academy of Child Psychiatry, 21, 262-267.

Shaheen, S.J. (1984). Neuromaturation and behavior development: The case of childhood lead poisoning. Developmental Psychology, 20 (4), 542-550.

Streissguth, A.P., Matin, D.C., Barr, H.M., Sandman, B.M., Kirchner, G.L., & Darby, B.L. (1984). Intrauterine alcohol and nicotine exposure: Attention and reaction time in 4-year-old children. Developmental Psychology, 21(4), 533-541.

Wilson, R.S. (1985). Risk and resilience in early mental development. <u>Developmental Psychology,</u> <u>21</u>(5), 795-805.

Chapter 11
Breadth and Depth of Training in Developmental-Clinical Psychology in Assessment and Interventions

Gloria R.Leon
University of Minnesota

Clinical training programs have typically approached training in the child area from an adult perspective. Specific course work and training in child psychopathology are not offered in many clinical programs, and there seems to be an assumption that students in the child clinical area will in some way be able to apply what they have learned regarding adults to working with children. The adolescent area has been even more neglected, with course instruction falling between the cracks of a focus on adults and what little specific education is available in the child area.

Where child clinical training is available, the crucial importance of developmental changes in defining and treating psychopathological disorders is frequently ignored. Students have not consistently been exposed to course material that could provide them with a developmental perspective, which shows that cognitive, behavioral, affective, and interpersonal processes change with age. Therefore students may lack specific knowledge of base rates of developmental phenomena (i.e., that psychological processes that are common at an earlier age and thus normal from a statistical perspective can be categorized as abnormal at later ages in terms of infrequency or developmental inappropriateness). Students also need a developmental background to provide them with an in-depth knowledge of cognitive processes; this information will help them appreciate that the type and expression of normal behavior or psychopathology in a given child will be influenced by cognitive changes occurring with maturation,as well as individual differences in cognitive abilities. Stroufe and Rutter (1984) discussed similar points in terms of individual patterns of adaptation and maladaptation.

In 1984, a special issue of Child Development was devoted to the topic of developmental psychopathology; the collection of papers defined and gave excellent examples of theoretical perspectives and clinical research in this area. Rolf and Read (1984) called for greater funding priorities for research training in developmental psychopathology, and discussed the need to enhance communication among researchers. Studies of risk, competence, and protective factors were proposed by Garmezy, Masten, and Tellegen (1984) as building blocks for a conception of developmental psychopathology.

Concerns about the quality of and models for training in the child clinical area have resulted in a call for the establishment of training programs with a developmental psychopathology perspective that combines current knowledge of normal child developmental and child psychopathology (Achenbach, 1987; Cicchetti, 1984). Locally and nationally, Norman Garmezy has been an energetic spokesperson, urging the creation of better training models for studying child and adolescent psychopathology (Garmezy, 1975). The formalization of the developmental psychopathology training program at the University of Minnesota has undoubtedly been spurred by Garmezy's strong commitment to this area.

The joint program we have developed at the University of Minnesota needs to be understood within an academic structure that is different from that of many other universities. The psychology faculty and courses and the PhD training program in clinical psychology are academically housed within the Department of Psychology in the College of Liberal Arts, whereas the child psychology faculty, courses in this area, and the PhD program in child psychology are located within the Institute of Child Development in the College of Education. Administrative matters become complicated because University of Minnesota regulations stipulate that the PhD degree must be obtained within a single college. In the past, students in child clinical psychology took a minor in child development, but there was no easy mechanism for child development students to receive clinical training. In meetings between interested faculty from the Institute of Child Development and the Department of Psychology, curriculum planning for what we eventually named the Joint Child Clinical/Developmental Psychopathology Program had to take into account the general PhD course requirements and examination procedures of the two departments. We developed a core curriculum for all students with a substantial child development and clinical psychology concentration. However, students who choose to obtain a relatively stronger background in child development enter the program and receive their degree through the Institute of Child Development. Those who desire a relatively more comprehensive background in adult as well as child psychopathology are admitted and receive the PhD through the Department of Psychology. The first official class of students entered the joint program in Fall, 1988, although students had been admitted on a more informal basis in previous years.

The first-year joint program curriculum covers the fundamentals of psychopathology, child development, assessment, and statistics. The second year focuses on developmental psychopathology and fundamentals of intervention. More specifically, the required curriculum for all joint program students consists of courses in intellectual and personality assessment, and interviewing. Two new courses, Comprehensive Assessment of Children and Child-Family Interventions with Underserved Populations, are being developed. Students take two quarters of a Developmental Psychopathology course sequence and an adult-centered Descriptive Psychopathology course; they are also required to take either Biological Bases of Psychopathology or Human Developmental Psychobiology. Two of the following three courses are required: Advanced Child Development, Advanced Cognitive Development, or Advanced Social Development. Students in the Department of Psychology take a total of 20-22 credits in child development, and ICD students of course have an even greater course and research concentration in child development. Practicum training and internship requirements follow APA standards, and focus on instruction in assessment and intervention techniques with children and adolescents.

In developing the joint program curriculum, we wanted to avoid requiring a course load that was so burdensome that students would not have time to conduct research, nor did we want the program to take an unreasonably long time to complete. On the other hand, we did not want to reflect the obverse of the training deficiencies of many adult-oriented programs by offering no training in adult clinical psychology. We feel that it is extremely important for students to be trained in understanding the psychopathology of a wide age range of persons, not only because those in the child and adolescent area have to deal with parents, but also because a developmental psychopathology curriculum should provide a perspective across the life span. We also feel that students should have knowledge about biological findings in psychopathology, including genetic ones.

It is important to emphasize that we do not view our current curriculum as "written in stone" but expect to make adjustments as students go through the program and as new faculty are hired. We will have more data in a year or two on whether the present version of the program is feasible in the five-year time period projected for its completion.

We are currently witnessing a tremendous explosion of interest in the field of child clinical psychology, and particularly in developmental psychopathology. Many universities are advertising for faculty in the child clinical area, and those with strong developmental backgrounds are eagerly sought. At present the demand far exceeds the supply of well trained psychologists with expertise in child clinical/developmental psychology, and it is not uncommon for universities to hold open searches for several years before hiring someone in this area. During the 1988 graduate school application period, we received a large number of applications from students with outstanding academic credentials who were applying for training in our joint program. We unfortunately could not accept all of them and still maintain a reasonable faculty/student ratio. If there is to be an improvement in services for children and adolescents with severe mental disorders, it is imperative that far greater training opportunities at both the predoctoral and postdoctoral levels become available to turn out future researchers and clinicians in developmental psychopathology. Greater federal and state funding is urgently needed to meet this goal.

References

Achenbach, T.M. (1987, April). What is "developmental" about developmental psychopathology? Paper presented at the meeting of the Society of Research in Child Development, Baltimore, MD.

Cicchetti, D. (1984). The emergence of developmental psychopathology. Child Development, 55, 1-7.

Garmezy, N. (1975). The experimental study of children vulnerable to psychopathology. In A. Davids (Ed.), Child personality and psychopathology: Current topics, (Vol. 2, pp. 171-216). New York: Wiley.

Garmezy, N., Masten, A.S., & Tellegen, A. (1984). The study of stress and competence in children: A building block for developmental psychopathology. Child Development, 55, 97-111.

Rolf, J., & Read, P.B. (1984). Programs advancing developmental psychopathology. Child Development, 55, 8-16.

Stroufe, L.A., & Rutter, M. (1984). The domain of developmental psychopathology. Child Development, 55, 17-29.

Chapter 12
The Integration of a Developmental Perspective
with Training in Clinical Child Psychology

Sandra W. Russ
Case Western Reserve University

A major challenge for clinical child training programs is to find the best way to integrate developmental theory with clinical child psychology core concepts and practica experiences. How can we help anchor the student so that a developmental approach guides that student's conceptualization of assessment, intervention, prevention programs, and public policy? At Case Western Reserve University, we do what many programs do, which is to have a Developmental Psychology course given during the first year of graduate training. A sequence in Child Assessment is also taught that year and we hope there is some transfer of knowledge from one course to the other. Training programs need to identify the key elements in the program that help facilitate this process of transfer and integration.

There has been increasing awareness in the field of the importance of developmental theory and research to clinical child training and vice versa. As Cicchetti (1984) states in the 1984 special issue of <u>Child Development</u> on Developmental Psychopathology, most great systematizers in psychology have "taken as a basic working principle, that we can learn more about the normal functioning of an organism by studying its pathology and, likewise, more about its pathology by studying its normal condition" (p. 1). Stroufe and Rutter (1984) in that same special issue point out that "perhaps the central proposition underlying a developmental perspective is that the course of development is lawful" (p. 21). These principles of child development should permeate the clinical child program. Serafica and Wenar (1985) eloquently state the importance of this:

> ...it is critical for clinical child psychologists to become familiar with the rate and emergence of various functions and of their maturation and integration. It is equally important for them to be aware of the environmental and intraorganismic factors which either facilitate or impede development so that the client may be understood in his or her totality (p.117).

<u>Key Elements in Graduate Programs</u>

<u>Developmental Approach to Child Clinical Courses</u>

One really cannot teach child assessment, psychopathology, or intervention without using a developmental approach. In child assessment, for example, Palmer, in his 1970 text, puts it very well when he conceptualizes the assessment process as determining in which areas and in what ways the child has veered off the normal developmental track. Palmer sees psychological assessment of the child as beginning with "assessment of the nature and rate of his development and proceeds to an investigation of possible factors that may be deterring...growth" (p. 15). Also, the entire process of assessment considers age-norms for a variety of dimensions and deviations from the norm. Often, a goal of treatment is to get the child back on the developmental track. One sign that it is time to stop treatment is that the child seems to be moving along fairly well in specific areas and the family and school are now functioning in ways that will enable the child to keep progressing. Either the obstacles and stresses that have interfered with development have been removed or the child is now coping in adaptive ways, or both.

One of my favorite exam questions in the child assessment course is "What is meant by a developmental approach and how does it influence your thinking about assessment?" Students sometimes complain about the global nature of that question, but it does give a sense of how the student is thinking about the issue at the end of the first semester. Perhaps we should ask the same question at the end of four years.

The role of graduate training is to establish the foundation for the ability to integrate a developmental approach with clinical child concepts and practice. The establishment of this foundation is a unique task of the graduate program. Graduate programs are better equipped than internship and postdoctoral programs to accomplish this goal because of the ability to develop a coherent course sequence over a long period of time. Different programs develop this foundation in different ways, depending upon the nature of the program and expertise of the faculty. If we can build this developmental base, then students are prepared to go into a variety of community settings and public sector programs. In order to build this foundation, the basic clinical courses must utilize a developmental approach. However, another key ingredient in achieving this kind of integration is the research experience in the program.

Research as a Bridge Between Developmental and Clinical Child Training

Research experience bridges the gap between developmental theory and clinical child training. For the student, research with children is an excellent integrator of developmental theory and clinical child issues. Research serves this purpose for several reasons. First, a research project usually focuses on a few specific variables intensively. Therefore, the student learns about the developmental course of a process such as self-esteem, or depression, or fantasy. Research will focus specifically on questions such as "What is appropriate for the age?"; "What is the developmental course?"; "How does this variable relate to other cognitive and affective processes?"; "How do family and environmental factors affect the developmental course of this variable?"; and "How is this process affected by specific interventions?" It is hoped that, the research supervisor will encourage the student to think about implications for intervention and prevention programs. By focusing so intensively on a few variables, the student really learns a developmental model.

Clinical and research supervisors should also be encouraging students to develop research questions from clinical experience. One real advantage of working with clinical populations day in and day out is that one gets a real sense of the cognitive and affective processes involved in child development. This clinical understanding should alter our development of research programs. That is, after all, what the Boulder model is all about--research and practice go hand-in-hand and each influences the other. We read many laments about the fact that research findings do not affect clinical decision making as much as they should. Equally important, but not often noted, is that research questions should evolve more than they do from clinical observations. Ross (1981) has stressed the need for a closer relationship between the clinic and laboratory. There should be a reciprocal relationship between the clinical case study and the experiment. We should encourage our students to trust their own clinical observations, delve into the area, develop a research project, and perhaps contribute to developmental theory. Students are especially ready to do this at the internship level. Because they now have sufficient clinical experience, they are able to generate important research questions that evolve from their clinical observations. Unfortunately, there is little time to carry out research during the internship year, and frequently the dissertation is already in the works. The Guidelines for Clinical Child Psychology Internship Training developed by the Section I Task Force on Internship Training encouraged some research activity during the internship year (Elbert, Abidin, Finch, Sigman, & Walker, in press). However, the research activity will necessarily be limited because of the clinical focus of the internship year. We need to find ways of encouraging and supporting research efforts of new PhDs (Russ, 1980) during postdoctoral and first job experiences.

Another reason that research experience contributes to the integration of developmental theory and clinical child training is that it so often involves normal populations. For example, there is no better way for a student to learn about fantasy play in 7-8 year olds than to observe play sessions of a large number of normal children. At Case Western Reserve University, we have a research clerkship in the first year of the program. The student serves an apprenticeship with a faculty member. This clerkship has worked very well in initiating the research experience in clinical child psychology. Ideally, the faculty member helps the student think about a particular variable, for example, fantasy play, in terms of normal development, deviations from a normal course, problems that deviations cause for a child, and implications for intervention and prevention.

<u>Student Perceptions</u>

I decided to ask several graduate students which elements of the program they thought had been most effective in helping them to integrate developmental theory with child assessment and intervention during the first two years of the program. Their response was an interesting one. They said that the presentation of case examples was most helpful in learning how to utilize a developmental perspective in approaching an individual child. Hearing the sophisticated clinician discuss what is appropriate for a 7-year-old, how normal development compares with this particular 7-year-old, how and why development has gone awry and implications for intervention was most helpful. The faculty, in essence, model the integration by discussing developmental issues in the context of the individual case. These students also mentioned the importance of access to normal populations as well as experience using lots of different tests with different child populations. Student feedback is important, and it might be worthwhile to carry out with students a systematic survey addressing the important questions in clinical child training.

Goals and Curricula of the Graduate Program

To summarize, for the purpose of integrating developmental theory and clinical child training, the following emerge as key elements in a graduate program:

1. Developmental theory course
2. Developmental approach to the child assessment, psychopathology, and intervention sequence
3. Early research experience with child populations
4. Experience with normal child populations
5. Frequent access to different faculty who utilize a developmental approach

The faculty need to repeatedly tie together developmental and clinical child concepts in teaching and in clinical and research supervision.

To think more broadly about general goals for clinical child training programs, for the Hilton Head Conference, Russ, Freedheim, and Kessler (1985) had outlined goals of training for clinical child students who were specializing in work with multiproblem children. We developed a model for a subspecialty within a clinical child track. That article outlines the specifics of the program. Our experience has been that a subspecialty within a clinical child program can be effective if careful thought is given to the balance of courses, if there is a general clinical child core utilizing a developmental perspective, and if the subspecialty is built on the strengths of the faculty and clinical-community opportunities in that program. With a few modifications for the more general clinical child training program, the goals are articulated here.

By the end of the first year, students should be able to:
- Decide when testing is necessary
- Competently put together an assessment battery that is relevant to the purpose of the testing
- Competently administer, score, and interpret standard tests used in child settings
- Make appropriate basic recommendations for intervention
- Write clear and accurate psychological reports for various purposes
- Give feedback to child, family, and school in an effective manner
- Be familiar with specialized assessment techniques for specialized populations
- Be aware of ethical issues in assessment
- Utilize a developmental approach in their approach to the assessment process

By the end of the second year, students should have:
- A basic foundation in child psychopathology and intervention
- Acquired basic intervention skills with children and families
- A developing integration of the assessment and intervention processes
- A basic foundation in research issues in the child area

The third and fourth years of graduate training should be a time for refinement of clinical skills; some specialization within the child area, if the student so desires; experience with adult populations; and the initiation and completion of research projects in the child area. Thus, at the end of four years of graduate training in clinical child psychology, students should:

- Have refined assessment and intervention skills with children and families.
- Utilize a sophisticated developmental approach to assessment and intervention.
- Have completed several research projects in the child area .
- Have a thorough knowledge of a particular child population, such as pediatric populations or multiproblem children, if they are specializing in that child population.
- Have some consultation skills for groups working with children and families.

These goals are consistent with the recommendations of the Hilton Head Conference (Tuma, 1985).

Conclusion

If students do acquire a solid developmental approach to child clinical issues, then we have a responsibility to prepare them for the realities of the marketplace (J. Kessler, personal communication, May 1, 1988). HMOs and third-party payers do not utilize a developmental approach. Wertleib (1985) has stressed the need for clinical child psychologists to recognize their responsibility to act as social change agents. We need to influence public policy to incorporate what we know, for example, about attachment, be it in regard to foster home placement or length of treatment with a therapist. Developmental theory holds that children are not "little adults." Our social policies often treat them as such. How do we help our students learn to deal with these issues, and find effective ways of speaking out?

In conclusion, the overall question for the training program is, How do we help the student to continue to see the larger picture?"-- the larger picture being the developmental context. Programs can help the student accomplish this end only if they keep raising questions that bring in the developmental perspective in a variety of ways and encourage the student to make the links between developmental and clinical child approaches.

References

Cicchetti, D. (1984). The emergence of developmental psychopathology. Child Development, 55, 1-7.

Elbert, J., Abidin, R., Finch, A.J., Sigman, M., & Walker, C.E. (1988). Guidelines for clinical child psychology internship training. Report of Section I Task Force on Internship Training. Journal of Clinical Child Psychology, 17, 280-287.

Palmer, J. (1970). The psychological assessment of children. New York: J. Wiley & Sons.

Ross, A.O. (1981). On rigor and relevance. Professional Psychology, 12, 318-327.

Russ, S.W. (1980). Graduate training in clinical psychology: Quality and beyond. American Psychologist, 35, 766-767.

Russ, S.W., Freedheim, D.K., & Kessler, J.W. (1985). Roles and responsibilities of trainees working with children with multiple problems. In J. Tuma (Ed.), Proceedings: Conference on Training Clinical Child Psychologists (pp. 60-63). Section on Clinical Child Psychology, American Psychological Association.

Serafica, F., & Wenar, C. (1985). A developmental perspective on training clinical child psychologists: The Ohio State University Clinical Child Psychology Program. In J. Tuma (Ed.), Proceedings: Conference on Training Clinical Child Psychologists (pp. 116-120). Section on Clinical Child Psychology, American Psychological Association.

Stroufe, L., & Rutter, M. (1984). The domain of developmental psychopathology. <u>Child Development</u>, <u>55</u>, 17-29.

Tuma, J. (1985). Recommendations: Conference on training clinical child psychologists. In J. Tuma (Ed.), <u>Proceedings: Conference on Training Clinical Child Psychologists</u> (pp. 168-169). Section on Clinical Child Psychology, American Psychological Association.

Wertleib, D. (1985). Clinical child psychology as an applied developmental psychology: Toward a redefinition of mission and training. In J. Tuma (Ed.), <u>Proceedings: Conference on Training Clinical Child Psychologists</u> (pp. 64-68). Section on Clinical Child Psychology, American Psychological Association.

Chapter 13
Family Training in Child Psychology

Robert E. Emery
University of Virginia

The first point that I want to make about family training in child clinical psychology is one that everyone will find trivial: We need to teach our students about different family forms, family functions, and family processes. Of course, we all agree with this goal, but I doubt that it is currently being achieved. I am sure that most child clinical training programs discuss the family in the context of courses in developmental psychopathology, child assessment, or family therapy, but I am not so sure that students are really learning about families in all of their complexity. What I am concerned about most is that many students are being taught only one perspective on families. Since there is no single "right" perspective, teaching one point of view may be worse than teaching no point of view at all.

This brings me to the second point that I want to make: We need to teach students objectivity about the family. Because of our closeness to the subject matter, there is the constant danger that our views about the family--both professional and personal--will become idiosyncratic and rigid. We run the risk of asserting that the ideal family is just like the one that <u>we</u> grew up in. Or perhaps the risk is that we insist that the ideal family is just the <u>opposite</u> of the one that we grew up in. As one example of the dangers posed by lack of objectivity, consider the literature on divorced or "father absent" families from 30 years ago and compare it with the literature today. To some theorists in the 1950s, families headed by a mother were pathological by definition. There was no need to support such an obvious assertion. To some of their contemporary counterparts, single parenthood or divorce is insignificant. It is sometimes even suggested to be a growth process. I do not think the extreme differences in these views reflect that research evidence has changed dramatically in 30 years. I think that it is a personal/professional/political issue. Ask the parent who wanted to get divorced how the children are adjusting. Just fine. Ask the parent who desperately wanted the marriage to continue. The children are a wreck.

Consideration of the changing psychological views of father absence, single parenthood, and divorce brings me to my third point about teaching students about "the family": We need to teach them that there is no such thing. There are many family forms and family practices that "work," not just one. If we expose students to cross-cultural research, they should come to appreciate that many of the family practices that we believe to be universally healthy or normal reflect, in fact, our cultural values. Of course, it is important to socialize children to value what is valued by their culture, but it is essential that psychologists recognize the cultural and subcultural limitations of these value systems. We can reinforce this lesson about cultural relativity if we teach students a little bit about history. History tells us that family forms and functions have changed dramatically over time, even in the West. The "good old days" for the family were not all that good. It has only been a couple of hundred years since infant morality rates dropped below 50%. Throughout most of Western history ,over half of all children never lived to become adults, and knowledge of this risk, along with a host of other factors, surely restricted parents' emotional investment in child rearing. And the specialized family worker and family caretaker roles that have been portrayed as the universal ideal seem to have developed as a result of the demands and rewards of industrialization in the West. I believe that the changing world economy is, and will continue to be, responsible for further changes in family roles and in family forms.

Lessons about diversity also need to be taught by educating students about the sociology of contemporary families. Right now, only 63% of all American children are residing with their two biological parents, and 45% of all married women with children under age 6 are employed outside of the home. Of course, the percentage of maternal employment is considerably higher for married mothers with older children and for single parents. Of American children 10% live with a biological parent and a stepparent, and most of the remaining 27% of children in the United States are living with a divorced, separated, widowed, or never-married parent. Nine times out of 10, the single parent is their mother. Among black children, single parent families are modal. Of all black children in America 49% live with one parent, a figure that exceeds the number living with two parents. Statistically then, single parent families are not abnormal. And students need to learn that they are not psychologically abnormal, either. Although psychologists need to be aware of the stresses involved in single parenting, they also need to know about alternative family structures, such as the role that the maternal grandmother often fulfills in black families.

In addition to teaching about the diversity of family structures, we need to teach our students about the diversity of family functions. This is the fourth point that I want to make. Families are not merely psychological units. They provide children with education, community status, and economic support. The economic function of families is perhaps the most important, or at least the most obvious. Of all families receiving public assistance through Aid to Families with Dependent Children (AFDC) 90% are single parent families. Although a two-parent family is not inherently or universally better than a one-parent family, it is clear that, on average, the two-parent family is a more adaptive economic unit. Child clinical psychologists need to concern themselves with the economic situation of single-parent families, because single parents certainly are worried about their financial circumstances, and socioeconomic factors clearly influence children's development.

Of course, child clinical psychologists are primarily concerned with the psychological functions that families serve, and this brings me to my fifth point: we must guard against losing the forest or the trees when we teach students about family psychology. Family relationships are fascinating and complex, and the possibility that subtle differences in family interaction have dramatic, life-long effects on children's personality development is an assertion that is both scientifically challenging and personally appealing to many psychologists. But we must not forget the central psychological functions that families fulfill-- providing affection, socialization, and stimulation to children. Students need to learn about basic attachment processes in infancy, childhood, and throughout the family life span. They need to know about socialization through various discipline practices and as a result of parental example. They need to recognize the cognitive stimulation, direct education, and specialized values that families impart. Once these basics are appreciated, more attention can be paid to subtleties.

In learning more about the subtle complexity of families, it is essential that students be able to think about the family as a system. On the one hand, teaching students about the family as a system is a lesson in simplicity. If we can think of the family as an organization--like we think of a business as an organization--we can begin to detach ourselves from the subject matter and appreciate some of the straightforward benefits of things like hierarchical organization and clear, caring, yet firm leadership. We can also see some of the obvious problems created by lack of commitment, ambiguous goals, and conflict in the organization. Thinking about the family as a system also offers exciting new complexities, however, and child clinical students need to know about reciprocal influences, homeostatic processes, family subsystems, and implicit and explicit interpersonal boundaries. As they come to think of the family as a system, students also should appreciate that, like individuals, families have developmental histories and developmental trajectories.

The final point that I wish to make about educating child clinical psychologists about families is that we be sure to sensitize them to the limits of family or parental influence. There are numerous extrafamilial influences on children, most notably in schools and the peer group, and as much as we might want to believe the Jeffersonian ideal, children do not come into the world with equal capacities. Parents can influence children, but they also are profoundly influenced by them. Researchers have begun to document the strains involved in the transition to parenthood, and we are finally starting to recognize the tremendous challenge faced by parents with children who are chronically ill, hyperactive, or autistic. Students typically have not yet faced the humbling task of trying to rear their own children, and they need to be educated intellectually and emotionally about the limits of parenting. In so doing, we can train psychologists who will work to support and educate families about possibilities rather than blame them for failures.

Chapter 14
Clinical Training for Services to Children and Families: The Case for
Family Contexts and for Mission-Oriented Specializations

Robert A. Zucker and Gary E. Stollak
Michigan State University

Introduction

Psychology as a discipline has had a long heritage of liberalism, with strong commitments to social justice and to the protection of the underprivileged and the victimized. These involvements are embedded within the structure of APA (at least the way it currently exists!) by way of a host of divisions that have missions with a central concern for the melioration of social and personal damage and injustice. And these commitments are not just found within the clinical divisions, but are shared with a variety of nonclinical colleagues who are also concerned with the identification and solution of such difficulties.

At the level of concern with children and their welfare, psychologists have an old as well as a more recent heritage of involvement, going back both to Lightner Witmer's Pennsylvania Clinic and to G. Stanley Hall. In recent years we have, as a profession, been heavily concerned with the potential victimization of children that an overinclusive diagnostic system would bring, especially when this might start to label as permanent what is more appropriately regarded as developmentally both stage specific and epiphenomenal (cf. Achenbach, 1988; Garmezy, 1978).

It is for these reasons that it is still puzzling why an understanding of and teaching about the most immediate set of contextual factors for the child--namely, these concerning the family--should be comparatively slow to enter the mainstream of training for child clinicians. In the first section of this paper, at the risk of restating the obvious, we take the opportunity to again make the case that learning about the family and being able to operate clinically within this context is as essential to child clinical training as is an understanding of and ability to apply developmental data and concepts to one's clinical work.

The Case For Family Contexts

The family is the principal context in which early human development takes place; it is the system thatimpinges upon and relates to the external world of school, work, neighborhood, community, and culture (Bronfenbrenner, 1986a). And as Bronfenbrenner (1986b) also notes, "compared to other influences, the family plays the dominant role in the development of competence and character." It is therefore, the most logical context in which to interact if our concerns are the prevention of the disruptive and sometimes later irreversible processes of older ages. It is clearly one of the most central matrices within which heightened biological as well as social risk unfolds. And even when the focus of intervention is the psychopathology of adulthood, evidence continues to mount that the family is one of the most appropriate units within which to moderate the effects of chronic disorder (Goldstein, 1988). Thus, long-term outcome studies on chronic schizophrenia in recent years have highlighted the importance of this system of organization as critical in either the exacerbation of chronic adult disorder or in effectively managing and reducing the social damage of this profound human malady (Brown, Birley, & Wing, 1972; Doane, Goldstein, Miklowitz, & Falloon, 1986).

All childhood chronic illnesses are implicitly a family affair (Rolland, 1987). The family is the unit within which the signs are first noted of the child's distress; the family is the unit that puts social meaning on the physician's label, and thus either moderates or exacerbates the child's stress; the family is the unit that manages aftercare, and maintains (or fails to maintain) whatever long-term regimens may be called for in managing the illness; and the family is the unit within which any stigma about chronicity and/or disfigurement is managed and within which the possibility of death is faced.

There are a number of other reasons why family work is central to clinical child training:

1. Any work with children involves contact with adults, at the very least simply to obtain information. The first level of this contact is the family, and it is essential that child clinicians know how to relate to and negotiate in this context.

2. The understanding of systems has increasingly led to the discovery that child troubles are highly correlated with other troubles in adjacent parts of the child's world. Child trouble is often connected to parent difficulty and tragedy. Poverty, membership in the underclass, or having a parent who is an alcoholic or a child abuser is but one marker of an already troubled system. On these grounds, from the simple perspective of efficiency, the family is the logical unit for contact and intervention.

3. The family is the systematic ecological link between childhood and the child's later adulthood. It is also the entry context for school experience, and the background against which school experience is played out. It is therefore the logical first locus within which to operate if our interests are truly preventive.

Criteria for Training

These points are not new; they may in one way or another be found in various parts of the Hilton Head proceedings (Tuma, 1985), but they bear repeating. With this factual and conceptual base as background, we would like to briefly articulate a set of criteria against which the success of particular training programs may be judged, and then move on to a description of the evolution and current functioning of our own doctoral program. In developing such a list of criteria, we have retained Boulder Model training as the ideal, for the reason that it requires the clinician to stay more tuned in to the knowledge base, and demands a more steady assault on questions concerning where the field should evolve than is the case within a professional practice training model. We suggest the following as an appropriate training mission for clinical child psychology programs:

Training for the understanding, remediation, and prevention of disorders and troubles of childhood, including but not limited to (1) an understanding of and an ability to work within the ecological and developmental contexts where many disorders emerge and are maintained, (2) the development of competency in assessment, (3) the development of competency in intervention, and (4) systematic contribution to the body of knowledge and the professional skill base pertaining to these issues.

*   *   *   *

Evolution of a Mission-Oriented Doctoral Program

Within this larger context, the Child and Family Clinical Psychology program at Michigan State has taken seriously the case for working within contexts; it has, as its programmatic mission, the training of doctoral level psychologists to work with the problems of children and youth from the joint perspective of the child and the family--that is, the child and the system in which the child is most heavily embedded during the formative years. The present organization of training reflects a series of developments that have evolved in a program that has been in existence since 1949, that has had a steady commitment to the Boulder Model of training, and that has produced approximately 500 Ph.D.s since that time. By late in the 1970s it had become clear to a significant number of our core faculty that the expansion and specialization of both the knowledge base and the professional practice base had made it literally impossible for any "generalist" program to train psychologists who were good at practically everything. Given that the minority in such programs--including our own at that time--typically are (and were) psychologists whose specialization is the training of child clinicians, it became clear that a generalist solution would more often than not favor training that had a heavier focus on the issues of adult functioning. The way we solved the problem was to develop several specialized sets of curricula, centering around particular content-oriented training missions that have some common core but are also heavily differentiated. Such was the resolution that was reached in 1980, which was the forerunner of the present doctoral program in Child and Family Clinical Psychology, as well as of the other differentiated program (involving training to work on prevention with adults) .

We mention this brief bit of personal history because we believe that what we experienced on a small scale is in fact the problem of the field and that the most effective model of training is one that recognizes and grapples with this need for differentiation of domains of training at the outset. We suspect that there will be more variation in how programs deal with across-domain commonality (i.e., what the core experiences across adult and child clinical, or between community and child, should be) than there will be in dealing with this common fact of across-area difference. In the remainder of this paper we outline a curriculum that has worked very effectively for us and that seems to share many common characteristics with other clinical child programs.

No program can find the time for all desirable content, and any effective solution is bound to involve some curriculum compromise. The direction our program has taken is to adopt a mission-oriented model of training, that first offers a general core in three different spheres: there is the basic science core, what has also been called the general psychology core, which in our program has been defined to include developmental psychology, statistics, and the APA distribution requirements; there is the core of generic clinical psychology (sometimes identified as the generic health service provider core), which includes courses in assessment and psychopathology, and in ethics; and there is the child/family clinical psychology core--that is, specialty training--which includes courses and practica focusing on the theory and practice of assessment, psychopathology, and intervention that is specifically child and family focused (see Table 1).

TABLE 1
Mission-Oriented Doctoral Program, Michigan State University

THE CORE

      I. Basic Science Core (Statistics, Developmental Psychology, APA Distribution Requirements)
     II. Generic Clinical Psychology Core (Assessment, Psychopathology, Ethics)
   III. Child/Family Clinical Psychology Core (Child and Family Focused
          Assessment,Intervention,Classification, and related garden variety practica)
   IV. Research Apprenticeship (in Specialty Area)

EMPHASIS AREA (SUBSPECIALTY) TRAINING

      Specialized Emphasis Area Seminars in:
          Classification and Etiology of Disorder
          Specialized Theories of Intervention
          Specialized Emphasis Area Assessment Techniques and Technology
          Specialized Advanced Practica and Clerkships
          Specialized Emphasis Area Related Research Involvements

---

MISSION TRAINING RELATED INTERNSHIP EXPERIENCE

      Specifically Selected Internship Experience that will supplement and/or complement
          university based training

Core training only begins the process of training for professional practice. Thereafter, we have made a deliberate programmatic decision to train for competency in a limited number of mission areas selected with particular regard for faculty interests and with an awareness at the epidemiologic level of what problems appear to be in most pressing need of a solution. This subspecialization focus, what we call emphasis area training, has been in two areas of special faculty interest and competence: (1) the problems of severely behavior-disordered children and those children known to be at high risk for such disorder but who are not yet so described, and the families in which such trouble and risk take place (we call this the severe problems area), and (2) the problems of pediatric psychological practice (the pediatric psychology area). The general core of the first two years incorporates a sensitivity to family system issues and begins to incorporate mission focused content, but emphasis area subspecialization is most heavily dealt with in the third and fourth year of the program. Subspecialization of course requires a resource base, both academic and experiential, that may not be available in a small clinical program. Thus, it is not uncommon to advocate beginning of subspecialty training at the postdoctoral level, usually in internship sites. Our own experience, however, clearly indicates that one can effectively mount such a program in a robust way at the predoctoral level if the resources are available.

A word about research: the Boulder model can be expected to work only when faculty also practice it. Clinical students will have less incentive to continue some research involvement after their doctoral degree is completed when their within graduate school mentors are involved in activities that have no direct bearing on the activities that they become engaged in after they leave graduate school. Our experience of the obverse in also true; when faculty are involved in problems of immediate relevance to the student's ultimate educational goals, enthusiasm and involvement are high. A mission-oriented approach to training makes this melding of research and practice easier to accomplish. At the same time such a commitment puts constraints on faculty interests and requires that there be some direct relationship between ongoing programmatic research by core academic staff and the training/educational mission of the program. But with a cooperating faculty who engage in vigorous dialogue, it is not only possible but also quite energizing.

Table 2 describes how these multiple educational demands may be integrated into a coherent educational endeavor.

One last point; given our emphasis on contexts, we want to underscore our awareness of the interdependence of the training program and its environment. The mission-oriented training we are able to pursue could not occur without a significant connection to neighboring programs, communities, and populations that are supportive of it, allow it to carry out its mission, are nurtured by the program, and in turn nurture it. Without such a network of interrelationships, our work would not succeed. With it, both the training and the community are enriched.

TABLE 2

A Program Involving Core and Specialty Area Training in Child/Family Clinical Psychology

FIRST TERM	SECOND TERM	THIRD TERM
	FIRST YEAR	
Psychopathology I (Clinical core)	Psychopathology II (Clinical core)	Psychopathology III (Special Topics in Psychopathology) (Child/Family core)
Clinical Assessment I (Clinical core)	Clinical Assessment II (Clinical core)	Clinical Assessment III (Specialized Techniques in Assessment) (Child/Family core)
Research Apprenticeship Statistics I	Research Apprenticeship Statistics II	M.A. Thesis Research Statistics III
Clinical Psychology Seminar	Clinical Psychology Seminar	Clinical Psychology Seminar
	SECOND YEAR	
Theories of Intervention I (Clinical core)	Theories of Intervention II (Child/Family core)	APA Required Course
Practicum I (Child/Family Core)	Practicum II (Child/Family Core)	Practicum III (Child/Family Core)
Thesis Research	Thesis Research	Thesis Research
Developmental Psychology I	Developmental Psychology II	Seminar on Ethics
Clinical Psychology Seminar	Clinical Psychology Seminar	Clinical Psychology Seminar
	THIRD YEAR	
Advanced Practicum I (Emphasis area)	Advanced Practicum II (Emphasis area)	Advanced Practicum III (Emphasis area)
APA Required Course	APA Required Course	APA Required Course
Advanced Seminar in Emphasis Area	Advanced Seminar in Emphasis Area	Advanced Seminar/Elective (in any area of psychology or other discipline)
Dissertation Research	Dissertation Research	Dissertation Research
Clinical Psychology Seminar (optional)	Clinical Psychology Seminar (optional)	Clinical Psychology Seminar (optional)
	FOURTH YEAR	
Advanced Practicum (optional)	Advanced Practicum (optional)	Advanced Practicum (optional)
Dissertation Research	Dissertation Research	Dissertation Research
Comprehensive Exams	Comprehensive Exams	Comprehensive Exams
Seminar/Elective (optional)	Seminar/Elective (optional)	Seminar/Elective (optional)
Clinical Psychology Seminar (optional)	Clinical Psychology Seminar (optional)	Clinical Psychology Seminar (optional)
	FIFTH YEAR	
Internship	Internship	Internship

NOTE: The Clinical Psychology Seminar is a vehicle that allows for doing program business and for the sharing of research and clinical content on a program-wide basis. It meets for 1-1/2 hours/week, and the meetings rotate through the three types of content.

References

Achenbach, T.M. (1988, May). Developmental psychopathology as a conceptual framework for training in multiple settings. Paper presented at the National Conference on Clinical Training in Psychology: Improving Psychological Services for Children and Adolescents with Severe Mental Disorders, Herndon, VA.

Bronfenbrenner, U. (1986a). Ecology of the family as a context for human development: Research perspectives. Developmental Psychology, 22, 723-742.

Bronfenbrenner, U. (1986b). A generation in jeopardy: America's hidden family policy. Testimony presented at a hearing of the Senate Committee on Rules and Administration on a Resolution to Establish a Select Committee on Families, Youth and Children, Washington, DC, July 23. (Also published in Division 7-Developmental Psychology Newsletter, Fall, 1986).

Brown, G.W., Birley, J.L.T., & Wing, J.K. (1972). Influence of family life on the course of schizophrenic disorders: A replication. British Journal of Psychiatry, 121, 241-258.

Doane, J.A., Goldstein, M.J., Milkowitz, D.J., & Falloon, I.R.H. (1986). The impact of individual and family treatment on the affective climate of families of schizophrenics. British Journal of Psychiatry, 148, 279-287.

Garmezy, N. (1978). DSM III: Never mind the psychologists; is it good for the children? Clinical Psychologist, 31(3-4), 1, 4-6.

Goldstein, M.J. (1988). The family and psychopathology. In M. R. Rosenzweig & L. W. Porter (Eds.), Annual Review of Psychology. (pp. 283-299). Palo Alto: Annual Reviews, Inc.

Rolland, J.S. (1987). Chronic illness and the life cycle: A conceptual framework. Family Process, 26, 203-221.

Tuma, J.M. (1985). Proceedings: Conference on training clinical child psychologists. Washington, DC: American Psychological Association.

SECTION V

BREADTH AND DEPTH OF TRAINING IN SCHOOL PSYCHOLOGY, APPLIED DEVELOPMENTAL PSYCHOLOGY, AND PEDIATRIC PSYCHOLOGY

Chapter 15
School Psychology as a Specialty Within a Group of
Specialties in Professional Child Psychology:
Education and Training Issues

Nadine M. Lambert
School of Education
University of California at Berkeley

Before I discuss the role of school psychology in identifying, intervening, and providing services to SED children, whether one is an individual practitioner or a member of a coordinated service delivery system, some preliminary comments may help to show how school psychology fits into clinical child psychology, child clinical psychology, or a general framework of psychology professionals who serve children.

What is a School Psychologist?

In my view a school psychologist is the cognitive, social, and behavioral scientist in the school setting who supervises and/or participates in a school psychological services delivery system. The school psychologist has acquired an appropriate theoretical and empirical knowledge base sufficient to guide the appraisal of the psychological and educational needs of children and youths and the design of educational and psychological interventions, and in turn for the design of a school psychological service delivery system. In his or her efforts to apply psychological knowledge to education, school psychologists consult and collaborate with teachers, parents, and administrators, and together they set objectives for service delivery. School psychologists provide a variety of direct and indirect services during the elementary and secondary school years to promote educational and psychological development and to prevent educational failure and mental disorders of all school age children from the normal functioning to the seriously handicapped, including the seriously emotionally disturbed child.

Brief Historical Perspective on School Psychology as One of Several Professional Psychology Specialties

School psychology was the first professional psychology concerned exclusively with children and the first identified professional specialty concerned specifically with the mental health of the childhood population. Among all of the psychological specialties, school psychologists, in their advantageous position of advocacy for the individuality of children, have enjoyed the best empirical basis for making generalizations about the interaction of children's psychological resources with educational processes. Having accountability for serving the whole range of individual differences from normal functioning to the seriously emotionally disturbed and the developmentally disabled provides them with a perspective to assign priorities for psychological interventions from modification of the classroom curriculum, to behavioral management, to counseling, and to referral to community mental health or community health resources.

Any discussion of the field of professional child psychology should be grounded firmly in the history of professional psychology at the time a particular developmental milestone occurred. For school psychology and general clinical psychology that historical period occurred when school psychology and clinical psychology emerged as distinct areas of professional practice from their common professional psychology origins at the conclusion of World War II.

After the mid-1940s (Fagan, 1987; Lambert, 1987b) the common path of education and training for generic professional psychologists divided into two major directions: (a) a school psychology track aimed toward studies of individual and developmental differences among children and youths and research applications to regular and special education programs, and (b) a clinical psychology track requiring knowledge of the etiology of mental disorders and their treatment, principally for adult interventions.

School psychology first became a recognized psychological specialization by state level certification to practice in the middle 1940s, often years earlier than licensure statutes for independent psychological practice. At least two historical factors accounted for the emerging identity of clinical psychology--one was the emigration of psychiatrists and psychoanalysts from Europe to the United States in the 1930s and the other was the establishment of the Veterans Administration's (VA) internships for clinical psychologists following the end of World War II. Clinical psychology's early clientele were principally adults, leaving to school psychology concern for children and adolescents.

Early Contributions of School Psychology to Recognize and Accommodate Individual Differences Among Children

In their early years, school psychologists extended theories and research on the psychology of individual differences in development and cognitive abilities. They applied the tradition from the teachings of early psychologists such as Thorndike (1911), who pointed out that teaching all children the same thing at the same time had a stultifying effect on development and that some type of accommodation to individual differences was a requisite to learning and development. Largely as a result of the efforts of school psychologists, teachers and principals began to accept variation in learning ability and other individual differences as a given and recognized the need to modify the educational programs to accommodate individual children. And as children's learning and behavior problems exceeded the capacity of regular education programs, school psychologists advocated even more specialized accommodation by supporting special education efforts. School and clinical psychology both recognize Lightner Witmer (Strickland, 1988; Witmer, 1897) as their predecessor. Even though he introduced the term "clinical psychologist," he obviously had school problems in mind when one of the first clients in the Psychological Clinic at the University of Pennsylvania (French, 1984) was an elementary school child who had problems learning to spell.

Long before child mental health was a national priority, school psychologists investigated the educational needs of children with emotional problems and were instrumental in the design of legislation to provide state subsidies for local programs to meet the needs of pupils with emotional handicaps. The language of Federal regulations for seriously emotionally disturbed children first appeared in California legislation in 1961, following a three-year-long field research initiative sponsored by the California legislature, conducted by school psychologists (Simpson & Bower, 1961), to determine how to meet the needs of emotionally disturbed children in the schools and the community. The legislation provided for a continuum of service from regular to special class instruction to home and hospital treatment. The California criteria were then published in the Federal Register and have persisted with some slight changes in eligibility qualifications to the present day.

Early on, school psychologists were the principal architects of the special education framework for the seriously emotionally disturbed, and knowledgeable about the needs of such children and adolescents. They have been foremost among proponents of more effective school as well as community service delivery systems. In these roles school psychologists have been in the forefront of the leadership movement to improve services to seriously emotionally disturbed and developmentally disabled children and to eliminate biased and prejudicial treatment of them in the schools and communities.

School Psychology as a Developing Professional Speciality

In spite of its long-standing history and commitment to professional psychology and child mental health, school psychology was not recognized by the American Psychological Association for accreditation until leaders in the field were able to negotiate with the American Board of Professional Psychology to recognize school psychology for diplomate status early in the 1970s. Recognition of school psychology by access to accreditation of doctoral level programs occurred shortly after, in 1972. Clinical psychology, on the other hand, had been recognized by APA for accreditation since 1947, almost simultaneously with the establishment of the VA internship program. The 25-year difference in APA recognition and the challenges of coping with state legislatures and state departments of education to institute appropriate levels of education and training for school psychologists resulted, in part, in the initiatives by the National

Association of School Psychologists to develop guidelines for training programs and service provision. At present both education and training standards as well as APA specialty recognition and standards for professional practice (American Psychological Association, 1981) have been established, and the policies of both the American Psychological Association and the National Association of School Psychologists are mutually consistent in recognizing doctoral as well as specialist level school psychologists.

School Psychology and Clinical Child Psychology

Earlier in this paper I have used the term "professional child psychology." This was a deliberate effort to recognize that among professional psychologies with an interest in serving children, there are at least three identifiable specialties at this time: school psychology, child clinical psychology, and pediatric psychology. And each of these specialties can be differentiated on several dimensions: the setting for service delivery, the clientele served, the emphasis on diagnostic and intervention services offered, and the scientific and professional foundations for the child practice specialty. All of the professional child psychology specialties share an interest in the necessity for coordinated service delivery, both within the setting in which they work as well as between settings and/or agencies.

The settings for service delivery. For the child population, the usual settings for psychological service delivery are the schools, community mental health agencies, hospitals and clinics, and the independent practice setting. Each of these settings has administrative structures for service delivery, and they can be differentiated as well by the types of client problems referred to them, diagnostic procedures utilized, and variations in intervention planning. Knowledge of the administrative structures and traditions, as well as training in the application of one's psychological knowledge to interventions supported by the intervention goals of a service delivery setting, become a necessary education and training emphasis in whatever program a graduate student is engaged.

The clientele served. Variations in range of client problems, from those encountered within schools, presented by children seen in hospital or clinic practice, and those referred to community mental health agencies or independent mental health practitioners, also define differences among the professional child specializations. School psychologists are concerned primarily with the educational process and promoting the mental health of children by ensuring opportunities for continuity of academic and social competence and identity development in childhood and adolescence, regardless of the severity of any handicapping condition.

Child clinical psychologists and pediatric psychologists serve a portion of the general child population usually centered on child and family factors affecting mental health and functioning, or psychological, behavioral, and biological factors interacting with the physical health of the child, for example. If we are to promote the mental health of the childhood population, careful study of the prevalence of various critical needs and/or risk factors and their age-specific manifestations must be made, along with an analysis of the availability of needed service delivery systems and coordination among them as well as the range of needed professional child psychological specialties. In my view, such prevalence data would indicate that more than one type of professional child psychologist is needed, and that the education and training of professional child psychologists would become preparation for specializations that are distinct from the preparation of the general adult clinical psychologist.

The services offered. Among the three professional child psychologies that I have mentioned, while all may share some common diagnostic and professional competencies, there are distinctions to be made about the differences in diagnostic and assessment procedures used, and the range of direct and indirect interventions that they offer.

The scientific basis for practice. In my definition of a school psychologist I mentioned that he or she is the cognitive, social, and behavioral scientist who has acquired an appropriate theoretical and empirical knowledge base sufficient to guide the appraisal of the psychological and educational needs of children, to explain the origins of children's problems encountered in schools, and to propose appropriate psychological and educational interventions. Within my perspective of specializations within professional child psychology, a first priority in developing these specializations is to begin the process of laying out the common and specific scientific preparation necessary for practice as well as the common and specific professional knowledge that each specialization requires. With the enormous psychological literature available to us for application to children's psychological needs, I believe that professional child psychology specialties draw from subsets of the applicable body of knowledge and acquire specialized knowledge that distinguishes among the child specializations as well as from adult professional psychology.

We give lip service but little attention to the scientific knowledge base necessary for practice with particular client problems in the several service delivery systems with which we are concerned. But to promote both scientific and professional child psychology, identifying the relevant theoretical orientations, as well as their scientific support, and being prepared to show their applications to psychological services would go far to improving education and training as well as ensuring high level professional practice. In short, I am dedicated to preparation of school psychologists who can identify and apply relevant psychological theory and science to the problems of children and adolescents in school. The educational foundation for professional training for school psychologists is that subset of psychological science and professional knowledge that is relevant to promotion and protection of the mental health of children in schools (Lambert, 1965; Lambert, 1987b). We already have such an ideal in our current education and training models as reflected in accreditation and licensure statutes. But is it detailed enough?

A Proposal for Education and Training of Professional Child Psychologists

Taking some liberties with the diagram from the recent proposal from the APA Task Force on the Future Scope of Accreditation, I envision education and training elements for professional child psychology specialties to incorporate differences in scientific and professional knowledge in educational preparation, differences in predoctoral training experiences in different settings with varying client problems, and differences in postdoctoral experiences. Such differences should distinguish professional child psychology programs from those for adult clinical psychologists, as well as distinguish among the child specializations.

We can assume that there is a basic scientific and professional core of knowledge that is common to all professional psychologists. Over and above this basic educational preparation, there should be advanced scientific and professional education appropriate for those aiming for professional practice with adults, as well as advanced preparation for those aiming for different specializations within professional child psychology. In Figure 1 I have indicated that there is a difference between an advanced school core of scientific and professional knowledge and an advanced child psychology core, but I envision that there may be more than two distinctions between school and clinical. I also have not taken into consideration specializations within adult clinical services.

Next are the practicum and laboratory settings in which a student gains professional practice experience. Again, these can be differentiated by setting and clientele. For convenience, I have labeled these very generally, but I assume that we could develop a variety of schemes to portray the types of child practicum training sites, clientele, and service. At this level, as well, there are differences in the training of adult clinical professionals from the professional child psychologists. Also, you will note that in the figure, I have suggested that education and training for adult clinical psychology does not prepare the student to apply to or practice in a setting in which psychological services are delivered to children. I have made this distinction because I have strong beliefs in the valid distinctions between both scientific and professional knowledge necessary for practice with children. The rest of the figure should be self-explanatory.

Conclusion

Obviously, I am committed to the importance of school psychology as a distinct professional psychology specialization serving the childhood population. But I also have firm beliefs in the important contributions

FIGURE 1

Education and Training Components for
Specializations in Adult and Child Professional Psychology

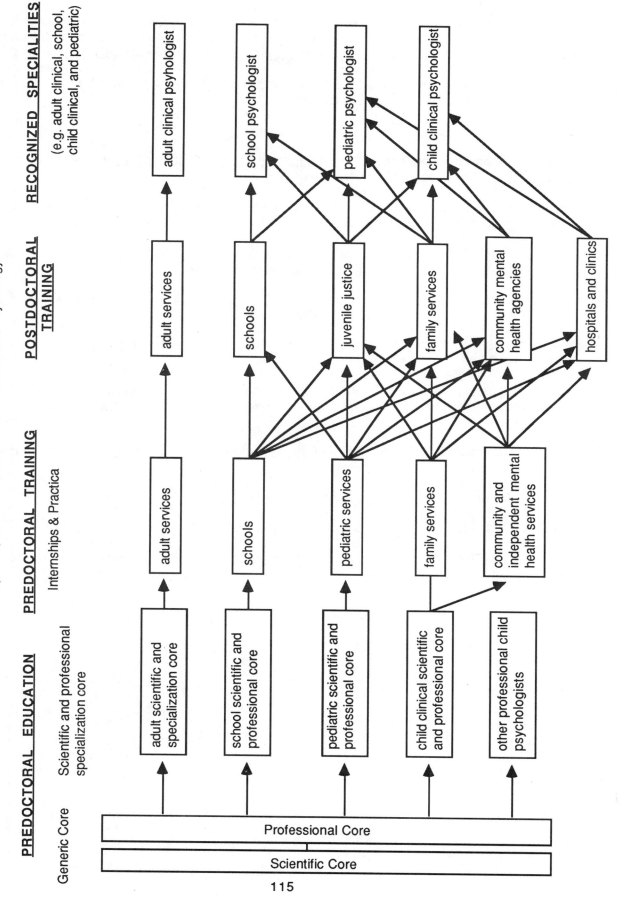

of child clinical psychologists as well as those in the field of pediatric psychology. We all have the welfare of the child and adolescent population as a common basis for interaction and exchange. And if we are to be successful in establishing coordinated service delivery systems, we should know a great deal about one another, at least enough to collaborate successfully. And finally, I hope to have made a case for the education and training of professional child psychologists as having important distinctions from the education and training of adult clinical psychologists.

References

American Psychological Association. (1981). Specialty guidelines for the delivery of services by school psychologists. Washington, DC: Author.

Fagan, T. K. (1986). School psychology's dilemma: Reappraising solutions and directing attention to the future. American Psychologist, 40, 851-861.

French, J. L. (1984). On the conception, birth, and early development of school psychology, with special reference to Pennsylvania. American Psychologist, 39, 976-987.

Lambert, N. M. (1965). The protection and promotion of mental health in schools (USPHS Mental Health Monograph No. 5). Washington, DC: U.S. Government Printing Office.

Lambert, N. M. (1987a). Comments on T. K. Fagan's school psychology's dilemma. School Psychology Review, 16, 27-30.

Lambert, N. M. (1987b). Conceptual foundations for school psychology: Perspectives from the development of the school psychology program at Berkeley. Professional School Psychology, 1, 215-224.

Simpson, R.E., & Bower, E.M. (1961). The education of emotionally handicapped children. Sacramento, CA: California State Department of Education.

Strickland, B. R. (1988). Clinical psychology comes of age. American Psychologist, 43, 104-107.

Thorndike, E. L. (1911). Individuality. Boston: Houghton Mifflin.

Witmer, L. (1897). The organization of practical work in psychology. Psychological Review, 4, 116-117.

Chapter 16
Dual Diagnosis--Mental Retardation and Mental Illness:
A Critical Training Need

Lynda Geller
SUNY, Stony Brook

With the deinstitutionalization movement, more and more mentally retarded children and adults are remaining with their families and living in the community. Their heightened visibility, coupled with the awareness of the more complex challenges that community integration brings, has led to the realization that mental health services for mentally retarded individuals are woefully lacking. Often, a large part of this service delivery problem derives from the fact that mental health professionals have little expertise in the diagnosis and treatment of mental illness in mentally retarded individuals, while mental retardation professionals have little understanding of psychopathology in this population. This gap is exacerbated by the dualism that exists throughout the country, separating mental health care systems from mental retardation care systems, and the lack of knowledge each system has about the resources of the other. This fragmentation can be an enormous impediment to establishing integrated services for the individual with mental retardation and mental illness.

A number of important training issues are raised by this problem. For one, the need for psychologists who are prepared to deal with so-called dually diagnosed children, adolescents, and adults will continue to increase on a nationwide basis as more and more institutions (mental retardation and mental health) close and contract, in favor of community placement. Individuals who have been ignored or treated primarily by psychotropic medications will now be living in the community, with the attendant stresses that this brings. Because behavioral problems and poor social skills are the primary causes for failure in community placements for mentally retarded individuals, the need for accessible mental health services is obvious. Thus, in our consideration of training needs, we need to develop programs for graduate study, internship, and continuing education that prepare new psychologists solidly in mental retardation _and_ mental illness, and that retrain current psychologists in areas to which they were not exposed in the past, in order to develop a large number of professionals who can competently cope with the specialized psychological problems that mentally retarded individuals present.

The training emphasis should be twofold:

1. A specialization in mental health work with children, adolescents, and adults with mental retardation.

2. For generalists, a sufficient knowledge of the special diagnostic and treatment issues involved so that these psychologists have the expertise to deal with the occasional cases they may encounter or to appropriately refer those they cannot serve.

Because the emphasis of this conference is on improving psychological services for children and adolescents with severe mental disorders, the following training recommendations will deal primarily with gaining expertise to provide mental health services for mentally retarded children and adolescents. However, it should be emphasized that there should be a thorough understanding of the special problems and therapeutic needs that mentally retarded individuals present throughout their life span in order for there to be true insight into childhood and family issues, emerging psychiatric problems, transition needs at adulthood, and chronic behavioral problems.

Graduate Training

Any psychologist who plans to provide services for children and adolescents (or adults) with severe mental disorders should be well trained in developmental disabilities because of the frequency of common etiologies, the high occurrence of psychological problems, the predisposing constitutional factors, and the family and community stressors. As developmentally disabled children increasingly are remaining in homes, schools, and communities, they will come to be a larger portion of a child psychologist's case load. In order to competently address the needs of clients who will appear in practice, the following areas of knowledge (many of which are already included in clinical training) form the basis of understanding of mental illness in individuals with mental retardation:

- Human growth and development
- Physiological psychology
- Mental retardation and developmental disabilities
- Assessment--intellectual, personality, and specialized child
- Psychopathology (child and adult)
- Psychotherapy (including behavior modification)
- Professional Issues (including least restrictive environment, legal competency)
- Psychopharmacology
- Practicum (an exposure to children and adults in a variety of community settings of various levels of restrictiveness)

For those who make the mental health problems of mentally retarded individuals a specialty, a more thorough and specific preparation is needed in order that they have the full understanding necessary to prepare to be an advocate, a referral source for others, an expert in specialized assessment and treatment, and a change agent in the community in resolving the many problematic systems issues these clients face. In addition to the above academic background, a greater breadth of knowledge and specialization needs to be achieved for concentration. The following areas of knowledge should be included:

- Neuropsychology (including biological bases of psychiatric disorders)
- Psychotherapy (including parent training, family dynamics, and social skills training)
- Behavior intervention
- Professional issues (ethics of aversive therapies, legal advocacy, and bioethics)
- Medical bases of developmental disabilities (including genetic perspectives)
- Social and educational systems and services

In order for graduate students to gravitate toward a specialization in mental retardation and mental illness, the field needs to be seen as valuable and dynamic and not as a stepchild among clinical psychologists. Until clinical psychology departments make an effort to recruit faculty with research and service interests in mental retardation, in general, and mental retardation-mental health problems, in particular, it is unlikely that sufficient interest among students will be generated to meet the need for psychological expertise in the coming years.

Internship Training

Internship offers the opportunity for trainees to gain exposure to a wider array of clients and develop their specialty area. For those planning a practice or career in clinical child psychology, it is crucial that the internship provide the trainee with supervised experiences with a variety of developmental disabilities and emotional disturbances, as children and adolescents with more severe disabilities will be making up a larger portion of most child psychologists' practices as the community integration movement continues to expand. For trainees who are planning a specialty in "dual diagnosis," the following area of experience would provide a solid background.

Assessment

- Experience with all ages through adulthood (even for child specialists) to gain a longitudinal perspective on mental retardation and mental illness

- Learning specialized techniques for individuals with sensory impairments and challenging test behaviors
- Experience with all levels of metal retardation
- Instruction in the adaptation of intellectual and personality assessment tools for individuals with varying disabilities

Intervention

- Dealing with family issues (adjustment to disability, training procedures, behavior management)
- Experiences with an array of specialized behavior therapy techniques
- Experiences in adapting standard therapy techniques to adults and children with mental retardation
- Practice with social skills training, an important tool for those with adjustment problems and to those with chronic psychiatric problems
- Instruction in the psychologist's role in medication management

School and Agency Interactions

- School placement - The trainee needs to gain a perspective for recognizing quality educational services by visiting a variety of special education settings, public and private
- For trainees who will have adults or adolescents in their practice, some exposure to the array of services for mentally retarded adults is vital, including group homes, sheltered workshops, job coaching programs, institutions, therapeutic day programs, and agencies sponsoring competitive employment
- Opportunities for trainees to have interactions with child welfare, court, mental health, and mental retardation agencies should be sought to gain an introduction to advocacy

Professional Development

- Ethics (aversive technologies, consent, least restrictive environments, behavior therapies, bioethics)
- Allied medical issues (etiology, prevention, early intervention, medical/behavioral interactions)
- Developing research questions of value

Continuing Education/Cross Training

Because problems in dual diagnosis have received so little attention in the past in either graduate or internship training, there is not a large cadre of competent psychologists who have expertise in assessing, treating, and advocating for individuals with mental retardation and mental illness. Because there are some psychologists who have specialized in developmental disabilities and others who have specialized in severe emotional disturbances, the training perspective for practicing professionals should be cross training. As members of each group have some relevant expertise, continuing education in areas of lesser knowledge can be provided to those interested in serving individuals with dual diagnosis. Federal and state agencies have recognized the dualism in service delivery that exists in most areas and the limited numbers of psychologists and other professionals who have expertise in both mental retardation and mental illness. Funds for the development of comprehensive cross training programs have been made available in many states and through the Department of Health and Human Services. Thus, the need has been recognized and appropriate continuing education opportunities should be emerging in the near future. Following is a listing of knowledge areas typically in need of development.

For Mental Retardation Specialists

- Manifestations of psychiatric illness among mentally retarded children and adults functioning at different cognitive levels
- Diagnosing emotional disturbances

- Psychotherapuetic approaches for mentally retarded children and adults and their families
- Psychotropic medication use (indications, side effects, interactions)
- Community and school mental health services
- Personality assessment (direct and informant)
- Legal rights and the mental health system

For Mental Health Specialists

- Levels of retardation and expectancies
- Community and school mental retardation services
- Manifestations of psychiatric illness as they may present in mentally retarded individuals
- Behavior management
- Social skills training
- Typical behavior problems and differentiation from psychiatric symptoms
- Learning and habilitation
- Adapting assessment procedures for individuals with cognitive impairments
- Legal rights (sexuality, parenting, competency)

Estimates of the incidence of mental health problems among mentally retarded individuals vary from 10% to 80%, depending on sample selection and disorder definition (Russell, 1988). Because of the ambiguity of these figures, members of the President's Committee on Mental Retardation have proposed a nationwide epidemiological study to help clarify the extent of the needs of this population in order that decision making and funding can rest on reliable data (Scott, 1988). In the meantime, there is general agreement that mentally retarded individuals are at far greater risk for developing mental health problems because of a number of factors, including a common etiology (CNS damage), genetic and metabolic dysfunctions, environmental stressors (family adjustment, community prejudice, inappropriate expectations), developmental influences (delayed individuation, underdeveloped social skills, poor language skills), and constitutional factors (hyper- and hyposensitivity, attention deficits) (Parsons, May, & Menolascino, 1984). The enormous gap between needs and services has not gone unrecognized by government, However, until the academic world responds by valuing the field sufficiently to develop graduate, internship, and continuing education training and to seek out as faculty and supervisors individuals with a commitment to the field, governmental funding and restructuring will not be sufficient to establish integrated and competent services for this population.

References

Parsons, J.A., May, Jr., J.B., & Menolascino, F.J. (1984). The nature and incidence of mental illness in mentally retarded individuals. In F.J. Menolascino & J.A. Stark (Eds.), Handbook of mental illness in the mentally retarded. New York: Plenum Press.

Russell, A.T. (1988). The association between mental retardation and psychiatric disorder: Epidemiological issues. In J.A. Stark, et al. (Eds.), Mental retardation and mental health. New York: Springer-Verlag.

Scott, K.G. (1988). The need for a national epidemiological study. In J.A. Stark et al. (Eds.), Mental retardation and mental health. New York: Springer-Verlag.

Chapter 17
The Breadth and Depth of Training in School Psychology

Howard M. Knoff
University of South Florida

There are many psychological and educational specialists who interact together to serve severely emotionally disturbed children and adolescents. School psychology has a long history of service to these individuals as well as to the students with learning and developmental problems (Alpert, 1985; Fagan, 1986). In this paper, I describe the training of school psychologists, focusing on the various roles that they engage in and on consultation as a critical role necessary to fully enact our training and utilize our skills.

Background

There are currently about 22,000 school psychologists working nationwide in the field and approximately 200 school psychology training programs (Brown & Minke, 1986). Most school psychologists have been trained at the 60-hour Educational Specialist (EdS) level or beyond, with about 20% having attained the doctoral level. Organizationally, there are two national groups representing school psychology: APA's Division 16 and the National Association of School Psychologists (NASP). NASP has approximately 12,000 members at the present time and has four major standards documents to guide the profession: the Standards for Professional Ethics, Standards for Training and Field Placement in School Psychology, Standards for the Credentialing of School Psychologists, and the Standards for the Provision of School Psychological Practice (1984-1985). These standards guide the training and practice of school psychology and are the cornerstones of our profession.

Relative to the training of child clinical psychologists, I would like to focus on the training and credentialing process of school psychologists, presenting a model that has been professionally derived and that can be applied--either in process or content--to this conference's task at hand. First, however, I would like to discuss the uniqueness of school psychology in serving children with severe emotional disturbances.

School Psychology in Practice

School psychologists work from a conceptual model that substantially differs from other child clinical professionals. This model involves the interaction between psychology and education, where school psychologists apply the psychology of learning, socialization, self-concept, school and family systems, and organizational development to the presenting educational and psychological problems of referred children (Knoff, 1986a). In addition, school psychologists must reflect children's psychological needs in a setting that emphasizes educational/academic progress. This often makes the school psycholgist a somewhat lonely voice in the school setting but a critical one relative to comprehensive service delivery.

Diagrammatically, Figure 1 applies Bronfenbrenner's ecosystem conceptualization to schools and school psychology. With the school building as the unit of analysis, this figure shows the referred child as part of a systems problem. School psychologists use this model to remind them that there are many possible reasons why a child presents with a problem--some that do not directly involve the child. For example, some children are identified as "problems" when the real problem is ineffective teaching, a poor student-curriculum match, or a trauma (e.g., a divorce) at home that carries into the school setting.

Another implication of Figure 1 is that school psychology has grown beyond the specific public school setting. School psychologists now work in hospitals, community mental health centers, developmental and institutional centers, and in private practice. School psychology, beyond the generic psychology literature, has its own research base, literature, and conceptual and pragmatic models. Driven by this base, school psychologists now work wherever the need for a Psychology X Education perspective exists. Clearly, as more school psychologists exist in nonschool settings, the opportunity for greater

FIGURE 1
The ecomap, adapted from Bronfenbrenner's ecological
systems model, showing possible environmental systems

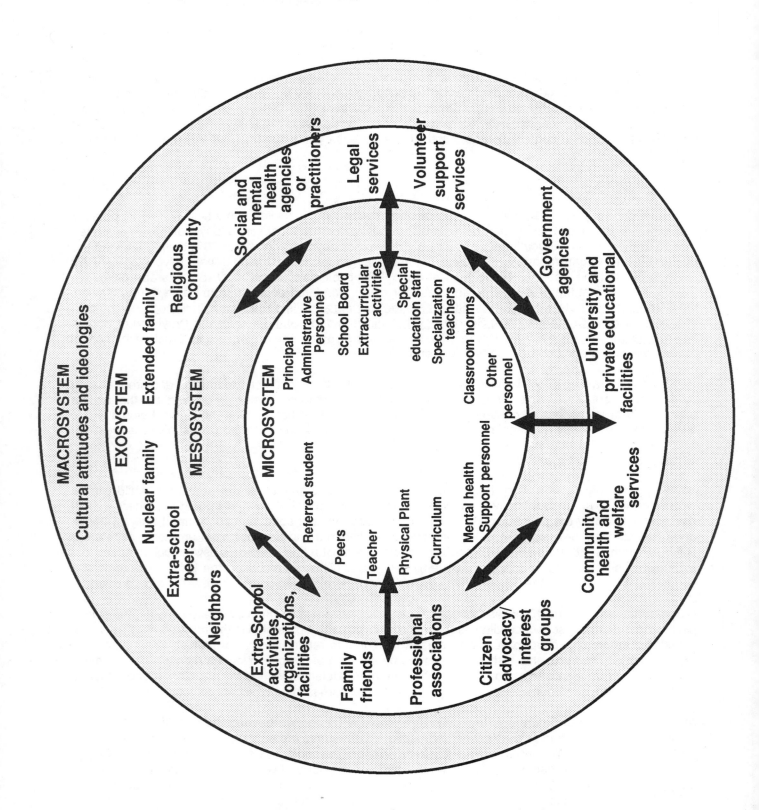

From "Personality Assessment in the Schools: Issues and Procedures" by
Howard M. Knoff, 1983, School Psychology Review, 12, p. 394. Copyright 1983
by National Association of School Psychologists. Adapted by permission.

interactions with other professionals will also increase--all for the benefit for the children whom we serve.

Training and Credentialing in School Psychology

As noted above, NASP has two standard documents that drive the training and credentialing process. Table 1 reveals aspects of these standards that are important to clinical training of school psychologists. Descriptively, it is important to look at the scope of course work that is required for all EdA level school psychologists. In addition, the full-year internship, primarily in a school setting, is critical in reinforcing the didactic course work and practice that school psychologists are initially trained in, as well as providing an integrated experience in the comprehensive delivery of school psychological services within a real organizational context. Beyond the internship, NASP requires three years of postcertification supervision of at least one hour per week before a permanent state-authorized credential (i.e., certificate) may be awarded. Thus, completion of the course work and experiences in Table 1 results in state certification at the Entry Level, whereas three years of job-related experience and supervision qualifies one for certification at the Independent Practice Level.

Recently, NASP initiated the National School Psychology Certification System. In this system, a nationally certified school psycholgist is one who has completed a 60-graduate-hour EdS (or equivalent) program as outlined in Table 1 and has passed the National School Psychology Examination given by the Educational Testing Service. This system will ensure that quality school psychological training occurs across the country, so that quality school psychology practice is similarly commonplace. An important aspect of this registry program is that ongoing membership will require 75 contact hours of continuing education (or university course work) every three years. This requirement will facilitate a process whereby school psychologists are continually maintaining and upgrading their skills.

It is important to note, finally, that school psychological credentialing and entry into the national system occurs at the 60-hour specialist or equivalent level. This level is the accepted level of certification and entry for the profession of school psychology; it is the most prevalent level for the thousands of school psychologists across the country.

A Model of Training and Practice

Beyond the training criteria derived above, a model of supervision that guides both training and practice has been suggested by Knoff (1986b). This model, revealed in Figure 2, consists of three components. The status component recognizes that school psychology training and practice involves both preservice and postcredentialing levels and ongoing continuing professional development. The supervision component identifies five areas of training across the status levels. These five areas are testimony to the complexity of sound professional training and practice, that is, a reinforcement of the notion that simple knowledge is not enough for appropriate practice. Finally, the functions components recognize that school psychologists engage in assessment, indirect, and direct services to SED children.

At this point, I would like to expand briefly the notion of indirect services because school psychologists spend much of their intervention time in indirect or consultation service delivery rather than in the direct or psychotherapeutic service done in the community mental health sector. More specifically, school psychologists often work with teachers and parents in such a way that the psycholoigists' actions will positively affect SED children (see Table 2). This indirect service delivery (see Figure 3) is a conscious focus of training for school psychologists at the preservice level.

There are seven models of consultation (see Table 3) that can be used to serve SED students. Some of them focus on child-specific services and some on program-related services (see Table 4 and 5). While space limitations preclude an expansion beyond this point, it is critical to emphasize that school psychologists must be proficient in facilitating individual child change as well as systems change. We can train school psychologists in all sorts of direct service skills, but if they are unable to get resistant systems to accept these services, then all the training is for naught. Training consultation processes, therefore,

TABLE 1

<u>NASP TRAINING AND CREDENTIALING STANDARDS</u>

<u>Educational Coursework/Qualifications Required</u>

<u>Psychological Foundations</u>

      Biological Bases of Behavior
      Cultural Diversity
      Child and Adolescent Development (Normal and Abnormal)
      Human Exceptionalities
      Human Learning
      Social Bases of Behavior

<u>Educational Foundations</u>

      Education of Exceptional Learners
      Instructional and Remedial Techniques
      Organization and Operation of Schools

<u>Assessment</u>

<u>Interventions</u> (Direct and Indirect)

      Consultation
      Counseling
      Behavior Management

<u>Statistics and Research Design</u>

<u>Professional School Psychology</u>

      History and Foundations of School Psychology
      Legal and Ethical Issues
      Professional Issues and Standards
      Roles and Functions of the School Psychologist

From "Standards: Training Programs, Field Placement Programs, and Credentialing Standards" (booklet) by Howard M. Knoff, 1984, p. 10-11. Copyright 1984 by the National Association of School Psychologists. Reprinted by permission.

FIGURE 2

A Model for the Professional Development of School Psychologists

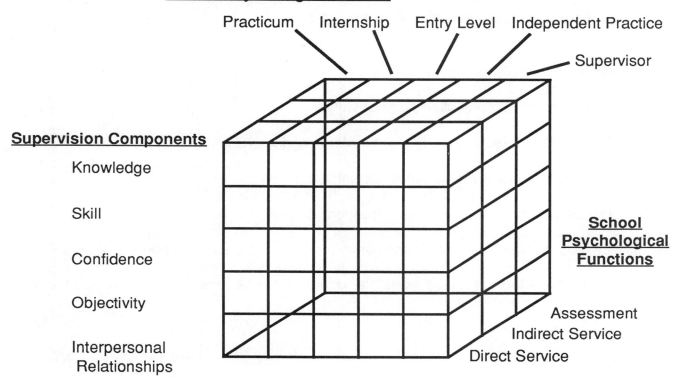

School Psychological Status:

Practicum   Internship   Entry Level   Independent Practice

Supervisor

Supervision Components

Knowledge

Skill

Confidence

Objectivity

Interpersonal
Relationships

**School
Psychological
Functions**

Assessment
Indirect Service
Direct Service

TABLE 2

Consultation Processes

The Primary Goals of Consultation:

1. To resolve identified referral problems

2. To improve consultee's understanding of and ability to respond effectively to problems similar to those referred in the future--and to hopefully prevent them from becoming problematic in the first place

Other Goals:

A. To provide an objective point of view

B. Help to increase consultees' problem-solving skills

C. Help to increase consultees' coping skills

D. Help to increase consultees' freedom of choice

E. Help to increase consultees' commitment to the choices made

F. Increase the resources available to the consultee to resolve persistent problems

FIGURE 3

Consultation Processes

Diagrammatic Representations of Consultation and Assessment

Consultation

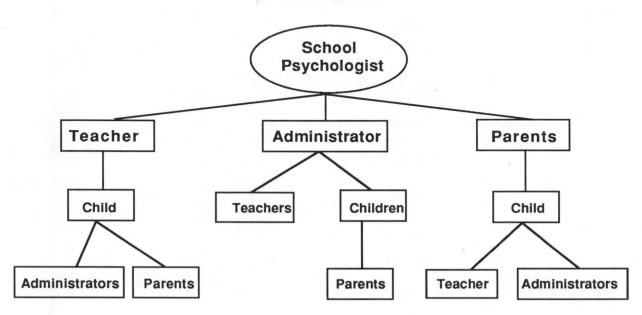

Assessment

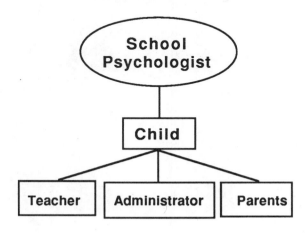

From "The School Psychologist-Client Relationship: A Heuristic Model Based on Service Delivery Roles and Organizational Factors" by Howard M. Knoff, 1986, School Psychology Review, 15, p. 298. Copyright 1986 by the National Association of School Psychologists. Reprinted by permission.

TABLE 3

INTERVENTION

Indirect Approaches

MULTIMODAL CONSULTATION

Acronym: PROBLEMAPS

PR   ocess consultation

O   rganizational development consultation

BLE   havioral consultation

M   ental health consultation

A   dvocacy consultation

P   sychoeducational consultation

S   trategic consultation

TABLE 4

<u>CONSULTATION PROCESSES</u>

The four types of consultation approaches:

1. Client-Centered Case Consultation

   Focus on work with consultees to remediate the difficulties of a child or group of children

2. Consultee-Centered Case Consultation

   Focus on consultee to provide skills and knowledge such that future problems with students can be prevented

   Primary Prevention
   Secondary Prevention
   Tertiary Prevention

3. Program-Centered Administrative Consultation

   Focus on administrative remediation of school-based programs that are not providing quality educational opportunities for students

4. Consultee-Centered Administrative Consultation

   Focus on consultee to provide skills and knowledge such that system-wide programmatic changes can be organized that prevent school-based problems <u>before they happen</u>

TABLE 5

CONSULTATION PROCESSES

Relating the Consultation Models with the Four Primary Consultation
Types/Approaches

Model	Client-Centered Case	Consultee-Centered Case	Program-Centered Administrative	Consultee-Centered Administrative
Process			XXX	XXX
O.D.			XXX	XXX
Behavioral	XXX	XXX		
Mental Hlth		XXX		
Advocacy				XXX
Psychoed.	XXX			
Strategic				XXX

must be required for all school psychologists and for all child clinical psychologists.

Summary

In this chapter, I have described the training and certification process that is already in place in school psychology. This process was then put into the context of supervision and professional development. A final emphasis was then placed on training in consultation or indirect services along with the more traditional assessment and direct intervention services.

School psychology is a necessary and important profession in the delivery of services to SED students. Unfortunately, school psychologists are often trained separately from other child clinical psychologists. Joint training, where appropriate, would not only maximize the use of university personnel but also begin a process of collaboration and understanding across the major psychological professions dealing with SED services. I encourage this joint training and collaboration as an important way to ensure quality training and service delivery in this most complex and interesting area of child psychology.

References

Alpert, J.L. (1985). Change within a profession. American Psychologist, 40, 1112-1121.

Brown, D.T., & Minke, K.M. (1986). School psychology graduate training: A comprehensive analysis. American Psychologist, 40, 1328-1338.

Fagan, T.K. (1986). School psychology's dilemma: Reappraising solutions and directing attention to the future. American Psychologist, 40, 851-861.

Knoff, H.M. (1986a). The assessment of child and adolescent personality. New York: Guilford Press.

Knoff, H.M. (1986b). Supervision in school psychology: The forgotten or future path to affective services? School Psychology Review, 15, 529-545.

Chapter 18
Training of Psychologists in Autism and Related Severe Development Disorders

Lee. M. Marcus

Director of Psychology Training, TEACHH Division, University of North Carolina School of Medicine

This paper describes a training model for psychology interns and postdoctoral fellows developed by the TEACCH program (Treatment and Education of Autistic and related Communication-handicapped Children) in the Department of Psychiatry at the University of North Carolina School of Medicine. Since 1984, TEACCH has had funding from NIMH for multidisciplinary training involving the training of two psychology interns and two social work students a year. The training of psychologists has evolved over the past 15 years and has paralleled the growth of the TEACCH program as an internationally recognized comprehensive diagnostic, treatment, consultation, and research center in the area of autism and other severe developmental disorders (Schopler, 1987). The training provided by TEACCH is a part of the general internship program at the University of North Carolina. TEACCH interns participate in a wide range of pediatric, child psychiatry, and developmental settings along with their TEACCH experiences.

Goals of Training at TEACCH

TEACCH provides a broad range of services to autistic children, adolescents, adults, and their families, including diagnostic evaluation, individualized treatment, special education, school and other agency consultations, parent training and counseling, and facilitation of parent group activities. TEACCH also maintains an active research program and provides a wide range of multidisciplinary training and dissemination activities for professionals. Interns have the opportunity to participate in all aspects of the TEACCH program. Specific goals include:

1. To develop and expand knowledge of concepts and issues in autism and related disorders.

2. To develop and apply principles of normal child development and social learning theory to the understanding and treatment of autism and related disorders.

3. To learn the process of diagnostic evaluation as well as of psychoeducational, developmental, and cognitive behavioral assessment of autistic and other communication-disordered individuals (Schopler & Reichler, 1979; Schopler, Reichler, & Renner, 1986).

4. To develop an understanding of the process of individualizing educational and cognitive behavioral programs for autistic children, adolescents, and adults (Schopler, Reichler, & Lansing, 1980).

5. To learn the process of adapting teaching programs to needs, concerns, and capacities of the family and help parents to live more effectively with their children (Schopler, Mesibov, Shigley, & Bashford, 1984).

6. To understand and facilitate the relationship of the child and family to larger social networks, including public school classrooms and consultation activities (Marcus & Olley, 1988).

7. To assess and develop interventions for adolescents and adults with autism, including individual counseling and participation in social skills training groups (Mesibov, 1986; Mesibov, Schopler, Schaffer, & Landrus, 1988).

8. To become familiar with the activities of the statewide advocacy network, the Autism Society of North Carolina.

Methods and Features of Training

The TEACCH intern spends approximately half of his/her time with TEACCH during the year and half in other clinical training activities that will be described later. Several features of the training approach are unique to this setting.

Generalist Model

The emphasis is on training the intern as a staff therapist using the generalist model. This model focuses primary attention on the needs of the child and the family rather than on the needs of the various professional disciplines, which has traditionally occurred in mental health and other systems that emphasize specialization. Clinic staff are designated as psychoeducational therapists and serve on diagnostic teams, providing whatever treatment or services are needed by the child and family. These therapists have educational backgrounds in diverse fields, including special education, early childhood education, social work, speech pathology, occupational therapy, and psychology. Their knowledge base is broad because of the intense initial and ongoing training provided by TEACCH. An underlying principle is that teachers, therapists, and others dealing with the autistic individual, like parents, have to deal with all aspects of the child's life, regardless of the degree of expertise. Only generalists and parents, unlike specialists, are willing to relate to all aspects of the child's functioning and to communicate on behalf of the entire child, as well as advocate for the psychology intern and provide primary supervision on assessment, treatment, and consultation activities. The clinical director, a licensed clinical child psychologist, coordinates the overall training and provides additional supervision in the areas of diagnosis and treatment.

Collaborative, "Hands-On" Training

In all training activities the intern is assigned a clinic therapist. During the course of the year, the intern works with and has been supervised by the entire clinic staff. Thus the intern has an opportunity to gain knowledge and techniques from individuals representing a wide range of perspectives, although these professionals share a common set of basic strategies and a core philosophy. In addition, the intern has a mentor, an experienced therapist, who meets with him or her regularly to discuss general issues and conceptual aspects of treatment beyond the particulars of an individual case.

The overall training strategy of closely monitored and hands-on supervision stems from the recognition that although interns usually have a strong background in assessment and knowledge of child psychopathology, they are typically inexperienced with autism and with TEACCH methods of diagnostic evaluation and treatment. For example, training in diagnosis and assessment requires the intern to learn the major test instruments, the Psychoeducational Profile (PEP) (Schopler & Reichler, 1979), the Adolescent and Adult Psychoeducational Profile (Mesibov et al., 1988), and the Childhood Autism Rating Scale (Schopler, Reichler, & Renner, 1986). During the first four-month rotation, the intern initially observes a therapist administer these instruments, scores and reviews the scoring, and becomes a member of the staff meeting. On subsequent evaluations the intern is given increasingly more responsibility for the administration of the PEP. Most interns are fairly independent by the fifth or sixth evaluation, although a therapist supervisor or the clinical director continues to work with the intern throughout the course of training.

Treatment cases are similarly supervised. Interns assume one of the two roles in the parents-as-cotherapists model: as child therapist, the intern has responsibility for developing a teaching program for the child and training the parent in it; as a parent consultant, the intern provides emotional support as well as helps with behavior management problems and self-help issues. Therapists provide immediate and close case supervision. Typically a case has a therapist assigned to one role and the intern and supervisor assigned to the other role. Thus an intern is not only well supervised but has the opportunity to learn from the other therapist assigned to the case. Interns also collaborate with therapists on consultation activities, whether on an individual case or a program such as a classroom or group home. They observe the therapist initially and later take on greater responsibility for making suggestions to the consultee. Thus, the principle of collaboration or partnership, central to the philosophy of TEACCH work with families and community agencies, is extended to internship training.

Encouragement of Individual Interests

Although all interns are expected to follow the core curriculum outlined above, each has an opportunity to pursue a specialized clinical interest within the framework of the program. These individualized activities tend to evolve or occur naturally as situations arise. To give some examples, one intern with a particular interest in parent support issues helped establish a group of mothers of young autistic children. She codirected the group along with the clinical director, facilitated the development of the structure and methods of the group, and was largely instrumental in the success of the program, which has become a regular part of intern training. Another intern had a strong interest in a diagnostic test that had been used in a research project at TEACCH. Although not a routinely administered test at the clinic, the instrument was useful for certain higher level children and adolescents. The intern found opportunities to give the test, helped in the modification of the score forms to improve the administration, and stimulated interest in the test at the clinic. As a third example, an intern who came with strong classroom consultation skills, although limited experience in autism, became quickly involved with a new case in which an autistic child was beginning second grade, a precarious mainstream situation. Because the classroom was nearby, the intern, just beginning training, had time available, and she was able to make frequent visits to the school and communicate closely with school staff, the parents, and TEACCH. The consultation went well and the mainstreaming was successful. This was an instance of capitalizing on the interests and background of the intern, while providing a meaningful learning experience in understanding the problems of autism.

Related Training Opportunities

Although the primary training setting for the intern is with TEACCH, half of the time is spent in other child programs that enhance the breadth and depth of the internship experience. The major rotations are briefly described.

Clinical Center for the Study of Development and Learning (CDL). This is an interdisciplinary program offering services to children with developmental disorders. Assessment and treatment programs are carried out by 11 disciplines. CDL offers training in assessment, treatment, and consultation skills for working with diagnoses such as mental retardation, cerebral palsy, learning disability, epilepsy, and other developmentally disabling conditions. The age range extends from infancy through adulthood and includes work with the individual, family, school, group homes, day care centers, and other community settings. Training is provided through one-to-one supervision of clinical activities, planned seminars, interdisciplinary staff conferences, grand rounds presentations, and workshops. A special emphasis is placed on working with and learning from other disciplines represented in the center, particularly in the assessment and treatment of multihandicapped clients. Other disciplines include pediatrics, pedodontics, physical therapy, occupational therapy, nutrition, audiology, communicative disorders, social work, nursing, and special education.

Pediatric Psychiatry/Psychology Liaison Program. The major program objective is to teach pediatric residents, interns, and medical students the diagnosis and management of developmental, psychological, and social problems of childhood, particularly those that arise secondarily to chronic and acute illnesses. To this end, the faculty has established ongoing consultation-liaison teaching relationships in a variety of pediatric settings, including (a) pediatric inpatient hospital wards, intensive care units, and nurseries; (b) primary care and screening clinics, which reflect pediatric office practice; (c) subspecialty clinics such as pediatric endocrinolgy, neurology, rehabilitation, oncology, pulmonary, gastroenterology, allergy; and (d) conferences on case management, child abuse, and so forth. Duties depend on the specific area of the liaison service in which the intern elects to work. The intern takes full responsibility for case management, compiling and synthesizing diagnostic material in the consultation, collaboration with physicians and interdisciplinary team members, and, when appropriate, presenting material at case conferences.

Child Psychiatry Inpatient Unit. This unit provides services to latency-aged children with severe behavior disturbances and their families. Services include intensive diagnostic evaluation, intensive treatment through individual sessions with the child, planned and controlled ward management, work with the parents, and school and other agency consultation. The intern is given primary responsibility for the overall coordination of the program of at least two children from admission to disposition. Responsibilities include individual therapy and behavior management, participation in family work and in the medical management of the child's disorder, and general case management responsibility. The intern participates in diagnosis and team conferences, refers for appropriate consultations, and plans and presides over disposition decisions.

Related TEACCH Training

In addition to the training program for TEACCH interns described above, other interns and postdoctoral fellows have the opportunity to rotate through the TEACCH program. Although the experience is briefer and less intense (i.e., usually one day a week for four months), the trainee learns the concepts and methods of assessing and diagnosing autistic children. The same generalist and collaborative training model is utilized. Often, two trainees, backed by therapist-supervisors, work together on a diagnostic evaluation. One will do the parent interview while the other assesses the child. This arrangement provides a supportive learning environment for the trainees, who learn from one another and the clinic staff.

Concluding Comments

The training opportunities provided through the TEACCH program as part of psychology internship training in the Department of Psychiatry at UNC constitute an effective approach to meeting some of the manpower development needs in the area of autism and related severe developmental disturbances. Psychology trainees master critical diagnostic, assessment, and treatment skills that can be generalized to other settings and other child populations. They are exposed to and learn a service delivery model at TEACCH that has been demonstrated to be efficient and relevant to the needs of the severely disordered individual and the family.

While being trained in this model, interns also are gaining valuable and diverse experiences in other excellent settings in the medical school. The total range of experiences links the training to the core concepts that have been recommended as basic to clinical child training (Tuma, 1985): understanding of developmental processes and sequences, dealing with the life span of developmental problems, multiple methods of assessment and intervention based on empirically validated approaches, recognition of the central role of the family, involvement with community agencies, and learning issues in advocacy and confronting and working with various social systems. This combined training represents a unique and successful approach to improving psychological services for this historically underserved group.

References

Marcus, L., & Olley, J. (1988). Developing public school programs for students with autism and related developmental disabilities. In M. Powers (Ed.), Severe developmental disabilities: Expanded systems of interaction (pp. 179-197). Baltimore: Paul H. Brookes.

Mesibov, G.B. (1986). A cognitive program for teaching social behaviors to verbal autistic adolescents and adults. In E. Schopler & G.B. Mesibov (Eds.), Social behavior in autism (pp. 165-283). New York: Plenum.

Mesibov, G., Schopler, E., Schaffer, B., & Landrus, R. (1988). <u>Individualized assessment and treatment for autistic and developmentally disabled children. Vol. 4 Adolescent and adult psychoeducational profile (AAPEP)</u>. Austin, TX: Pro-Ed.

Schopler, E. (1987). Specific and nonspecific factors in the effectiveness of a treatment system. <u>American Psychologist, 42</u>, 376-383.

Schopler, E., Mesibov, G.B., Shigley, R.H., & Bashford, A. (1984). Helping autistic children through their parents: The TEACCH model. In E. Schopler & G.B. Mesibov (Eds.), <u>The effects of autism on the family</u> (pp. 65-81). New York: Plenum.

Schopler, E., & Reichler, R.J. (1979). <u>Individualized assessment and treatment for autistic and developmentally disabled children. Vol. 1. Psychoeducational profile</u>. Austin, TX: Pro-Ed.

Schopler, E., Reichler, R.J., & Lansing, M. (1980). <u>Individualized assessment and treatment for autistic and developmentally disabled children. Vol. 2. Teaching strategies for parents and professionals</u>. Austin, TX: Pro-Ed.

Schopler, E., Reichler, R., & Renner, B. (1986). <u>The childhood autism rating scale (CARS)</u>. New York: Irvington.

Tuma, J.M. (Ed.). (1985). <u>Proceedings: Conference on training clinical child psychologists</u>. Washington, D.C.: American Psychological Association.

Chapter 19
Current Status of Graduate Training in Pediatric Psychology:
Results of a Survey

Donald K. Routh and Annette M. La Greca
University of Miami

Results of a Telephone Survey

Almost two decades ago, surveys were carried out of psychological training in medical school departments of pediatrics (Routh, 1970, 1972). In 1968-69, practicum training for graduate students in psychology was reportedly available in 24 of the 100 medical school pediatrics departments; by 1970-71, such practicum training was found to be available in 32 of these departments. These surveys found that unlike psychology interns (who were almost all trained in clinical psychology), students at the practicum level frequently had some other background than clinical, for example, developmental, abnormal, social, personality, counseling, educational, or experimental psychology. One thing that was not clear from these surveys was how many psychology departments placed their practicum students in pediatric settings. In large cities, for example, it is possible for a given psychology department to place its students in more than one medical school pediatric setting. Also, universities located in smaller communities may place psychology students in settings such as private pediatric offices or community hospitals not affiliated with any medical school. Ottinger and Roberts (1980) described a university-based predoctoral practicum in pediatric psychology of just this kind at Purdue University. This approach must be judged as successful, in that Purdue has probably turned out a larger number of pediatric psychologists than any other university (La Greca, Stone, & Swales, 1989; Routh, 1988).

The present study was carried out in preparation for the National Conference on Clinical Training in Psychology: Improving Psychological Services for Children and Adolescents with Severe Mental Disorders. We were asked to speak on the topic of graduate training in pediatric psychology, specifically the "nuts and bolts" of such training programs and how much can be taught or learned in a finite period of time. It seemed to us that the best way of attacking this topic would be to find out, in some detail, what training graduate programs were actually providing in pediatric psychology at present.

La Greca, Stone, and Swales (1989) recently compiled data on the universities that produced the most doctoral graduates who subsequently joined the Society of Pediatric Psychology (SPP) (Section 5, Division 12, of the American Psychological Association). Their survey included 89% of the SPP members for 1985. Twelve universities were identified as producing the most pediatric psychologists; each of these predoctoral programs had eight or more graduates who subsequently became members of SPP. In addition, efforts were made to pinpoint newer graduate programs producing pediatric psychologists. To this end, 29 additional universities were identified (a) that produced at least four graduates who were SPP members, and (b) whose average year of graduation (1974 or later) was more recent that the mean graduation year for the entire SPP sample (1973-1974). These 41 universities together accounted for 54.7% of the SPP members in the La Greca et al. survey sample and were the focus of the telephone survey reported here.

Method

During April and May, 1988, telephone calls were completed to informants in the 41 universities listed in Table 1. These were all of the institutions reported by La Greca et al. (in press) in their survey of SPP members for 1985. For each university, one or more knowledgeable informants was contacted. In most cases, the informants were directors of clinical psychology training or faculty members with a known interest in pediatric psychology. Informants were asked the following questions: (a) whether their university had an APA-approved clinical psychology training program, (b) whether there was an identified track in pediatric psychology within this (or any) graduate program, (c) whether a graduate course in pediatric psychology or equivalent topic was offered, and (d) whether a practicum in a child health setting

TABLE 1
Results of Survey of Graduate Programs with 4 or More Graduates Who Were
Members of the Society of Pediatric Psychology, 1988

University	Number of Graduates Who Became SPP Members	APA-Approved Program in Clinical Psychology	Practicum in Child Health Setting	Graduate Course in Pediatric Psychology	Separate Track in Pediatric Psychology
Purdue University	19	x	x	x	
University of Iowa	13	x			
University of Texas	13	x			
Case Western Reserve Univ.	11	x	x	x	x
University of Pittsburgh	11	x	x		
Vanderbilt University	11	x	x		x
Boston University	9	x	x		
Ohio State University	8	x	x	x	
Temple University	8	x	x		
University of Maryland	8	x	x		
University of Minnesota	8	x	x		
University of Virginia	8	x	x	x	
UCLA	7	x	x	x	
University of North Carolina	7	x	x		
University of Washington	7	x	x		
Oklahoma State University	6	x	x		
SUNY-Stony Brook	6	x	x		
University of Nebraska	6	x			
University of Utah	6	x	x		
Yeshiva University	6	x	x	x	
SUNY-Buffalo	5	x	x		x

Table 1, continued

University	Number of Graduates Who Became SPP Members	APA-Approved Program in Clinical Psychology	Practicum in Child Health Setting	Graduate Course in Pediatric Psychology	Separate Track in Pediatric Psychology
University of Alabama	5	x	x		
University of Georgia	5	x		x	
University of Wisconsin	5	x	x .		
Baylor University	4	x			
DePaul University	4	x	x		
Duke University	4	x	x		
Emory University	4	x	x		
Kent State University	4	x	x		
Loyola University	4	x			
Michigan State University	4	x	x		x
Southern Illinois University	4	x		x	
University of Arizona	4	x			
University of Arkansas	4	x			
University of Connecticut	4	x			
University of Miami	4	x	x	x	x
University of North Dakota	4	x	x		
University of Oklahoma	4				
University of S. California	4	x			
University of Mississippi	4	x			
University of Tennessee	4	x	x		

From "Pediatric Psychology Training: An Analysis of Graduate, Internship, and Post-Doctoral Programs" by A.M. LaGreca, W.L. Stone, and T. Swales, 1989, Journal of Pediatric Psychology, 14(1), p. 106. Copyright 1989 by Plenum Press. Reprinted by permission.

was available. Additional questions were asked as indicated to try to clarify what kind of graduate training experiences were likely to have been received by doctoral students subsequently identifying themselves as pediatric psychologists.

Results and Discussion

The principal results of the survey are provided in Table 1. This table lists the 41 universities, the number of doctoral graduates of each who were subsequently members of the Society of Pediatric Psychology (from La Greca et al., in press), and information about whether each university offers a child health practicum, a graduate course in pediatric psychology, or specific track in pediatric psychology.

As can be seen in Table 1, 40 of the 41 universities have APA-approved programs in clinical psychology (the informants' statements about this were confirmed by the listings of their universities in the December, 1987 American Psychologist). It now seems that, somewhat in contrast to the situation reported in the surveys almost 20 years ago (Routh, 1970,1972), graduate training in pediatric psychology is taking place almost entirely within clinical psychology programs. The only university on the list that does not have an APA-approved program in clinical psychology (the University of Oklahoma at Norman) is reported not to be producing any further pediatric psychologists at the moment.

However, the above information may be a little misleading. At three of the universities surveyed, the pediatric psychologists are reported to be emerging from training programs other than those in clinical psychology. At Boston University, although there is a clinical program and a child clinical track within it, the pediatric psychologists seem to be coming from the developmental psychology program. Although no practicum is required within this program, a number of these developmental psychology students have reportedly been able to arrange informal practicum experiences at the Children's Hospital Medical Center in Boston and then go on to do internships at the Developmental Evaluation Clinic there.

Similarly, at UCLA, there is an APA-approved clinical program with a number of child-oriented graduate students in it. However, it is reportedly the developmental psychology graduate students in this department who end up in child health practica. No child health practica currently seem to exist for clinical students at UCLA because psychologist supervisors with clinical credentials are evidently unavailable in these settings.

Finally, the situation at Yeshiva University seems to be a unique one. This psychology department does have an APA-approved clinical program, but its pediatric psychology offerings, including a course in preventive intervention with children as well as hospital-based child practicum experiences, are part of the APA-approved school psychology program instead. These psychology programs are unusual in that the department housing them is on the medical campus of the university (Albert Einstein Medical Center in the Bronx) rather than on the arts and sciences campus in Manhattan.

A notable feature of Table 1 is the number of universities offering practica in child health settings. There are 28 of them, or 68% of the departments. Thus, child health practica seem to be the predominant mode of graduate training in pediatric psychology today. Ottinger and Roberts' (1980) training model thus seems to have stood the test of time. Moreover, our findings are consistent with a recent survey of pediatric psychologists, conducted by the Training Committee for the Society of Pediatric Psychology (La Greca, Stone, Drotar, & Maddux, 1988), that indicated that most individuals first became interested in pediatric psychology via applied experiences with pediatric populations.

When we compare our current data with the survey results obtained 20 years ago (Routh, 1970,1972), the relative percentage of available practica seems substantially higher (i.e., 32% of the medical school pediatrics departments offered practica then, whereas 68% of the surveyed graduate psychology departments offer child health practica now). Of course, the present survey was restricted to programs that have been identified as producing pediatric psychologists; the percentage of all psychology programs offering child health practica would presumably be lower. Perhaps that more notable change from the earlier surveys is the fact that now a larger proportion of the graduate students in these practica are from clinical training programs.

Nine of the departments, or 22%, have a graduate course in pediatric psychology, usually with that exact title. These courses are often taught every other year and thus are considered to be rather specialized ones with limited enrollments. It is interesting that some of the universities that offer these courses are ones that do not offer child health practica. The informants from such programs (such as the Southern Illinois University or the University of Georgia) in fact indicated that although the absence of nearby medical centers made it difficult for them to offer child health practica, they considered the course a good substitute. Students taking such graduate courses would undoubtedly be better prepared thereby for later experiences in child health settings on internship or in a postdoctoral year.

Only five of these universities, or 12%, reported actually having a separate track in pediatric psychology. A special graduate training program in pediatric psychology, with a particular emphasis on producing researchers to be faculty in departments of pediatrics and psychology, is reported by Case Western Reserve University, which has NIMH funding for this endeavor. In some ways, this seems similar to the original Iowa training program in pediatric psychology (Routh, 1969). However, the Iowa program was funded by NICHD rather than NIMH and thus perhaps emphasized physical illness more. The Iowa program aimed to produce not only PhD psychologists but also pediatricians with a PhD in psychology in addition to their MD degrees (it never found any appropriate candidates for the MD-PhD program, however). Instead, the Case Western Reserve pediatric psychology program is linked up with a more streamlined fellowship program in behavioral pediatrics (funded by the U.S. Maternal and Child Health Service). As Table 1 shows, there are also special tracks in pediatric psychology in the clinical psychology training programs at Vanderbilt University (Peabody), SUNY at Buffalo, Michigan State University, and the University of Miami. Thus, it does not yet seem that the idea of a special graduate training program in pediatric psychology had caught on strongly around the country. Indeed, respondents to the previous survey conducted by the Training Committee for SPP (La Greca et al., 1988) considered the ideal preparation for a pediatric psychologist to be a combined program in clinical child and developmental psychology rather than specialized graduate training in pediatric psychology per se.

Some of the universities listed in Table 1 appear at present to be producing pediatric psychologists without offering either a child health practicum or a special course in the area. One might wonder how this happens. The tentative answer we arrived at through talking to informants from those universities (such as the University of Iowa and the University of Texas) was simply the lack of availability of child health research opportunities there. Even in the absence of any special formal program elements, a graduate student and a faculty mentor may come up with feasible research plans addressing child health issues. An example that comes to mind is Ann Deaton's (1985) dissertation at the University of Texas, sponsored by Ellen Olbrisch, on adaptive noncompliance among the parents of asthmatic children--an award-winning piece of research done in a department without a child health practicum, a pediatric psychology course, or a special program. The zeitgeist of the field may be sufficient to generate a certain number of instances of this kind.

Two practical questions need to be considered. First, what advice does our survey imply should be given to NIMH regarding graduate training in pediatric psychology? We suppose that it would be to encourage psychology departments who wish to do productive training in this area to "follow the leaders" and offer child health practica, perhaps special course work in pediatric psychology, and relevant research opportunities to interested students. One caveat to this advice, however, is that one also must consider the context in which these pediatric experiences are provided. Integrating our present findings with those that emerged from the SPP Training Committee's survey (La Greca et al., 1988), it would appear that predoctoral training in clinical child and developmental psychology is the preferred model for training in pediatric psychology. Exposure to pediatric populations and child health issues, through practica, coursework, and/or research opportunities, serves to supplement this more basic training and prepares the individual for a more specialized pediatric experience during internship and/or postdoctoral years.

Second, how is such training relevant to the problem of providing psychological services for children and adolescents with severe mental disorders? We believe such training is very important. It is often the case that child mental health problems initially surface in medical settings. Studies examining referral patterns, for example, have found that mental health problems present in pediatric medical practice at a rate that is five times greater that the referral rate to psychiatric outpatient and inpatient services (Goldberg, Regier, McArarny, Pless, & Roghmann, 1979). Furthermore, children's medical problems have psychological consequences for the affected children and their families. Along these lines, an investigation of the types of problems encountered in outpatient pediatric practice disclosed that only 12% of the child patients presented purely physical problems, but some 52% evidenced a combination of medical and psychological concerns (Duff, Rowe, & Anderson, 1972). For many children and their families, the existence of a chronic disease, or an acute but serious medical condition, can set the stage for problems in coping, adjustment, and mental health. Let us, therefore, consider the training of pediatric psychologists as an important aspect of providing psychological services to children and adolescents with severe mental disorders.

References

Deaton, A.B. (1985). Adaptive noncompliance in pediatric asthma: The parent as expert. Journal of Pediatric Psychology, 10, 1-14.

Duff, R.S., Rowe, D.S., & Anderson, F.P. (1972). Patient care and student learning in a pediatric clinic. Pediatrics, 50, 839-846.

Goldberg, I.D., Regier, D.A., McArarny, T.K., Pless, I.B., & Roghmann, K.J. (1979). The role of the pediatrician in the delivery of mental health services to children. Pediatrics, 63, 898-909.

La Greca, A.M., Stone, W.L., Drotar, D., & Maddux, J.E. (1988). Training in pediatric psychology: Survey results and recommendations. Journal of Pediatric Psychology, 13, 121-139.

La Greca, A.M., Stone, W.L., & Swales, T. (1989). Pediatric psychology training: An analysis of graduate, internship, and postdoctoral programs. Journal of Pediatric Psychology, 14(1), 103-116.

Ottinger, D., & Roberts, M.C. (1980). A university-based predoctoral practicum in pediatric psychology. Professional Psychology, 11, 707-713.

Routh, D.K. (1969). Graduate training in pediatric psychology: The Iowa program. Pediatric Psychology, 1, 4-5.

Routh, D.K. (1970). Psychological training in medical school departments of pediatrics: A survey. Professional Psychology, 1, 469-472.

Routh, D.K. (1972). Psychological training in medical school departments of pediatrics: A second look. American Psychologist, 27, 587-589.

Routh, D.K. (1988). A places rated almanac for pediatric psychology. Journal of Pediatric Psychology, 113-119.

SECTION VI

BREADTH AND DEPTH OF TRAINING IN THE INTERFACE OF THE JUVENILE JUSTICE SYSTEM, SOCIAL WELFARE SYSTEM, AND CLINICAL CHILD PSYCHOLOGY

Chapter 20
The Legal System, the Social Welfare System, and Child Clinical Psychology

Murray Levine
Research Center for Children and Youth
State University of New York at Buffalo

We are not usually aware of the degree to which the law states boundaries for our actions, and therefore our feelings and beliefs as well, until we encounter legal limits. The point is most obvious in criminal law, but it is equally true for every area of life affecting children and families. Legal rules fix our responsibilities when we enter into relationships, marry, procreate, abort pregnancies, raise our children, educate them, and when we divorce; after we die, the distribution of property to spouses and children is governed by legal rules. The relationships of individuals to institutions and organizations that provide social necessities such as education, medical care, income maintenance, employment, and housing are governed by legal rules. The issues are no different for the middle class than for those less well off, except that the lives of those less well off are shaped more directly by encounters with agencies designed to assist or to control. It is a safe assertion that the events, the behaviors, and the associated feelings that lead to the encounters with legally constituted agencies and the encounters themselves constitute stressful life events of a kind that are correlated with psychological disorder. A substantial number of our clients are involved with the social welfare system, the courts, the family courts, and special education programs. The targets for prevention programs are undoubtedly the same people.

Some examples will illustrate the number of people whose lives are directly affected by their relationship to systems and agencies that provide both social assistance and social control (see Levine & Perkins, 1987, for sources and further detail). The bulk of the approximately 11 million recipients of welfare payments are children. All of these children and their families are in direct and regular contact with welfare workers who oversee many aspects of their lives and who control access to income, medical care, training, day care, and employment, among many other matters. Hundreds of thousands of families are investigated each year because of allegations of abuse, sex abuse, and neglect. These allegations are called to the attention of the police or child protective services by physicians, educators, psychotherapists, and other child care workers who have a legal duty to report suspected child abuse. These reports at a minimum result in investigations but may result in the transfer of custody of the child to the state for placement outside the home, and in some instances the termination of parental rights. In addition, the families may be subject to criminal prosecution. Very often such families are referred to mental health professionals for diagnosis or for care.

Courts and lawyers have an impact on over 2 million persons involved in divorces each year, and over 1 million children. Persons in the throes of separation or divorce are frequent users of clinical services. The lives of children, their parents, their grandparents, and their reconstituted families are governed by legal rules regulating custody, visitation, support payments, enforcement of custody and support, adoption, and inheritance. The ramifications may endure for a lifetime. Many estranged spouses and many within intact families are subject to episodes of domestic violence. The reactions of the police and the courts, and the usefulness and limits of orders of protection all influence the sense of well-being and safety of children and their parents. A clinician cannot fully understand the actions, the emotions, and the attitudes of participants independently of the legal contexts in which our clients' problems arise and are worked out.

Over 1 million children and adolescents a year are processed through the juvenile courts. They are referred by their parents because the parents cannot control them or have given up on them, by the schools because they are truants, and by the police because they are alleged to have committed crimes. These children may be diverted to social agencies for care, may be placed on probation, or may be placed outside of the home, but in each instance they are under the supervision of the family court or some other agency with legal power over their destinies. These figures do not include the thousands of adolescents who may be placed in private psychiatric hospitals against their own wills, but with legally sanctioned procedures, for care for alcohol, drug, and other behavior problems.

About 4 million children a year are involved in special education services through the schools. Educational dispositions for these children are governed by elaborate regulations that define disorder, that define parental rights for participation in educational decisions affecting their children, and that define the services that may be provided. School psychologists are routinely involved in these decisions, as are psychologists in residential settings that treat many thousands of children each year. Psychologists in other clinics or in private practice can get involved in helping parents to press for their views of what special educational services their children should or should not receive.

The clinical enterprise is affected directly and indirectly by the legal framework within which we function. I shall skip over the direct and indirect power of legal licensing to shape graduate curricula, to limit entry into the field, and to affect practice by rules governing unprofessional conduct. Because of third-party payments, clinical records are less than fully confidential. Diagnoses and record keeping are shaped by the economic necessity to meet the requirements of third-party payers, to say nothing of how our anticipation of subpoenas also influences what we record about our clients. Even though legal privileges presumably protect the client against undesired disclosures of personal matters, there are so many exceptions and waivers, particularly in the context of custody battles, that the privilege is almost worthless. Although the Tarasoff rule is not followed in all jurisdictions, we are all familiar with its stricture that we take due care when a client reveals an intention to harm an identifiable victim. In addition, licensed psychologists have a legally mandated duty to report child abuse. The psychologist cannot guarantee absolute confidentiality to the client. Our inability to do so must affect how we communicate those matters to the client, how the client may limit disclosures to us, and how we may inquire or fail to inquire for fear of learning something that would trigger a legal duty.

I can best illustrate the training implications by describing our own doctoral program in child clinical psychology and law. In recognition of the direct and indirect influences of law on the lives of our clients and on the practice of clinical psychology, our PhD program in child clinical psychology at SUNY Buffalo now includes a concentration in law for graduate students electing to pursue that program. It is not a joint degree JD-PhD program. We opted for a concentration in legal studies because curricular restrictions imposed by APA accreditation, departmental doctoral requirements, the internship, and law school accreditation were such that little time would be saved in a joint degree program. Moreover, experience with joint degree programs shows that a large number do not finish the PhD but take advantage of the marketability of their JD degrees to leave without completing the PhD. Although experience is as yet too limited to say, graduates of joint degree programs tend to pursue either a career in psychology or a career in law and do not typically enter employment where integrated training is used or required. All of that may change in the future, but we shaped our program with those facts in mind.

Our program, which was supported initially by a three-year NIMH Clinical Psychology Training Grant, is now entering its fifth year. We have graduated our first PhD student, and several other dissertations are progress. The program has attracted substantial attention from students even through it is more demanding in its requirements than other tracks in our clinical program. We have started to present our research at professional meetings. Charles Ewing, on the SUNY Buffalo law faculty, is receiving increasing national attention for his work as an expert witness, and for his integration of legal and psychological issues in an analysis of the battered spouse defense to homicide. Gail Goodman, a leading developmental psychologist who is best known for her research on the child as a witness, recently joined our faculty. As the program gains a reputation, faculty at other colleges and universities are sending us students who want this track.

All students are admitted to our core clinical program, which follows a Boulder model, and elect options or tracks. Those in the child clinical psychology and law program take the same first-year courses as the other clinical students: assessment, statistics, and research methods. In addition, they take the introductory developmental psychology graduate course. In the second semester, they continue with statistics and research methods, and they take the child and adolescent section of our assessment sequence. They also take child psychopathology. In subsequent years, they will also complete an additional practicum in behavior modification with a family focus and complete courses in prevention and in child development. Beginning in the second year, students take three regular law courses in the law school. Each semester, they are placed for a day a week in a clinical psychological setting in which they see how some of the legal issues they are studying play themselves out in clinical contexts. They take family law first. The course covers marriage and the definition of family, separation, divorce, domestic violence issues, reproduction issues and parental rights. The students take juvenile law next. The course covers the status of children under private law and the emancipation of minors (e.g., ability to contract and parental responsibility for the support of minor), children's constitutional rights, the juvenile justice system, including delinquency and status offenses, juvenile offender laws, and state intervention into the family. The students enroll in the law school's School Law Clinic in the first semester of the third year. In the didactic portions of the clinic meetings, they study laws, regulations and procedures governing the education of handicapped children. The curriculum centers on Section 504 (prohibiting discrimination against the handicapped) and PL 94-142, the Education for All Handicapped Children Act. In addition to studying the basic laws and regulations and judicial interpretations of these, the course includes simulated hearings in which law students examine and cross-examine psychology graduate students who play the role of expert witness. The psychology graduate students consult with the law students in interpreting educational, psychological, and psychiatric data in cases the law students are representing through the clinic. We also have a psychology and law colloquium series, which is attended by students in all years of the program.

While taking the family and juvenile law courses, the students are placed for one day a week in either the Child and Adolescent Mental Health Clinic, which serves the Family Court, or they are placed with the West Seneca Children's Psychiatric Center. In addition to providing inpatient care to involuntarily committed children, West Seneca has a school, outpatient and day care facilities, and a school consultation program. The Western NY Children's Psychiatric Center also has a Mobile Mental Health Team, which provides consultation and other mental health services to all children in the region who are wards of the state. That means services are provided to children in group homes, in foster care, and in facilities for juvenile delinquents, including juvenile offenders (youth under age 16 who have been convicted of one of several designated felonies in adult criminal proceedings and are incarcerated). Students rotate through the Family Court clinic and the Children's Psychiatric Center.

Students observe family court sessions, undertake some evaluations, and on occasion have been asked to present their findings to a family court judge. The students are supervised by a staff psychologist in each setting. The students tour various group homes and other facilities that house children who have been committed to the state's care, including a maximum security facility for juvenile offenders. They also have the opportunity to observe the school program in the Western NY Children's Psychiatric Center, and they observe team meetings.

They obtain some understanding of the strengths and weaknesses of dispositional alternatives, an understanding that is lacking when clinical training is limited to observation in the examining or therapy room. When taking the school law clinic, students are placed in an alternative high school that provides them with the opportunity to interact with and to understand educational approaches to difficult-to-manage adolescents. The students have undertaken a variety of projects, including testing and counseling and other group work activities. The school also houses a program that trains the severely and profoundly retarded in skills for everyday living and does vocational evaluations of retarded adolescents. The psychology students take roles such as teacher aide and have assisted in conducting the complex and extensive vocational evaluation battery. The students come to understand educational approaches and learn to appreciate the problems of working with adolescents who are not particularly interested in being in school.

The students take second- and third-year law courses in competition with advanced law students. Because the psychology students have not had the benefit of the first-year law curriculum, I meet with the students weekly in a tutorial group to help them to learn to read and analyze cases, to understand legal terminology, and to help them to understand legal modes of analysis. The students need this assistance in the first semester. They take regular law course examinations on a pass/fail basis. However, feedback from the law professors indicate the students are well able to handle themselves in the examinations. In some instances psychology students have scored near the top of their classes. By the second semester, students feel comfortable with the legal materials and I meet with them on a monthly basis. The law professors enjoy having the psychology students in their classes. They frequently call on them to contribute to the discussion from a psychological perspective.

We encourage the students to do their preliminary qualifying papers and their predissertation research (MA thesis) in appropriate areas. We also encourage dissertations on psychology and law topics. Students have completed research on the child as a witness in a simulated sex abuse case, on factors correlated with the amount of visiting of children by noncustodial fathers, on the effect of reports of suspected child abuse on the subsequent development of psychotherapy cases, and on the degree to which family court judges follow a statute that requires referral to the school's Committee on Special Education whenever an educational handicap is suspected and an out-of-home placement is under consideration. We expect our research output to increase with the addition of Gale Goodman to our faculty.

There are some special conditions that made it possible for us to develop the program at SUNY Buffalo. The SUNY Buffalo Law School is unusually receptive to interdisciplinary work. It has a large number of faculty members with PhDs in social sciences in addition to their law degrees. Charles Ewing, JD, who is Professor of Law and Adjunct Professor of Psychology, teaches the juvenile law course. He is an experienced PhD clinical psychologist who has done and continues to do extensive child clinical and forensic work. Isabel Marcus, JD, and Louis Swartz, JD, who have taught our students in family law, have PhDs in political science and in sociology, respectively. Ronald Hager, JD, who teaches at the school law clinic, has worked extensively with psychologists and educators, and has an interest in empirical research. I completed my law degree at SUNY Buffalo about a year before the program began. I know many of the faculty and they know me. I have also been in the Buffalo area for a number of years and I was familiar with the various services and facilities in our community. All of these conditions, and the cooperation of the clinical psychology program faculty made it possible to develop the program within the psychology department.

It is too soon to evaluate long-range results in terms of jobs and careers. The program is growing. We are accepting four to five students a year. We are encountering some vexing problems of growth in terms of field supervision, research supervision, scheduling, and field placements. With good will, the problems are being solved. The number of students opting for the program reflects not only its reputation in the professional community but also the enthusiasm that students in the program show for it. It is their enthusiasm that draws in new students.

I offer this description of our program not as the model for other programs, but as an example of a program that takes seriously the necessity to understand the interaction between our clients, the legal and welfare systems, and clinical services and to train child clinical psychologists accordingly. I can think of many other models that would serve as well as ours, but I think that if we review our own clinical experiences, we cannot fail to conclude that a modern program in child clinical psychology must include some orientation to the law.

References

Levine, M., & Perkins, D.V. (1987). Principles of community psychology: Perspectives and applications. New York: Oxford University Press.

Chapter 21
Children as Objects of Social Control:
Implications for Training in Children's Services

Gary B. Melton
Center on Children, Families, and the Law
University of Nebraska-Lincoln

Organizationally and philosophically, perhaps the major difference between child and adult mental health services is that services for (or perhaps I should say to) children are almost uniformly coercive. Children and youth usually are legally impotent to seek or refuse services, and "voluntary" treatment is rarely the product of a minor's own choice. Particularly in more restrictive forms of services (even those that professionals assess to be of good quality), the likelihood is that a randomly selected child-client[1] not only would prefer not to be in treatment (Bush, 1980; Kaser-Boyd, Adelman, & Taylor, 1986; Lidz, Gross, Meisel, & Roth, 1984; Rivlin & Wolfe, 1985; Roth & Roth, 1984; Taylor, Adelman, & Kaser-Boyd, 1985) but also evaluates the problem as more a matter of family or community dysfunction than personal mental disorder (Small & Teagno, 1979).[2] The concept of blaming the victim is not foreign to most youth who are the objects of therapeutic services. As Achenbach (1980) tersely noted, "Children do not share the disease model of treatment for psychopathology" (p. 397).

To make matters worse, in many states a child may be "volunteered" for incarceration for the purpose of treatment by a social worker whom the child has rarely seen but who has legal authority to act on his or her behalf. The odds are low that the guardian social worker will have had even a conversation with the child about treatment and placement alternatives, despite the evidence that such involvement by the child in decision making not only is ethically desirable or even mandated (Division of Child, Youth, & Family Services, 1982; Melton, 1987a), but also that it is therapeutic (Bush, Gordon, & LeBailly, 1977; Melton, 1987a; Tremper & Kelly, 1987). Nonetheless, the social worker's action may bear the blessing of a guardian ad litem, who is charged with protecting the child's interests but who often has not even met him or her (Landsman & Minnow, 1978).

To secure coercive treatment, the guardian social worker typically will have had a number of bureaucratic avenues from which to select, literally, the path of least resistance. The child may enter the same therapeutic program through one of number of systems (e.g., juvenile justice, mental health, child welfare) historically and, to a large extent, ideologically derived from the juvenile court (Levine & Levine, 1970; Platt, 1977). Moreover, the court itself often still acts as authority for, or broker or direct provider of, children's services.

---

[1]Actually, the "child" is more likely to be an adolescent. However, for convenience, I will continue to use the former label rather than the more awkward construction of "child or adolescent." In any event, legal policy generally fails to distinguish among minors of various ages (see Melton, 1987c; Zimring, 1982).

The term "client" presents similar difficulties, especially given that the minor is per se incompetent to consent to services and usually even will be denied the opportunity to give or refuse assent to services. Nonetheless, I will use the term to connote that the child's interests are purportedly those at stake.

[2]A substantial body of research shows that parents and children typically disagree about the child's level of disturbance and the level of restrictiveness of treatment that he or she needs. When important third parties (e.g., teachers) are added, the reliability of opinion decreases still more. (See, e.g., Costello, Edelbrock, & Costello, 1985; Green, Beck, Forehand, & Vosk, 1980; Kashani, Holcomb, & Orvaschel, 1986; Kazdin, 1986; Kazdin, Esveldt-Dawson, Unis, & Rancurello, 1983; Kazdin, French, & Sherick, 1981; Rickard, Graziano, & Forehand, 1984.)

In such a sociolegal context, it should not be surprising that children's services now--just as in the early days of the juvenile court about three-quarters of a century ago--usually are aimed at youth whose most salient social attributes are that they are nonconforming and difficult to control--modally, conduct-disordered male adolescents from impoverished, fractured families (for an epidemiological review, see Melton & Hargrove, in press). In that regard, it is important to recognize that children's services generally are not directed toward protection of parental control, despite commentary that often frames child mental health policy as a struggle between the interests of children and parents (Melton & Spaulding, in press). Rather, they are expressions of social control, indeed state control.

Whatever the contemporary verbiage about both family privacy and children's rights, the evidence is clear that intrusions on children's privacy and restrictions on their liberty have steadily escalated in the past three decades, with the curve becoming ever steeper (Jackson-Beeck, Schwartz, & Rutherford, 1987; Lerman, 1980; Melton, 1987b). Most often, such coercive interventions in the lives of youth have involved concomitant intrusions into family privacy. Moves to reform children's services to emphasize services that are intensive but relatively unrestrictive would show respect not only for the autonomy and privacy of youth but also for the integrity of their families (see generally Gilgun, Schwartz, Melton, & Eisikovits, in press; Melton & Spaulding, in press).

The picture that I have painted of children's services is admittedly stark, but it is a realistic portrayal of many of them. Consider, for example, that efforts to provide youth with legal authority to seek treatment independently have served more to free clinicians from liability than to decrease the coercive nature of the child mental health system (Melton, 1981). Power of consent usually has not been accompanied by an increase in the economic, social, or geographic accessibility of services to youth. Consider also that the most outrageous mistreatment of youth often has been undertaken in the name of treatment (Melton & Davidson, 1987). Consider also that the majority of public funds for children's services have continued to be consumed by residential programs, despite the lack of any evidence that such programs are superior to less restrictive treatment models (Melton & Hargrove, in press).

I do not mean to suggest that child clinicians typically are authoritarian or that children's services are inherently antithetical to their clients' interests. To the contrary, CASSP has demonstrated that even a small commitment to care in planning child mental health services can result in significant positive change (Melton & Hargrove, in press). Also, at their best, children's services effectively leverage children by providing them with the skills and sense of personal control that ultimately promote their autonomy. Nonetheless, I see no signs that the primary function (and, therefore, the primary clientele) of the children's services will change substantially in the foreseeable future. I also do not foresee that the ethical and policy issues in children's services will become any easier.

In considering the training of clinical child psychologists, it is important to look straightforwardly at the tradition and presence of social control as the ultimate purpose of children's services. That reality has several implications for the design of training programs in children's services.

First, consciousness-raising is a critical aspect of training for future providers of children's services. Simply identifying the interests at stake in services to children and family often is quite difficult, and the prevailing law about which interests are paramount often is even more obscure (Ehrenreich & Melton, 1983; Melton, 1983). As I have noted elsewhere, the ethical problems ultimately become even stickier decisions about the allocation of authority and the degree of intrusiveness of treatment: "Amid these multiple and often confused interests, advocates with apparently noble intentions will use children--even their own children--to promote other interests" (Melton, 1987a, p. 359).

Second, consideration of ideological underpinnings of children's services should obscure neither (a) the conflicts of interest that are inherently a part of such programs nor (b) the practical problems of designing effective services that are respectful of the autonomy and privacy of youth (Melton, 1987c). Adults who work with children need to be aware of their own perspective on childhood and the social and political values that are wrapped in various approaches to children's rights. Self-awareness is not enough, though.

Professionals in children's services need to have analytic skills that permit identification of the politics of the situation and realistic planning (including adoption of legal and fiscal structures) for services to children, whether individually or as a class. Service providers also should be capable of identifying threats to due process that may be raised by blurring of lines between legal and therapeutic setting and purposes (cf. Melton & Limber, in press).

Third, training should be broad, with a primary focus on interventions that integrate educational/vocational, affective, family, and community components. With the emphasis on social control so deeply embedded in children's services, the recipients of such services are almost certain to continue to be primarily "multi-problem" youth and families, whose problems are both persistent and pervasive. As outcome research confirms (see, for review, Melton & Hargrove, in press), when the range of problems is as broad as that which most clients of children's services bring, it is unrealistic to expect substantial lasting impact of either 50 minutes a week of psychotherapy or a residential placement that fails to change the community setting or to build skills in adapting on the street. To be successful, new workers in children's services must be prepared to leave the office and structured units of service and to abandon rigidly defined boundaries of professional practice.

Fourth, training should include instruction in advocacy, including political and legal action, as well as more clearly psychological interventions (Melton, 1985). Such education should go beyond injunctions to be "nice to kids" to systematic application of social science research to the stimulation of social change on behalf of children and families, whether at a micro or macro level (see Melton, 1983).

Finally, training for direct service providers probably should be nondisciplinary.[3] I am continually struck by how insightful and forward-looking the work of Nicholas Hobbs (1975, 1982) was. In that regard, Hobbs's innovation of teacher-counselors was an inspired, if seldom adopted, approach to human resource development.

Both outcome research and policy analysis of the goals of children's services lead to the conclusion that providers of services to children and families should by prepared, as noted above, to integrate service components. The traditional model of coordination of services among various professionals is probably unrealistic in most communities, where a full complement of child specialists in the various professions is unlikely to appear. More fundamentally, such a multidisciplinary approach simply does not work for the youth and their families with pervasive and persistent social and behavioral problems who are, and are likely to continue to be, the focus of most programs across the major therapeutic service systems.

The mission and content of such services do not differ appreciably. If social control itself is to be controlled, professionals in children's services should be prepared to move across settings--to work as comfortably in a public welfare office or a juvenile detention center as a mental health center--and to conduct planning for all child service systems together.

We currently are developing such a nondisciplinary training program as part of a plan for radical reform of children's services in Nebraska. The highest level in the new training program (a Specialist [MA plus 30 credit hours] degree) will involve training in a mix of skills usually variously acquired by clinical, community, and school psychologists, social workers, family life educators, community planners, and special educators. Using a training-the-trainers model, the primary market for the new program will be community college faculty, extension agents, and bachelor's and master's level counselors who are in a position to

---

[3]In arguing that training should be nondisciplinary, I am referring to the identity of trainees. Programs should be interdisciplinary in content.

develop an integrated approach to seriously troubled and troubling children and families.[4] We aim to train specialists in children's services, not psychologists, social workers, or other traditional discipline-based professionals.

Admittedly, the conclusions that I have drawn are somewhat paradoxical. On the one hand, I have argued that children's services are designed primarily to exert social control on maladapting children and families and that such a purpose is likely to continue to be paramount.[5] On the other hand, I have advocated development of training programs that are designed ultimately to minimize intrusiveness and of services and to maximize efficacy. In the end, these conflicting thrusts can be at least partially reconciled. Professionals in children's services must have sufficient understanding of the law, ethics, politics, and sociology of the various service systems to plan services that reflect an understanding of the forces acting on those systems and that accommodate them accordingly but that preserve respect for the personal dignity of children and families.

References

Achenbach, T.M. (1980). DSM-III in light of empirical research on the classification of child psycholopathology. Journal of the American Academy of Child Psychiatry, 19, 395-412.

Bush, M. (1980). Institutions for dependent and neglected children: Therapeutic option of choice or last resort? American Journal of Orthopsychiatry, 50, 239-255.

Bush, M., Gordon, A.C., & LeBailly, R. (1977). Evaluating child welfare servies: A contribution from the clients. Social Service Review, 51, 491-501.

Costello, E.J., Edelbrock, C.S., & Costello, A.J. (1985). Validity of the NIMH Diagnostic Interview Schedule for Children: A comparison between psychiatric and pediatric referrals. Journal of Abnormal Child Psychology, 13, 579-585.

Division of Child, Youth, and Family Services, American Psychological Association. (1982, March). Standards regarding consent for treatment and research involving children. Resolution adopted by the executive committee.

Ehrenreich, N.S., & Melton, G.B. (1983). Ethical and legal issues in the treatment of children. In C.E. Walker & M.C. Roberts (Eds.), Handbook of clinical child psychology (pp. 1285-1305). New York: Wiley.

Gilgun, J.F., Schwartz, I.M., Melton, G.B., & Eisikovits, Z. (Eds.). (in press). Rethinking child welfare. Lincoln: University of Nebraska Press.

Green, K.D., Beck, S.J., Forehand, R., & Vosk, B. (1980). Validity of teacher nominations of child behavior problems. Journal of Abnormal Child Psychology, 8, 397-404.

---

[4]The particular audience chosen is not directly a product of the analysis in this paper. Rather, it reflects the ecology of rural communities such as those common in Nebraska.

[5]I have intentionally not argued that such a purpose is illegitimate. Although the application of control is questionable in some instances, for the purpose of argument, I will assume that such a function will continue to be viewed as legally and ethically justifiable. In any event, I expect that assumption to continue to underlie child mental health policy.

Hobbs, N. (1975). <u>The futures of children: Categories, labels, and their consequences</u>. San Francisco: Jossey-Bass.

Hobbs, N. (1982). <u>The troubled and troubling child: Reeducation in mental health, education, and human services programs for children and youth</u>. San Francisco: Jossey-Bass.

Jackson-Beeck, M., Schwartz, I.M., & Rutherford, A. (1987). Trends and issues in juvenile confinement for psychiatric and chemical dependency treatment. <u>International Journal of Law and Psychiatry</u>, <u>10</u>, 153-165.

Kaser-Boyd, N., Adelman, H.S., & Taylor, L. (1986). Children's understanding of risks and benefits of psychotherapy. <u>Journal of Clinical Child Psychology</u>, <u>15</u>, 165-171.

Kashani, J.H., Holcomb, W.R., & Orvaschel, H. (1986). Depression and depressive symptoms in preschool children from the general population. <u>American Journal of Psychiatry</u>, <u>143</u>, 1138-1143.

Kazdin, A.E. (1986). Acceptability of psychotherapy and hospitalization for disturbed children: Parent and child perspectives. <u>Journal of Clinical Child Psychology</u>, <u>15</u>, 333-340.

Kazdin, A.E., Esveldt-Dawson, K., Unis, A.S., & Rancurello, M.D. (1983). Child and parent evaluations of depression and aggression in psychiatric inpatient children. <u>Journal of Abnormal Child Psychology</u>, <u>11</u>, 401-413.

Kazdin, A.E., French, N.H., & Sherick, R.B. (1981). Acceptability of alternative treatments for children: Evaluations by inpatient children, parents, and staff. <u>Journal of Consulting and Clinical Psychology</u>, <u>49</u>, 900-907.

Landsman, K., & Minow, M. (1978). Lawyering for the child: Principles of representation in custody or visitation disputes arising from divorce. <u>Yale Law Journal</u>, <u>87</u>, 1125-1190.

Lerman, P. (1980). Trends and issues in the deinstitutionalization of youths in trouble. <u>Crime and Delinquency</u>, <u>26</u>(3), 281-98.

Levine, M., & Levine, A. (1970). <u>A social history of helping services: Court, clinic, school, and community</u>. New York: Appleton-Century-Crofts.

Lidz, C.W., Gross, E., Meisel, A., & Roth, L.H. (1984). The rights of juveniles in "voluntary" psychiatric commitments: Some empirical observations. <u>Bulletin of the American Academy of Psychiatry and the Law</u>, <u>8</u>, 168-174.

Melton, G.B. (1981). Effects of a state law to permit minors to consent to psychotherapy. <u>Professional Psychology</u>, <u>12</u>, 647-654.

Melton, G.B. (1983). <u>Child advocacy: Psychological issues and interventions</u>. New York: Plenum.

Melton, G.B. (1985). Training child clinicians as child advocates. In J.M. Tuma (Ed.), <u>Proceedings: Conference on Training Clinical Child Psychologists</u> (pp. 51-55). Baton Rouge, LA: American Psychological Association, Section on Clinical Child Psychology.

Melton G.B. (1987a). Children, politics, and morality: The ethics of child advocacy. <u>Journal of Clinical Child Psychology</u>, <u>16</u>, 357-367.

Melton, G.B. (1987b). Law and random events: The state of child mental health policy. <u>International Journal of Law and Psychiatry</u>, <u>10</u>(2), 81-90.

Melton, G.B. (1987c). The clashing of symbols: Prelude to child and family policy. American Psychologist, 42(4), 345-354.

Melton, G.B., & Davidson, H.S. (1987). Child protection and society: When should the state intervene? American Psychologist, 42, 172-175.

Melton, G.B., & Hargrove, D.S. (in press). Planning mental health services for children and youth. New York: Guilford.

Melton, G.B., & Limber, S. (in press). Psychologists' involvement in cases of child maltreatment: Limits of role and expertise. American Psychologist.

Melton, G.B., & Spaulding, W.J. (in press). No place to go: Civil commitment of minors. Lincoln: University of Nebraska Press.

Platt, A.M. (1977). The child savers: The invention of delinquency (2nd ed.). Chicago: University of Chicago Press.

Rickard, K.M., Graziano, W., & Forehand, R. (1984). Parental expectations and childhood deviance in clinic-referred and non-clinic children. Journal of Clinical Child Psychology, 13, 179-186.

Rivlin, L.G., & Wolfe, M. (1985). Institutional settings in children's lives. New York: Wiley.

Roth, E.A., & Roth, L.H. (1984, April). Children's feelings about psychiatric hospitalization: Legal and ethical implications. Paper presented at the meeting of the American Orthopsychiatric Association, Toronto.

Small, A.C., & Teagno, L. (1979, November). A comparative study of children's and their parents' expectations of psychotherapy. Paper presented at the meeting of the American Association of Psychiatric Services for Children, Chicago.

Taylor, L., Adelman, H.S., & Kaser-Boyd, N. (1985). Exploring minors' reluctance and dissatisfaction with psychotherapy. Professional Psychology: Research and Practice, 16, 418-425.

Tremper, C.R., & Kelly, M.P. (1987). The mental health rationale for policies fostering minors' autonomy. International Journal of Law and Psychiatry, 10, 111-127.

Zimring, F.E. (1982). The changing world of legal adolescence. New York: Free Press.

Chapter 22
Clinical Psychology Training and Delinquency:
A Multidimensional Approach

Alexander J. Rosen
University of Illinois at Chicago

For the most part, clinical psychology has focused on the development and delivery of interventions to individuals. Psychodynamic, behavioral, and cognitive perspectives, whatever their differences, tend to agree that the proper targets of therapy are internal malfunctions that result from a strained interaction with a stressful environment. This assumption has led to the emergence of a wide variety of techniques of proven worth for dealing with a broad range of problem behaviors, including those that characterize many delinquent youths. Delinquency as a field, however, appears to require an expansion of this basic model that entails a significant shift in emphasis. The intersecting dimensions, to which the title of this chapter alludes, reflect this requirement. The first, a methodological dimension, includes a continuously evolving practice that is informed by theory and research and is directed toward prevention as well as intervention. The second, an ecological dimension, expands the individual focus to include the family and the community.

This multidimensional approach is not, of course, a new one. But the field of delinquency provides a particularly elegant example of the many ramifications of this approach for both practice and training. Indeed, it was in the field of delinquency that the Chicago School of Sociology produced the first comprehensive research and prevention program emanating from an integrated, multilevel conceptual analysis (Keys, 1987). Although this program, which led to the founding of the Institute for Juvenile Research, existed over 50 years ago, its pioneering approach can still be used to inform current efforts that continue to grapple with similar issues.

At the close of the first World War, the sociology department at the University of Chicago developed the concept of the city as a laboratory for the investigation of social behavior. Clifford Shaw and Henry McKay, in particular, focused their attention on the problem of juvenile delinquency and emphasized the importance of developing an empirical strategy that was linked to social reform. Their analysis included assumptions about the continuity of deviant behavior and about the importance of the social context. The former assumption enabled an humanitarian view that contained the possibility of change. The latter broke with the historical precedent of concentrating on the individual and provoked a shift to the community, which these investigators saw as the cause, the preventive agent, and the cure for delinquency. Their research involved both life history and epidemiological methods to examine the ways in which communities that lacked indigenous leadership, viable economic institutions, effective voluntary organizations, and stable family patterns contributed to the initiation, toleration, and perpetuation of juvenile crime. Social disorganization was assumed to create delinquency and, as communities became more effective, delinquency rates were expected to drop.

Their data and concepts were put into practice in the 1930s with the advent of the Chicago Area Project. Three high-delinquency areas of the city, the near north side, the near west side, and the south side steel mills area, were all targeted for interventions designed to discourage and ultimately prevent delinquent behavior by changing the social ecology of the local communities. Community forces were mobilized to combat social disorganization and indigenous workers were trained to develop local competencies. There were three primary components of the project. The first involved the development of recreational activities for youths in the community both during the school year and during the summer. The second consisted of neighborhood improvement activities that involved identifying a community problem and helping local adults and youths to address it. The third component attempted to prevent the transmission

---

I would like to thank my colleagues, Nancy Guerra and Chris Keys, for directing me toward the literature that guided my thinking about these important training issues.

of delinquency and to reduce the occurrence of more serious delinquent behaviors. This was accomplished by mobilizing a cadre of indigenous youth workers who met with groups of boys, encouraged them to get involved in positive activities, counseled them and their families when necessary, hooked them up with social service agencies for additional assistance, and developed, together with the local police and juvenile court, a supervison plan to help them stay out of jail. This latter effort was accomplished by visiting detention facilities and helping those incarcerated make the transition back into the community.

The Chicago Area Project is currently established as a United Way Agency with a $2 million annual budget and a set of community committees that are active in over 25 city neighborhoods. And although its conceptual framework appears dated, and its outcomes have not been rigorously evaluated, it has clearly provided us with a legacy that bears on all aspects of contemporary thought about delinquency. The development of a social ecological model for preventive interventions, the broadening of theoretical perspectives to envision cause, risk, and treatment as including social and community rather than just individual phenomena, the development of longitudinal methods to sample patterns of delinquency over time, and the insistence on a strong, theoretically driven, empirical analysis of delinquency prevalence and transmission prior to the planning of interventions are all relevant today. The Chicago School established that deviant behavior, such as delinquency, can be viewed in the context of a theory, research, and practice perspective that addresses individual, family, and community constituents, all of which have important implications for the training of concerned professionals.

With this as a backdrop I would now like to examine contemporary efforts that provide direction for the training of clinical psychologists to work with delinquent youth. What does the literature of the 1980s have to tell us about the way to design our training programs? Is the legacy of the Chicago School consistent with current knowledge regarding juvenile offender rehabilitation? Recent reviews (e.g., Gendrau and Ross, 1987; Kazdin, 1987) suggest that indeed it is.

In the 1950s and 1960s the prevailing and dispiriting view in the literature was that, in the case of delinquency, "nothing works." Fortunately this pessimistic outlook did not inhibit researchers in the 1970s and 1980s from examining a wide variety of rehabilitative agendas; fortunately because in fact many things do work, and some things even work rather well. Thus, while there is no compelling evidence for the effectiveness of biomedical procedures, the use of diversion, which was intended as an alternative to further processing by the justice system, can and does work when it is programmed with substance and delivered with integrity. An excellent example of this approach is contained in a study by Davidson et al. (1987, in Gendrau and Ross). A multifaceted intervention, delivered by paraprofessionals within a diversion format, was used to treat 213 juvenile offenders. University students, intensively trained for 8 weeks and supervised for an additional 18 weeks, worked in the juvenile's community (average age 14; 83% male; 1.5 average arrest rate in year before treatment, primarily for larceny and breaking and entering). The treatments themselves, which were randomized across subjects, consisted of (a) behavioral contracting and child advocacy, which occurred both out in the community and in the court system, (b) the above with an additional focus on the family of the delinquent, and (c) an individual relationship approach. Two years after the interventions were administered, self-reports and adult and juvenile police records were examined. The results were impressive; the community-based interventions led to significant reductions in recidivism, up to 29% compared with the individual-relationship controls. Other controls, randomly assigned to the usual court processing, did worst of all. Davidson et al. argue that treatment programs can be effective when they are well grounded theoretically and when they focus on positive rather than pathological or punitive processes. If this sounds familiar it is because this highly sophisticated contemporary approach so clearly resembles the work done by the Chicago School some 50 years earlier but with results that can now withstand rigorous methodological scrutiny.

The success of this diversion of juvenile offenders through community-based interventions is paralleled by the success of early intervention programs designed to prevent the onset of delinquency. A compelling literature now exists that documents the utility of family and school interventions, the value of developmental and longitudinal perspectives, and the viability of cognitive-behavioral strategies targeted to individuals at risk. A consensus seems to be emerging that suggests that the variables associated with delinquency are gradually being revealed. Kazdin et al. (1987, in Gendrau and Ross) provide one example of the way in which problem-solving skills training can be effective with high-risk children, supporting the contention that social skills deficits associated with cognitive and attributional processes may underlie antisocial behavior in general and poor peer relations in particular. The Perry preschool project (Berreuta-Clement et al., 1984, in Gendrau and Ross), part of Head Start, is an example of a school-based early enrichment program for disadvantaged black youths that 11 years later was found to have produced better grades, fewer absences, fewer special education services, a greater likelihood of continued education and employment, and fewer arrests. These results were similar to those reported in 11 other Head Start projects, indicating that a proactive policy that attempts to match potent interventions with known risk factors can be successful.

Perhaps the most convincing examples derive from the family intervention literature. Jim Alexander's functional family therapy, a behavioral/cognitive/systems approach that attempts to modify family communications and interactions based on the assumption that problem behaviors serve a function, and Gerald Patterson's parent management training (PMT), which attempts to modify maladaptive parent-child interactions that are assumed to initiate and maintain problem behaviors, have both produced impressive and convincing support for the effectiveness of early family interventions. For example, Alexander and his colleagues (Barton et al., 1985, in Gendrau and Ross) recently replicated an earlier study on a much harder core delinquent sample. Thirty adolescents received functional family therapy and were contrasted with a group of yoked controls. Each of the subjects had about 20 adjudicated offenses. A 15-month follow-up revealed that the treated youths were charged with committing 33% fewer offenses than the controls. An even more impressive replication on a poor, rural sample revealed 11% court adjudications for the treated group compared with 67% for the untreated, and in this case lower-risk, controls after a 2-1/2 year period. The evidence in support of Patterson's PMT approach, which by now has generated hundreds of outcome studies over the course of two decades, is in some respects even more impressive. Rather than reviewing it in detail, I will just quote from a recent article by Kazdin (1987), in which he says about PMT, "No other intervention for antisocial children has been investigated as thoroughly and shown as favorable results."

This applied literature is accompanied by another on basic processes associated with antisocial behavior in general and aggression in particular. In a series of carefully controlled, longitudinal studies my colleagues Len Eron and Rowell Huesman, for example, have demonstrated the importance of cognitive factors in mediating aggressive behaviors (Eron, 1987). Punishment often works with kids who identify with their parents, but this depends upon the child's interpretation. If this interpretation results in the encoding of the punitive interaction as an example of the successful use of aggression to solve a problem, then the likelihood exists that the child will subsequently model his or her behavior after that of the powerful and punitive parent. This basic research paradigm points the way to a variety of interventions with high-risk children that are currently being investigated.

What does all of this have to say about clinical training in the field of delinquency? To me the message is loud and clear and hearkens back to those early efforts in the city of Chicago. The only legitimate way to decide how to train is to know what works. The only way to find out what works is by doing empirical research guided by and anchored to scientific theory. But since what works invariably depends upon a multiplicity of changing conditions, the scientific analysis never really ends, and clinical psychologists should be able to contribute to its continued evolution. The real question seems to be, Do we want to train clinicians to help a few delinquent kids, or do we want to train them to make a dent in delinquency per se? For the former, clinicians might need to know only how to apply a variety of proven or promising individual techniques including problem solving, perspective taking, and self-control strategies (Little & Kendall, 1979). For the latter, however, it appears that clinicians need to do much more than sit in an office and wait for clients to show up. They have to understand the social ecology of the problem behavior, that is, how it articulates with the family and community in which it occurs. They need to develop the skills that will enable them to work in school and correctional settings as well as in homes, courthouses, and neighborhoods. They need to know as much about how to train paraprofessionals as they do about direct service delivery. They need to be skilled in program development and evaluation as well as in community organization and consultation. And finally, they need to be scientists, grounded in each of the relevant substantive areas of psychology, for example, developmental, social, and cognitive, that will provide the basis for newly emerging conceptualizations destined to shape future state-of-the-art technologies.

References

Eron, L.D. (1987). The development of aggressive behavior from the perspective of a developing behaviorism. American Psychologist, 42, 435-442.

Gendrau, P., & Ross, R.R. (1987). Revivification of rehabilitation: Evidence from the 1980s. Justice Quarterly, 4, 349-407.

Kazdin, A.E. (1987). Treatment of antisocial behavior in children: Current status and future directions. Psychological Bulletin, 102, 187-203.

Keys, C.B. (1987). Synergy, prevention, and the Chicago School of Sociology. Prevention in the Human Services, 5, 11-34.

Little, V.L., & Kendall, P.C. (1979). Cognitive behavioral interventions with delinquents: Problem solving, role-taking, and self-control. In P.C. Kendall and S. D. Hollon (Eds.), Cognitive behavioral interventions: Theory, research, and practice. New York: Academic Press.

Chapter 23
Juvenile Justice Treatment Programs: Opportunities for Subspecialization in Clinical Child Psychology

Eric M. Johnson
Director of Training and Research, Morrison Center

Juvenile justice treatment programs present a myriad of opportunities for the clinical child psychologist. These opportunities exist for both predoctoral training and ongoing practice. Morrison Center, located in Portland, Oregon, is a community mental health center serving children and families that has recently begun to develop juvenile justice treatment programs. This has allowed our predoctoral interns to expand into areas of service delivery beyond traditional child and family services. Over the past several years it has also become apparent that clinical child interns wishing to subspecialize in juvenile justice treatment programs require specialized skills and knowledge that are not typically provided during predoctoral training. The development of these skills and knowledge needs to be addressed at both predoctoral and internship levels.

To set the stage for discussing these issues, this chapter will briefly discuss Morrison Center, its juvenile justice treatment programs, and its predoctoral psychology Internship program. This chapter will also address some of the skills and knowledge required for subspecialization.

Morrison Center

Morrison Center is a child and family community mental health center in operation since 1947. Originally a child guidance clinic with a small staff and budget, today its staff exceeds 125, with a budget in excess of three million dollars. Throughout its history, psychology has played a key role. This is most evident through Morrison Center's commitment to an empirical orientation and to training. The commitment to empiricism is most evident through the development of Center-wide program evaluation. Five of Morrison Center's major treatment programs conduct extensive data collection efforts. These efforts enable the programs to characterize the populations they work with, assess risk factors predictive of mental illness and delinquency, assess treatment outcome, and guide program development by analyzing populations they are successful with and those they are not. This data collection includes historical and demographic information, multiple behavioral indexes, and psychological measures such as the Child Behavior Check List, Jesness Inventory, or MMPI.

The commitment to training is evident through the offering of training for psychology interns, social work students, psychiatry residents, and nursing students. In addition to providing a variety of staff and trainee seminars and inservices, Morrison Center regularly sponsors professional training with national and international authorities and has played a key role in influencing state and local policy and practice regarding mental health services or children and families. In addition, Morrison Center annually sponsors the Western Regional Summer American Board of Professional Psychology (ABPP) Institute, offering in-depth training on psychological issues presented by a large faculty of distinguished psychologists.

Development of Juvenile Justice Treatment Programs

As a child and family treatment agency, Morrison Center has always treated adolescents with a variety of serious problems, including conduct disorders, self-destructive behavior, and school-related problems. Historically, little differentiation was made between adolescents referred for treatment from the juvenile justice system versus those from other referral sources. It continues to be true today that youth in the juvenile justice system are to a large extent interchangeable with most other youth in the mental health system (Melton, Petrila, Poythress, & Slobogin, 1987) and that efforts to distinguish them tend to be arbitrary and/or are determined by how early they were identified. That is, an 8-year-old male identified as a victim of sexual abuse would most likely be referred for mental health counseling. If he were not identified, however, and six years later began to victimize others, he would most likely be referred for treatment by a juvenile justice treatment program. Probably the most distinguishing features among these youth are quantitative differences, not qualitative ones (Achenbach, Chapter 9, this volume). In our experience, however, the youth from the juvenile justice system present special problems. These problems ultimately led to the exclusion of most juvenile justice youth from traditional child and family services. They provided the impetus for the development of special treatment programs, in terms of self-destructive and violence potential, the liability such problems create when the agency is responsible for maintaining such youth in the community, the lack of staff specialization to deal with such problems, and treatment outcome data indicating existing programs were unsuccessful with this population.

It took little initiative, then, to seek out state and county contracts to develop specialized treatment programs for such youth when the opportunity presented itself. Such an opportunity arrived when the State of Oregon began to downsize its juvenile close custody system and to return youth to their county of origin for treatment and no longer sent as many adjudicated youth for custodial care. Out of such developments Morrison Center was able to create three new programs. Each of these programs will be briefly described below.

Adolescent Day Treatment Program. This program, initiated in 1984, serves the population of severely emotionally and behaviorally disturbed adolescents, ranging in age from 11 to 19. These adolescents represent youth who are too disturbed to function in the regular school system or in the community without close supervision but who do not require long-term institutionalization. Many of these youth previously have been placed in mental hospitals or penal institutions. All of these youth are designated as educationally handicapped under PL 94-142; all are categorized as "seriously emotionally disturbed" and 60 percent are also categorized as "learning disabled." Creative programming includes extended day coverage (9 a.m. to 9 p.m.), intensive family integrated educational and treatment services, positive peer culture milieu, vocational preparation, extensive transitional services to facilitate mainstreaming into schools, Outward Bound recreational programs, and so on. This program has achieved leadership recognition throughout the Northwest for the treatment of juvenile sex offenders. The Adolescent Day Treatment Program serves approximately 15 youth concurrently and from 15-25 youth per year.

Alcohol and Drug Treatment Program. This program, begun on March 15,1986, is funded by Children's Services Division as part of downsizing the state juvenile corrections facility. Services include residential, day treatment, and aftercare-outpatient services for adolescents who have serious alcoholism or drug dependency in combination with delinquency. Services also include intensive family involvement, special education, and alcohol and drug abuse treatment, with an emphasis on responsibility taking by the youth, family, and community. The treatment model emphasizes continuity of care and decreasing the level of restriction over 12 months.

Supervision-Network Program (SuperNet). This program is designed for the population of adolescents who are at high risk of being committed to the state correction school and who have two or more felonies and/or multiple misdemeanors. SuperNet represents an adaptation of a former program based on a more traditional therapy model but which, our outcome data showed, was ineffective with higher risk youth. A conceptual shift was made toward an emphasis on close supervision by a network of family, extended family, and community support systems. This network works in close collaboration with SuperNet staff and the probation counselor. Skills training also is emphasized in survival skills and family functioning. SuperNet serves approximately 90 youth per year.

In addition to these programs, Morrison Center was recently awarded a 40-hour psychological consultation contract with the state's largest juvenile correctional facility. In addition to providing traditional psychological assessments, this contract focuses on program development, staff training, and case consultation.

Training to maintain a state-of-the-art understanding of the field has also been important. Toward this end, Morrison Center's executive director, Orin Bolstad, completed a sabbatical leave with Michael Rutter in

London, England, and David Farrington was invited to Portland, Oregon, in 1985 to present a workshop on the prediction of delinquency.

<u>Predoctoral Psychology Internship Training</u>

A predoctoral psychology internship has been in existence at Morrison Center since 1957. The internship has been APA approved since 1963 and has received NIMH support since 1974. Since the inception of the internship, interns have had a traditional child and family mental health training experience. This training focused on assessment and intervention, dealing with the typical populations of abused, neglected, and behaviorally disturbed children, while networking with local child service agencies and institutions. Interns have been encouraged to develop special projects through electives of their choice (e.g., to develop a sex abuse prevention curriculum or a school-based family communication program), and most complete a six-month, 20-30 percent time rotation at an outside placement (e.g., at a private psychiatric hospital).

As Morrison Center has become more involved with the court and corrections systems, so too has the internship training program. Forensic evaluations are a primary focus of the Morrison Center's evaluation clinic. Interns are taught to understand and address forensic issues and, with few exceptions, most receive first-hand experience in courtroom testimony. Interns have also become increasingly involved with the juvenile justice treatment programs and have completed rotations at the state-run juvenile correction facility the Center currently contracts with. For example, of the five interns in 1987-1988, four of the five were involved in some facet of juvenile justice work. This work included the following projects or rotations:

1. Consultation to a preteen sex offender treatment program run by SuperNet to develop a group curriculum for male victims of sexual abuse.

2. Consultation to the same program to develop a group social skills curriculum.

3. Consultation to the Drug and Alcohol Treatment Program to provide psychological assessments and to assist in developing a chemical dependency questionnaire that predicts response to treatment.

4. Rotations completed by two interns at the state correctional school. Interns have provided case consultation and staff training, and have assisted in the development of three new treatment programs.

It is likely that interns will become increasingly involved in such activities. This will be possible, in part, because of the likely decrease or discontinuation of funding for interns to receive training in the provision of more traditional child and family services. In addition, it has meant that the agency has had to seek alternate sources to fund the internship. To date, it would appear these funds are most likely to come from the juvenile justice system.

<u>Skills and Knowledge Required for Subspecialization</u>

As noted earlier, there is significant overlap between youth in the mental health system and those in the juvenile justice system. Whereas the differences need to be highlighted, this fundamental similarity needs to be stressed. As such, many of these recommendations will apply to the clinical child generalist, as well as the subspecialist. Requisite skills and knowledge include conceptual underpinnings, intervention skills, assessment skills, issues of orientation, and personal factors related to "goodness of fit."

<u>Conceptual Underpinnings</u>. Historically, concepts originating in the study of adult psychopathology have tended to provide the guidelines for the diagnosis and treatment of children. As a result, these guidelines

tended to be downward extensions from adult psychopathology and overlooked the overwhelming significance of developmental processes for all aspects of child behavior. As a result, clinical child psychology in general needs to adopt a developmental approach to psychopathology in children (Achenbach, 1974). More specifically, for the purposes of subspecialization, there needs to be a focus on dysfunctional families. Many delinquent youth come from homes characterized by neglect, physical and/or sexual abuse, alcohol and drug dependence, and severe mental illness. Both the generalist and the delinquency specialist need to appreciate the role traumatization and victimization play in the lives of these children (Furman, 1986; Finkelhor & Browne, 1985; Sebold, 1985), and the resulting posttraumatic stress disorders many of these children suffer.

An appreciation of developmental psychopathology helps the delinquency subspecialist to better understand the resulting complex of self-destructive and compulsive behaviors that often ensues for these children. For many of these children there is a final common pathway characterized by distrust, low self-esteem, poor social and academic functioning, and acting out. The delinquency subspecialist needs training at the predoctoral level to understand the dynamics of drug abuse, sexual abuse and how victims often become victimizers, and of aggressive/assaultive behavior. The delinquency subspecialist also needs training to understand the runaway subculture, street life, and teenage prostitution. Considering we live in the age of AIDS, the delinquency subspecialist also needs an awareness of socially transmitted diseases.

Intervention Skills. Whereas the mental health field has tended to favor the development of internal sources of control, the corrections approach has emphasized external control and punishment. The delinquency subspecialist can most profitably focus on the development of cognitive-behavioral strategies that produce a blending of internal and external controls. Predoctoral training can profitably focus on teaching intervention skills that include social skills training, problem-solving strategies, anger management, and confrontation skills for treating psychopaths and sex offenders (Davis & Leitenberg, 1987; Doren, 1987; Feindler & Ecton, 1986). The delinquency subspecialist also needs training in alcohol and drug treatment, particularly treatment approaches that incorporate the disease model and twelve-step approach. Although psychologists as a group are not comfortable with the disease model, it is the treatment most chemically dependent youth will encounter in the community. Ideally, the delinquency subspecialist would also receive predoctoral training in minority issues and gangs. The juvenile justice system is disproportionately filled with minority youth, many of whom are in gangs or are likely to be recruited.

It is important to note that the delinquency subspecialist and, I think, increasingly the clinical child generalist will not, in most cases, be a direct provider of intervention services. It is important that we prepare such practitioners for a nontraditional treatment role. Such practitioners will be spending the bulk of their time providing supervision and case consultation, or assisting with program development and staff training.

Assessment Skills. Most issues pertaining to assessment apply equally well to both the clinical child psychologist and the delinquency subspecialist. Because both types of psychologists are likely to be evaluating clients referred by parties demanding answers, a host of issues confront the clinician. Specific predoctoral training in forensic matters can help the psychologist to (a) discern who the client is, (b) avoid coercing involuntary clients, and (c) understand legal issues without feeling pressured to answer ultimate legal questions (Melton, Petrila, Poythress, & Slobogin, 1987). Psychologists in training also need help to recognize the limits of their competence, need to exercise caution in the predictions they make (e.g., regarding dangerousness and likelihood of reoffending), and should be coached to inform consumers of their services on the limits of their knowledge (Monahan, 1980; Rappaport, Lamiell, & Seidman, 1980).

Many of these issues are ethical problems that continually confront professional psychologists of all persuasions. I am in agreement with Monahan (1980) that every predoctoral program granting professional degrees should offer a mandatory applied ethics course.

The delinquency subspecialist needs to be alert to several other issues as well. Psychologists are often stereotyped in the juvenile justice system as evaluators who briefly drop in to "x-ray" an adolescent's mind, supply a report that contributes to an already burgeoning chart, and quickly exit, having provided little relevant feedback. As a consequence, many juvenile justice workers see a limited role for psychologists and are not familiar with other services they can provide. Conversely, other juvenile justice workers will ask assessment questions that are beyond our competence. Rather than ask for a diagnosis or personal insights, more typically they are asking, "What should I do with this kid, when, and for how long?" The delinquency subspecialist needs to be mindful of these stereotypes and seek ways to expand his/her consultation role without going beyond the limits of competence.

Getting Oriented. Practicing psychologists need to take time to educate themselves in the concepts and operations of the system in which they plan to work. For the delinquency subspecialist this needs to occur both predoctorally during practica and throughout the internship year. The delinquency subspecialist may be confronted by corrections personnel who do not have an appreciation for mental health interventions. As noted, they may instead favor a punitive, custodial approach based on the premise that delinquent youth are irremediable. Some corrections personnel are likely to have a limited understanding of a psychologist's function and only refer clients for testing or evaluations, failing to take advantage of other consultation skills. Corrections personnel who are treatment oriented are likely to have their own theoretical or therapeutic model, such as reality therapy, and be quite doctrinaire, with limited understanding of other treatment approaches. The delinquency subspecialist may need to constantly prove that he/she is relevant and competent beyond just "x-raying the mind" before establishing credibility and a working relationship.

Personal Factors Related to "Goodness of Fit". Psychologists in training need assistance to determine if there is a good fit between their personal characteristics and the type of work they are likely to encounter in the juvenile justice system. Historically, working with delinquents, mandated or otherwise, was not considered feasible or glamorous and was overlooked in favor of more "attractive" practices. Choosing to work in the juvenile justice system requires that one has done some soul-searching and values clarification. One needs to also be prepared to deal with individuals who have committed crimes that are personally reprehensible (e.g., rape or murder) yet who nevertheless require services. Such clients can also be rude, offensive, and intimidating, requiring the psychologist to set limits and consider personal safety issues. Other clients will require that the therapist be directive and confrontational.

These examples highlight the possibilities for "culture shock" and the need to prepare psychologists in training for the personal distress they are likely to experience. Too often, graduate training does not address this experiential component, with the result that during internship interns are not prepared to deal with the disillusionment and dissatisfaction that inevitably arises from time to time. The graduate school and internship program need to work in concert to address these professional development issues to ensure that psychologists in training have considered "goodness of fit."

References

Achenbach, T.M. (1974). Developmental psychopathology. New York: Ronald Press.

Davis, G. E., & Leitenberg, H. (1987). Adolescent sex offenders. Psychological Bulletin, 101, 417-427.

Doren, D. M. (1987). Understanding and treating the psychopath. New York: John Wiley.

Feindler, E., & Ecton, R. (1986). Adolescent anger control: Cognitive behavioral techniques. New York: Pergamon Press.

Finkelhor, D., & Browne, A. (1985). The traumatic impact of child sexual abuse: A conceptualization. American Journal of Orthopsychiatry, 55(4), 530-541.

Furman, A. (1986). On trauma. Psychoanalytic Study of the Child, 41, 191-208.

Melton, G. B., Petrila, J., Poythress, N. G., & Slobogin, G. (1987). Psychological evaluations for the courts: A handbook for mental health professionals and lawyers. New York: Guilford Press.

Monahan, J. (1980). Report of the taskforce on the role of psychology in the criminal justice system. In J. Monahan (Ed.)., Who is the client: The ethics of psychological intervention in the criminal justice system, (pp. 1-17). Washington, DC: American Psychological Association.

Rappaport, J., Lamiell, J. T., & Seidman, E. (1980). Ethical issues for psychologists in the juvenile justice system. In J. Monahan (Ed.), Who is the client: The ethics of psychological intervention in the criminal justice system, (pp. 93-125). Washington, DC: American Psychological Association.

Sebold, J. (1987). Indicators of child sexual abuse in males. Journal of Contemporary Social Work, February, 75-80.

SECTION VII

TRAINING PROGRAMS DESIGNED TO MEET THE NEEDS OF CULTURALLY DIVERSE GROUPS

Chapter 24
Training Programs Designed to Meet the Needs of Hispanic Children, Youth, and Families

Martha E. Bernal
Arizona State University

The term <u>Hispanic</u> has been used by the U.S. Census Bureau as a generic term to refer to people of Spanish heritage, including people of Cuban, Mexican, and Puerto Rican descent, as well as others who come from various parts of Latin America. "Hispanic" emphasizes their European commonality, but there are few pure Spanish among them; they have become racial and ethnic blends with native people, Black people, or varying other racial groups. There are two interrelated reasons why we are attending to them here.

The first reason is that Hispanics are a young and rapidly growing population. Their median age in 1985 was 25 years as compared to 32.9 for the white non-Hispanic population (U.S. Bureau of the Census, 1986), indicating that a large proportion have just entered or will be entering their childbearing years. These Hispanic people are going to have children and form families. There were 15.8 million Hispanics in 1982, and that number of Hispanics will be added to the population approximately every 30 years: 31 million in 2010, 47 million in 2040, 60 million in 2080. There will be very large increases in the population of Hispanic children. With these increases in a young population will come increases in the need for services and programs that enhance and increase their competencies and skills. These services and programs have to be provided in sufficient quantity and quality so as to significantly impact problems created by poverty and inequitable access to societal resources.

The second reason this population merits our attention is because of its continuing migration to the United States. This migration results both in further population increases and in special needs for their children and families because of their cultural and linguistic differences and the stresses of acculturation that they undergo.

A Framework for the Study and Teaching of Ethnic Psychology

In addition to all the training that has been described as important for work with children and families, what else does psychology need to do to prepare trainees for work with Hispanic children and families? I will briefly describe a framework, adapted from Berry (1984), for thinking about two major sets of independent variables that must be considered in the study of ethnic psychology, and thus in training for work with ethnic groups. In this framework, the mental health or psychological adaptation of ethnic minority children and families is the dependent variable.

The first independent variable is enculturation. People of all cultures experience enculturation; they undergo the normative socialization experiences of their culture. These experiences lead to the development of living skills, behavioral competencies and values, as well as to cultural identity. Similarly, people who are members of ethnic groups are enculturated by their ethnic families and community, and develop appropriate skills. The important fact for minorities, however, is that they are members of an ethnic group that exists in another culture, and that they must acculturate to that group.

The second independent variable is the process of acculturation, or adaptation to the dominant cultural group. This process probably begins at an early age in ethnic minority children, whenever they first have contact with the dominant culture. That contact can occur through living in an interethnic community, but for most children entry into school brings a large increase in dominant group contact. Most ethnic minority people engage in acculturative adaptations throughout their lifetimes as their social environments change, and this adaptive process of fitting into the surrounding culture probably occurs on a daily basis. Some of these adaptations can produce highly stressful consequences when severe cultural conflicts occur among ethnic family or group members, or between the individual and dominant culture members.

Examples of such consequences include family dysfunction resulting from intergenerational culture conflict, antisocial adaptations in youths because of cultural marginality and alienation, serious psychopathology as a result of migration, and failure to develop competencies for living because of inadequate educational and vocational systems of the dominant society.

Two factors determine the nature of acculturation. The first factor consists of the characteristics of the dominant culture, such as their willingness to share resources, and their values and attitudes regarding other cultural and racial groups. The second factor is the nature of interactions that ethnic minorities have with the dominant group institutions and members.

Implications of This Framework for Psychology

What tasks does this conceptual framework generate for psychology in the preparation of trainees for work with Hispanic children and families? The enculturation/acculturation framework identifies key targets for training for both service and research. Each of the two independent variables suggests some answers about the kind of preparation needed.

Education about the enculturation of Hispanic children is necessary for psychologists to develop and render quality services and conduct appropriate research on Hispanic children. Psychologists need knowledge about the history, culture, and characteristics, including childbearing and socialization practices, of the Hispanic group or groups with which they will be working. They also need to know about intragroup variations resulting from the degree and nature of ethnic identity, and regional, urban/rural, and socioeconomic differences. They need to understand the life circumstances of group members, develop sensitivity to their culture, and communicate with them in their own language when necessary. Most likely, they will need to conduct research on the enculturation of Hispanic children, since very little exists.

Scientific study of the acculturation process is essential to the understanding of psychopathology and development of treatment and preventive interventions for Hispanics. The fruits of this research should be part of the training of psychologists for work with Hispanic children and families. It is useful for the trainee to understand psychological adaptation from the perspective of the social ecology of Hispanic children and their families, particularly the impact on acculturaion of the characteristics of the dominant group and the nature of interactions between dominant and Hispanic groups. Some of this information exists in the area of social psychology, in the knowledge base on intergroup relations and processes, prejudice, racism, and so on. However, little of this literature bears directly on dominant culture values and attitudes that affect Hispanic people, or on the contribution of such characteristics to Anglo-Hispanic group relations.

A review of the psychological literature on ethnic minority groups, including Hispanics, has shown that psychology has tended to interpret cultural differences of ethnic minority groups as deficits and to place the blame for these and other deficits on the ethnic minority group itself rather than on the social environment (Ryan, 1971). The time has come for our field to adopt an approach that values psychological knowledge about Hispanics and other ethnic minority groups and seeks to learn and teach about the influences of the dominant society of their acculturaion. The time has come, in other words, for psychology to approach the study of the mental health and psychological adaptation of ethnic minority groups in a manner that is devoid of ethnocentric or racist perspectives. This approach is vital in the preparation of psychologists for work with Hispanic children and families

The most obvious and urgent task that needs to be undertaken right now, as a first step toward cultural pluralism, is to increase the numbers of Hispanic graduate students and faculty in training programs. These professionals will know best how to train and serve other Hispanics. But the response must be quick and substantial, especially in areas of the country where these groups are concentrated. The proportions of Hispanic graduate students and faculty currently in training programs must jump noticeably from their meager current levels to numbers that are adequate for work with the increasing Hispanic population.

Then training programs need to take an inventory of their own houses to ascertain how they can develop the kind of curricula and training experiences that will prepare psychologists to address the independent variables of ethnic psychology that have been described here.

References

Berry, J. (1984, August). Cross-cultural and ethnic psychology: A comparative analysis. Presidential address presented at the 7th International Conference of the International Association for Cross-Cultural Psychology, Acapulco, Mexico, August 29 to September 1.

Ryan, W. (1971). Blaming the victim. New York: Pantheon.

U.S. Bureau of the Census (1986). Projections of the Hispanic population: 1983 to 2080 (Current Population Reports, Series P-25). Washington, DC: U.S. Government Printing Office.

Chapter 25
Training to Meet the Needs of Asian-American Children, Youth, and Families

Jean Lau Chin
Director of Mental Health/Social Services
South Cove Community Health Center, Boston

Just as the developmental process has been a core concept in clinical training, I believe that cultural diversity as a contextual variable that affects the delivery of psychological services will also be viewed as a core concept essential to clinical training in psychology. Most university training programs do not offer specialty training with child clinical or ethnic minority populations. If we are training to meet the psychological service needs of Asian-American children and families, we must examine several questions:

• What kind of training settings facilitate learning about the needs of Asian-American populations?

• What kind of academic curricula are needed to train culturally sensitive psychologists?

• What kind of skills are needed to provide culturally relevant services?

Training Setting

The community mental health movement over the last two decades led to the growth of community-based human service agencies. Most of these agencies have served low income, ethnic minority populations and have been fertile training sites for mental health professionals. Yet, training institutions have been slow to integrate issues unique to these community-based settings into academic curricula. When community agencies are used as training sites, they are often perceived as a field experience en route to private practice with a more desirable clientele.

The bulk of services to children are being provided in community mental health settings. Oftentimes, this requires a networking of community agencies and services geared to multiple problems of families, and results in mental health problems encumbered by social and economic stressors. Mental health service delivery to children and families in these settings is, by necessity, more time-consuming and comprehensive than services to adults. Psychotherapy to children in community-based settings, to be effective, must consider many contextual variables beyond the therapy room itself.

Community mental health settings typically have shown low utilization rates for Asian-Americans. Since many are non-English-speaking immigrants/refugees, service delivery issues are compounded by the need for, but limited supply of, qualified bilingual providers. These language barriers adversely affect the ability of families to access mental health services. Language barriers aside, Asian-American children and families are often confronted with a mental health system that is insensitive to cultural differences and unskilled in working with non-English-speaking minority clients. Traditional clinical practices are tailored to a majority norm rather than to a culturally diverse population, or to low-income minority groups. Consequently, this has exacerbated low utilization rates and unmet needs within mainstream mental health settings for Asian-American children and families.

Training settings must address these issues to facilitate learning about the needs of Asian-American populations. Training institutions often do not draw on the expertise of community-based agencies where ethnic minority populations are served to collaborate on training for minority populations. Junior faculty unfamiliar with service needs of ethnic minority populations are often recruited for ethnic content sources. Academic curricula are often limited to a single course on cross-cultural issues. Cross-fertilization of theory and practice relevant to ethnic minority populations is often limited by isolation of faculty from an ethnic minority network.

Academic Curricula

The first step in examining academic curricula needed to train culturally sensitive psychologists is to examine the assumptions held by training institutions. Does the academic curriculum stress the recognition of ethnocentric bias and the diversity of clinical populations? Most do not. Most clinical training programs continue to use frameworks that define mental health service delivery to Asian-Americans as deviations from traditional practice. Culturally relevant services are often viewed as short-term solutions to "plug the gaps" until Asian-American clients can access mainstream services. Theoretical frameworks used for diagnosis and psychotherapy do not emphasize the adaptive potential within cultural groups to define effective treatment strategies. Course content often emphasizes knowledge of ethnic content rather than cultural differences, which influence diagnostic and treatment outcomes. Service models often do not draw on community networking, psychosocial support systems, or outreach strategies found to be effective with minority and low-income communities.

To train culturally sensitive psychologists, academic curricula need to value the different perspectives and worldviews of a culturally diverse population. Supervision should emphasize the recognition of ethnocentric bias. Assumptions of the supervisor need to be challenged if he or she is not from the minority community being served. Ethnic role models should be available to further the professional development of ethnic minority students.

Critical to this examination are the criteria used for evaluating student performance. Does grading of clinical skills recognize value and permit differing cultural styles of coping and learning? Many minority psychologists have faced the problem of a mismatch in cultural styles between professor-student and supervisor-supervisee. Many have coped by sacrificing culturally syntonic styles for more acceptable majority behaviors.

Last, I will discuss a few of the skill issues to be addressed in training to provide culturally relevant services.

Child Assessment Skills

The differentiation of developmental phenomena from cultural differences becomes the major task in teaching child assessment that is relevant to Asian-American populations. Where cultural values and worldviews differ between Asian and Western cultures, a diagnosis that validates a cultural norm becomes inappropriate for Asian-American children. The delineation of typologies, common in diagnostic assessment, often have had the net effect of labelling Asian-Americans as deficient because they differ from white middle class norms.

Personality assessment, therefore, must be careful to avoid cultural stereotypes by eliminating the use of typologies and trait assessment of Asian-Americans. With regard to intellectual assessment, differential diagnosis of bilingual problems from language disabilities is particularly problematic. For Asian-Americans having English as a second language, assessment of verbal skills is confounded by developmental issues of bilingual acquisition and values of the prevailing sociocultural context. Data documenting a "verbal deficit" in minority groups or the "academic excellence of Asian students" lend a bias that makes assessment and its interpretation a challenge at best. Teaching child assessment must include the recognition of cultural bias and the inappropriateness of standardized norms for Asian-American populations.

Data on prevalence of mental health disorders among Asian-Americans must be interpreted with caution. Identity problems, for example, were once seen as a prevalent mental health disorder among second-generation Asian-Americans, that is, the "marginal man" concept. What did not happen was the acceptance of a bicultural identity as a normal developmental process for cultural minority groups. Whereas ethnic identity is critical to self-definition for most Asian-Americans, identity problems reflecting developmental failure must be differentiated from that which is reactive to the normal trauma of acculturation.

174

There is a tendency toward overinclusion of individuals in certain diagnostic entities when these fit with issues popular in the sociocultural context. The subjectivity and fluidity of mental health diagnosis in response to the sociocultural context needs to be recognized. More recently, for example, there has been an emphasis on posttraumatic stress disorder among Southeast Asians. We need to ask whether there is an overinclusion of Southeast Asians in this diagnostic entity, with a tendency to overlook other dynamic phenomena and whether developmental phenomena are being confused with psychopathology.

Treatment/Intervention Skills

Given the significance of worldviews and cultural values in governing social behavior and communication, we need to acknowledge that psychotherapy operates within a social and cultural context. For example, the impact of authority and hierarchy in interpersonal relationships has a different meaning in Asian culture. When this occurs between client and therapist, the potential for misalliance occurs. Unless differing worldviews are recognized in the framework and practices used by the therapist, psychotherapy is unlikely to be culturally sensitive. The basis for forming a therapeutic alliance, the nature of the presenting problem, different help-seeking behaviors, and the facilitative use of hierarchical relationships are but a few of the variables where the impact of culture is significant. How they differ within Asian -American populations needs to be carefully examined.

Consultation Skills

The role of the child psychologist as a consultant needs focused training to meet the needs of Asian-American children and families. Training often does not address interprofessional relationships, for example, working with teachers or community workers, while differentiating one's role as a psychologist. For low income immigrant/refugee families, multiple problems exist that draw on the psychologist as an advocate and liaison with other community and public agencies. Whereas this sometimes blurs boundaries between advocate and parental roles, this issue becomes critical to child clinical training. For Asian psychologists working with Asian clients, the tendency for other professionals to assume that the professional is the parent, translator, relative--anyone other than the psychologist--becomes a challenge to professional identity.

Strategies for Training

Two training strategies have been used at South Cove Community Health Center to address training and professional development needs. In both instances, they draw on the expertise of Asian-American professionals and integrate cultural perspectives with service delivery.

Interactive Forum

An interactive forum was sponsored in 1987 as a collaborative effort between the Psychology Department at the University of Massachusetts, Boston, and the Mental Health/Social Service Department at the South Cove Community Health Center in Boston to provide theorists and clinicians working with Asian-American populations with the opportunity to discuss two major issues, transference and empathy, as they occur in psychotherapy with Asian-American clients. The partnership bridged the public-private sectors, academician-practitioner roles, and university-community linkages, with the goal of developing clinical curriculum training materials relevant to low-income Asian-American populations. The uniqueness of the forum was that, for the first time, Asian-American professionals were gathered not to address the need for culturally sensitive services, but rather to determine how this could be done in the delivery of psychotherapy. In other words, rather than address the broad question of whether psychotherapy is effective with Asian-Americans, we addressed the questions of how psychotherapy is effective and how specific issues manifest themselves differently in Asian-American populations.

Staff Exchange Model

South Cove Community Health Center in Boston and Chinatown Service Center in Los Angeles embarked on a pilot staff exchange project. As immigrant service agencies with over a solid decade of service delivery experience, we felt a community-based exchange of staff would provide incentives for program development and reassessing service priorities as well as opportunities for professional training. While visiting scholars are models existing in academic settings, they do not exist in community-based settings. This model is unique because it attempted to address the limited supply of bilingual provider resources by developing a partnership under circumstances that would normally be competitive. A next step would be to develop such an exchange between academic and community-based mental health settings.

Recommendations for Training

In summary, the following are recommendations for training to improve psychological services for Asian-American children and families:

1. Training institutions should be developing partnerships with community-based mental health agencies serving Asian-American clients for training sites. There should be true collaboration, which could include Asian-American professionals as active participants/collaborators in policy development, course content, and program development of clinical training programs.

2. Training institutions need to address the assumptions underlying academic curricula and training goals if clinical training is to train culturally sensitive psychologists. Use of a majority-minority dichotomy is not acceptable. Emphasis should be on valuing differences and integrating cultural diversity into academic curricula.

3. Skills needed to provide culturally relevant services may be different from those currently being taught in training programs. Close examination of effective strategies must take into consideration the differing worldviews of diverse cultural groups and must value the differences and support the strengths inherent in each cultural group. For Asian-Americans, whose culture differs significantly and visibly, this becomes especially important in examining intraethnic as well as interethnic variables.

4. It is essential to include Asian-Americans and other ethnic minority psychologists serving minority populations from community-based settings in the formulation of accreditation criteria and setting of training standards. In doing so, Asian-American psychologists should be utilized not just as experts in Asian-American issues but also as contributors to the training of psychology in general.

5. Cost and the limited pool of Asian-American professionals are often reasons for noninclusion of services for Asian-American children and families. Oftentimes, this reflects the failure to draw on existing networks within Asian-American communities as well as the failure to use more creative options for integrating issues of cultural diversity into clinical training programs. For example, a consultant pool could be developed for training institutions to draw from when hiring minority professionals in every ethnic group for each specialty is truly unwarranted and financially unfeasible.

Finally, let me end by addressing the question of specialty vs. generic training for working with Asian-American children and families. I would argue for both. There are unique skills in which one needs intensive specialized training to be effective with low-income Asian-American populations. However, unless we begin to address generic assumptions that militate against valuing differences in the language of our policies and outcomes of our training, we will not be training to meet the needs of a culturally diverse population and our ethnic minority populations.

SECTION VIII

MODEL TRAINING PROGRAMS DESIGNED TO MEET THE PERSONNEL
NEEDS OF STATE AND LOCAL MENTAL HEALTH SERVICE SYSTEMS:
MODELS THAT ARE WORKING AND MODELS FOR THE FUTURE

Chapter 26
Project Wraparound: A State-University Partnership in Training Clinical Psychologists to Serve Severely Emotionally Disturbed Children

John D. Burchard, Richard T. Clarke, and Ruth I. Hamilton
Department of Psychology
Wayne L. Fox
Center for Developmental Disabilities
University of Vermont

Project Wraparound is an experimental demonstration project designed to maintain severely emotionally disturbed children in unrestrictive, mainstream settings through the provision of intensive services in the home, school, and community. The project involves a partnership between the State of Vermont (the Departments of Mental Health, Social and Rehabilitation Services, and Education) and the Clinical Psychology Doctoral Training Program at the University of Vermont. At present, Project Wraparound offers clinical psychology trainees state-funded predoctoral internships in either family-based or school-based services. A postdoctoral internship program is presently being planned.

With respect to the role of clinical psychologists in serving severely emotionally disturbed children, the direction of Project Wraparound is not "business as usual." The premise of Project Wraparound is that the existing service delivery system does not meet the many needs of severely emotionally disturbed children, their families, and schools. Recent reports have indicated that an estimated 70-80% of children requiring mental health services are not receiving the needed or appropriate level of service (U.S. Congress, 1986). Likewise, Knitzer (1982), in her influential report entitled Unclaimed Children, estimates that approximately 2/3 of the 3 million children with a serious emotional disturbance are not receiving adequate mental health services. Under the current service delivery system, the majority of severely emotionally disturbed children are not seen by clinical psychologists. When they are, it is more likely for assessment than for intervention. This is not only true for psychologists, it also applies to the entire mental health system (Knitzer, 1982). The only point along the treatment/intervention continuum where severely emotionally disturbed children have a high probability of seeing a mental health professional is at the most restrictive end, represented by psychiatric residential hospitals and institutions. Unfortunately, this is the end where treatment/intervention techniques are the most costly and the least effective.

In the absence of more appropriate services designed to meet the mental health needs of severely emotionally disturbed children and their families within the mainstream educational system, local schools and social service agencies tend to remove children from their home and school environments in the belief that residential care offers the most effective treatment modality (Behar, 1984). As a consequence, the existing service delivery system has too often utilized residential treatment options without an attempt to provide less restrictive and less costly intensive home and school intervention (Friedman & Street, 1985). This more traditional service delivery approach involves what we refer to as the "take-out continuum." Very few services are provided until the severity of the behavior problems reaches a magnitude where placement in a more restrictive school and/or residential program is either required or justified. To merely add more clinical child psychologists to the existing service delivery system would not solve the problem of unmet needs. In order to provide more effective services to severely emotionally disturbed children, changes need to occur in both the service delivery system and in the role of the psychologist within that system.

It has been suggested that a more comprehensive system of care is needed to provide services to severely emotionally disturbed children and youth in the "least restrictive environment" possible (Stroul & Friedman, 1986). Project Wraparound is an attempt to meet that need.

Setting and Services

Project Wraparound takes place in a relatively small, rural community in the Northwest corner of Vermont. The "Wraparound Community" is composed of four towns and includes approximately 10,000 residents. At the present time, there are approximately 2,300 students attending any one of five elementary schools or the high school. The Wraparound Community also includes the majority of Vermont's minority population. Of the 2,300 students (K-12), approximately 500 are native American Indians (Abenaki Tribe).

The philosophy of Project Wraparound is relatively simple: to identify those children who are the most severely emotionally disturbed, and then to "wrap" services around them to facilitate their adjustment to the mainstream. The mainstream is defined as the natural family, the home, the school, and the community.

Although the philosophy may be simple, the implementation is not. It requires a radical shift in a service delivery system that includes many agencies and has evolved over many years. Although a shift toward more intensive and comprehensive mainstream services has been advocated for quite some time, few changes have taken place (Joint Commission on the Mental Health of Children, 1969; President's Commission on Mental Health, 1978). Project Wraparound addresses this shift by emphasizing interagency case management and coordination, intensive mainstream psychological and family services, and training and consultation for teachers and parents. The Wraparound continuum of intervention involves increasing and decreasing the intensity of services as they are needed within the mainstream. For example, at the more intensive end of the continuum, project staff might spend five or more hours a day working within the home, providing direct teacher consultation and psychological service to the child within the school. In addition, there may be a full-time instructional aide to assist the child in control strategies, guide independent work, and help focus the child so that he/she might be better able to take advantage of the regular classroom instruction.

Our preliminary analysis of the most severely emotionally disturbed children in the Wraparound Community provided confirmation of our assumptions regarding the traditional service delivery system. We first asked the special education staff to identify those children they believed to be the most severely emotionally disturbed children in their school district. In order to provide some empirical basis for the type and severity of the behavior problems displayed by these children, behavioral checklists were administered to their classroom teachers and relevant special education staff (Achenbach & Edelbrock, 1986). All but two of the 22 children who were regarded as the most severely emotionally disturbed had behavior problem profiles that were within the clinical range. In those cases where we had behavior problem checklist data from parents, the profiles were also within the clinical range (Achenbach & Edelbrock, 1983).

The clinical range on the Achenbach Problem Behavior Checklist was established through profiles of children who were receiving clinical services. On examination, it was discovered that the population of children we had identified were receiving very few services. When services were provided, they took the form of academic remedial education. At the time these data were compiled (1986-87 school year), none of the 22 children or their families were receiving mental health services from either the local community mental health center or other mental health professionals in the community. Within the school, most of the children were regarded as having a handicapping condition, but in only two cases was the condition categorized as serious emotional disturbance (e.g., in accordance with the Education of the Handicapped Act, PL 94-142, 1975). While half of these children were receiving some tutorial or special resource room services, none of them were regarded by the special education staff as receiving adequate services, given the severity of their behavioral disorders.

In addition to these 22 children, preliminary data were obtained prior to the initiation of Project Wraparound on the severely emotionally disturbed children whose natural family resided within the Wraparound catchment area but were receiving services in restrictive residential placements outside of that community. According to officials from the Department of Social and Rehabilitation Services, there were five severely emotionally disturbed children from the Wraparound community living in group homes and institutions located either in other parts of the state or out of state. These five children were adjudicated as delinquent, unmanageable, or abused/neglected. The annual cost of these five placements was in excess of $150,000 per year.

Although a detailed description of the Wraparound service delivery system is beyond the scope of this paper, what follows is a brief outline of the essential components.

Organizational structure. The Wraparound service delivery system was developed and is coordinated by three psychologists at the University of Vermont in the Department of Psychology and the Department of Special Education, Social Work and Social Service. The major responsibilities of the psychologists include project development and administration, interagency coordination with the State Departments of Mental Health, Education and Social Rehabilitation Services, and staff supervision. The staff on site in the Wraparound Community primarily consists of Education Specialists, who work in the schools, and Family Support Specialists, who work in the homes.

Referral/assessment process. The target of Project Wraparound is those children in the Wraparound Community who are either (a) at risk of becoming severely emotionally disturbed and considered in imminent danger of being removed from their families, or (b) are regarded as handicapped under special education guidelines for severe emotional disturbance. The process for identifying a child as severely emotionally disturbed conforms to the requirements of the Education of the Handicapped Act (PL 94-142, 1975). The primary characteristics of those children who receive Wraparound services are behavioral problems that (a) place the child beyond the 98th percentile on both the teacher checklist and the parent checklist (Achenbach & Edelbrock, 1983; 1986), (b) have persisted over a long period of time, and (c) have adversely affected educational performance. The final decision regarding special education eligibility is made by a school-based basic staffing team.

Although standard psychological and educational data are incorporated into the assessment process, considerable emphasis is placed on behavior checklist data. The purpose of the checklist data is (a) to provide an empirical basis for the type and severity of the problem behaviors on a cross-situational basis, and (b) to enable the selection of comparable children in nearby school districts who are not receiving Wraparound services (control children).

Treatment/intervention. The two major locations for intervention are the family and the school. Within the family, the Family Support Specialist, in partnership with significant members of the family, develops a Family Service Plan (FSP) that outlines specific objectives and intervention strategies designed to promote improvement in critical areas of family functioning. In most cases, one component of FSP focuses on the improvement of behavior management skills. Other components designed to alleviate stress and increase coping skills might focus on improving the family social support network, helping a parent obtain a job, child care or Medicaid, or helping a family member relate more effectively with a human service agency. A more detailed description of this ecological approach to intervention is provided elsewhere (Barth, 1986). Family support specialists usually work with a family for a period of 12 weeks. Follow-up sessions occur biweekly for 8 weeks, followed by monthly visits for the next 6 months. A critical part of their work involves a close liaison with the school.

Within the school, the role of the Education Specialist is more diversified. The Education Specialist provides ongoing consultation and training to classroom teachers, resource personnel, and instructional aides. He/she designs, implements, and evaluates behavior management programs, provides interagency coordination, and assists the basic staffing team in the evaluation of the goals and objectives of the individualized education plan (IEP). In addition, the Education Specialist may provide direct services to the severely emotionally disturbed child. This might include intensive training in skills relating to social interactions, problem solving, anger control, or impulsivity control.

The Role of the Psychologist

The role of the psychologist in Project Wraparound can be separated into two functions: predoctoral training and doctoral-level administration and service.

Predoctoral training. The clinical psychology doctoral training program at the University of Vermont (UVM) was started in 1969 and accredited by the American Psychological Association in 1973. Like other Boulder model clinical programs, it is designed to develop competent professional psychologists who can function in applied, academic, or research positions. A distinctive feature of the clinical training program is the local internship experience. In addition to a required one-year APA approved internship (which exist only out-of-state), students are provided with a multiyear half-time rotating internship that utilizes a number of local training facilities. These training facilities include the more traditional inpatient and outpatient services to children and adults as well as the school and home-based services provided by project Wraparound. The model behind the UVM internship experience stresses early placement in a variety of nearby clinical facilities that provide simultaneous research and clinical training relevant to clinical problems.

The internships through Project Wraparound provide intensive training as an Education Specialist or a Family Support Specialist. In either case, the student spends 20 hours a week on the project for a period of 10 months. Individual supervision is provided on a weekly basis by clinical psychologists at the university. Although there is not a specialized program in clinical child psychology at the University of Vermont, students who are especially interested in working with children are encouraged to complete both the school and family-based internships in Project Wraparound before they graduate.

The internships that are provided by Project Wraparound are a supplement to the academic and other internship experiences that the student receives in the clinical training program. The only academic component that differs from most clinical training programs is that students who become interns in Project Wraparound are also encouraged to take a seminar on the topic of social policy and children. The seminar places a heavy emphasis on the role of the courts, the legislature, and human service agencies in the lives of severely emotionally disturbed children and their families.

The role of the doctoral-level psychologist. As described above, the role of the doctoral-level psychologist in the current Wraparound service delivery system involves both administration and direct service. With respect to further implementation of the model on a statewide basis, doctoral-level psychologists trained in the Wraparound philosophy and intervention process could be located both in the community mental health centers (family component) and the school system (school component). In general, their function would involve the development and coordination of an interagency Wraparound program in their catchment area, staff recruitment and supervision, and the delivery of some assessment and intervention services to severely emotionally disturbed children and their families.

At the present time, we are developing a postdoctoral program to pilot this phase of the Wraparound project. Should this effort be successful, postdoctoral psychologists would assume the administrative and service function presently being performed by the three doctoral-level psychologists at the University of Vermont.

The State-University Partnership

For the past seven years, the State of Vermont has focused on the unmet needs of severely emotionally disturbed children. In 1982, the Commissioners of the Departments of Education, Mental Health, and Social and Rehabilitation Services began meeting on a regular basis to revise policy to prevent those children from "falling through the cracks" in the service delivery system. In 1985, the Department of Mental Health obtained a three-year NIMH planning grant to ensure adequate services for children and adolescents with severe emotional disturbance (Child and Adolescent Services System Program, or CASSP).

Under the direction of a 25-member interdisciplinary and consumer-oriented steering committee, CASSP established local interagency teams in each region of the state, conducted a statewide needs assessment, and began to plan and advocate for more appropriate services for severely emotionally disturbed children. Because most families with severely emotionally disturbed children tend not to access traditional services, an interest developed among advocates and providers to bring services directly to the family. With the support of both the legislature and the state government, resources were appropriated to fund intensive, in-home services in several locations of the state.

Project Wraparound was one of the six programs that obtained state funding to provide intensive community-based services to severely emotionally disturbed children and their families. A unique component of Project Wraparound is the partnership between the state and the university. As with any partnership, the most critical component is the quid pro quo. Project Wraparound offers significant benefits to both parties of the partnership.

With respect to state interest, professional mental health services are being delivered to a much larger proportion of the severely emotionally disturbed children in the demonstration catchment area than in the past. In addition, because these services are being delivered in community-based, mainstream settings, the revised service delivery system has the potential to prevent the child from penetrating the more restrictive end of the service delivery continuum, where treatment is more costly and less effective.

The university's interest in the partnership consists of an increase in the breath and depth of training program for clinical psychologists. Since its conception in 1973, the program has provided excellent training for clinical psychologists, particularly in the provision of traditional services delivered in outpatient clinics. The vast majority of severely emotionally disturbed children, however, do not access those services. This was demonstrated in the preliminary needs assessment in the Wraparound Community, and we expect that it applies elsewhere. The challenge is, first, to identify the most severely emotionally disturbed children in a school system. An empirical definition of that population would be those children who are beyond the 98th percentile on the teacher behavior checklist (Achenbach & Edelbrock, 1986). The second step is to determine the services that are being received by those children and their families. Our bet is that the vast majority of those children are not being serviced by any mental health professionals, let alone clinical psychologists.

In summary, Project Wraparound represents an attempt to develop and implement a more meaningful and effective service delivery system for severely emotionally disturbed children and their families. It actively incorporates the clinical psychology training program in that objective. Clinical psychology trainees receive intensive training in the delivery of school-based services. Should the program be successful in its efforts to facilitate the adjustment of severely emotionally disturbed children within the mainstream, it is felt that doctoral-level clinical psychologists can play a critical role in the dissemination and administration of that service delivery system on a much broader basis.

References

Achenbach, T.M., & Edelbrock, C. (1983). Manual for the child behavior checklist and revised child behavior profile. Burlington: University of Vermont, Department of Psychiatry.

Achenbach, T.M., & Edelbrock, C. (1986). Manual for the teacher's report form and teacher version of the child behavior profile. Burlington: University of Vermont, Department of Psychiatry.

Barth, R.P. (1986). Social and cognitive treatment of children and adolescents: Practical strategies for problem behaviors. San Francisco: Jossey-Bass.

Behar, L.B. (1984, October). An integrated system of services for seriously disturbed children. Paper presented at ADAMHA/OJJDP State of the Art Research Conference on Juvenile Offenders with Serious Alcohol, Drug Abuse, and Mental Health Problems, Rockville, MD.

Friedman, R.M., & Street, S. (1985). Admission and discharge criteria for children's mental health services: A review of the issues and options. <u>Journal of Clinical Child Psychology</u>, <u>14</u>, 229-235.

Joint Commission on Mental Health of Children. (1969). <u>Crisis in child mental health</u>. New York: Harper & Row.

Knitzer, J. (1982). <u>Unclaimed children</u>. Washington, DC: Children's Defense Fund.

President's Commission on Mental Health. (1978). <u>Report of the sub-task panel on infants, children, and adolescents</u>. Washington, DC: U.S. Government Printing Office.

Stroul, B.A., & Friedman, R.M. (1986). A system of care for severely emotionally disturbed children and youth. Washington, DC: CASSP Technical Assistance Center.

U.S. Congress, Office of Technology Assessment. (1986). <u>Children's mental health problems and services - A background paper</u> (ATA-BP-H-33). Washington, DC: U.S. Government Printing Office.

Chapter 27
Training Clinical Child Psychologists to Serve SED Youth:
Delaware's Prospects and Hopes

Julian R. Taplin
Division of Child Mental Health Services, State of Delaware

The discussion of Delaware's prospects and hopes in the area of training clinical child psychologists to serve severely emotionally disturbed youth will be made in three sections:

1. An overview of Delaware's existing service system and its evolution,

2. Comments on curriculum and skills we will seek and seek in turn to develop more fully,

3. Comments on trainees' adaptation to the context of work in public sector services.

The Existing Service System and Its Evolution

Leaders in Delaware have been concerned about the quality of state services to children and families for a number of years. About four years ago, the state took the bold step of gathering a number of fragmented services to children together into a single cabinet-level department. Although the name is awkward--the Department of Services for Children, Youth, and Their Families--the concept of having juvenile justice, child welfare, and mental health services together in a unified department offers significant opportunities. With the opportunities come, of course, the inevitable risks of a new and untried type of organization.

Some of the opportunities are uniquely Delawarean: The state's population is a mere 620,000, smaller than many counties or catchment areas. Although spread out among inner city, suburban, and rural groups, the state offers a high degree of manageability because there is essentially only one level of jurisdiction, that of the state. The administration of Governor Castle is particularly supportive and interested in establishment of not just adequacy but excellence.

The integrated department has some inherent advantages that go beyond the obvious ones of improved coordination and better service planning:

Family focus. Where services are administratively divided by the child's presenting problem, that is, where children's services tag along as addenda in various adult departments, each department, be it mental health, justice, or welfare, has ample excuse to disclaim responsibility for the situation of the family involved. In the integrated department, family is not just a legitimate focus, but, happily, in Delaware a mandatory one. It follows, then, that in our mental health program design there can and must be family- and community-based strategies.

Prevention. Once improved coordination among child welfare juvenile justice and mental health appear, the logic of prevention becomes inescapable. Delaware's integrated department contains major, formal preventive efforts (though, it should be noted, psychologists play only a minor role in the present staffing).

Unserved population. The integrated department is more quickly confronted with populations that are unserved because the department is the known single source that is supposed to fix problems related to children. In Delaware's case, two groups' problems appear very badly addressed: first, "troubling" or "undersocialized" youth, who often have immature, handicapped, irresponsible, or even criminal parents, and second, youth with retardation and developmental disabilities, a group curiously omitted from the department in its initial synthesis.

Every organizational form has both its strengths and its weaknesses. Among the weaknesses of the integrated approach are:

1. There is no model for integrating cultures. Intercultural differences and competing expectations are a source of tension.

2. Reorganization has brought some loss of roles or boundaries and misunderstanding of professional standards, for example:

A juvenile court judge diagnoses from the bench and commits to his favorite hospital because at the time it seemed like a nicer idea than the state training school.

A Foster Care Review Board, composed predominantly of Junior League members, attempts to review the work of psychiatrists, psychologists, and social workers, and to call patients and families before them to find out if "the child's needs have been met" and to call for therapies or settings they prefer.

General Direction of the Division

The division has had a permanent psychologist director for just one year. To encourage a value-driven system, the draft statement was created. Next came the statement of a broad goal, which took the form of an outline for the eventual system (see Figure 1).

The figure shows the heritage of the Child and Adolescent Service System Project (CASSP), in particular the work of Friedman and Stroul (1986) and Behar & Kayyes (1987). It contains five levels of types of programs (there will be several kinds of program in each level), which range in intensity and restrictiveness (the division understands that intensity and restrictiveness are clearly not identical dimensions, but for simplicity they are shown on a single axis).

The present situation is unhappily typical. Only a small part of the eventual array of services is in place. Services are unevenly distributed geographically and across age. The majority of expenditures go to the residential treatment centers and inpatient hospitalization, with, at present, only small percentages for day treatment and for outpatient services.

Despite the incompleteness and unevenness, there are a number of most encouraging steps toward a more complete array of up-to-date services. For example, the state will open a community-based alternative to hospitalization project modeled on the Houston Child Guidance work (Gutstein, 1987). Together with the minority community, a community-based project for high-risk youth is being designed around the notions of modeling successful minority families, improved community support systems, and on-site family therapy.

As would be expected with the coming of the former director of Oregon's Morrison Center, Delaware will shortly open a replication of Morrison's development of the Perry Preschool project aimed at severely emotionally disturbed preschool age children, typically those who have been severely abused. Drawing further on work from Morrison, Delaware will emphasize day treatment approaches for young children and for adolescents.

Changes in the residential treatment center network will allow the state to bring chronically mentally ill youth back from the out-of-state hospitals. Finally, psychiatric hospital admissions, now much overused, will be regulated by an independent quasi-judicial board reviewing against stated criteria. The presently excessive average length of stay will be managed by a series of increasingly demanding screenings, culminating in hearings by a citizen ethics board.

FIGURE 1
CHILD MENTAL HEALTH OVERVIEW

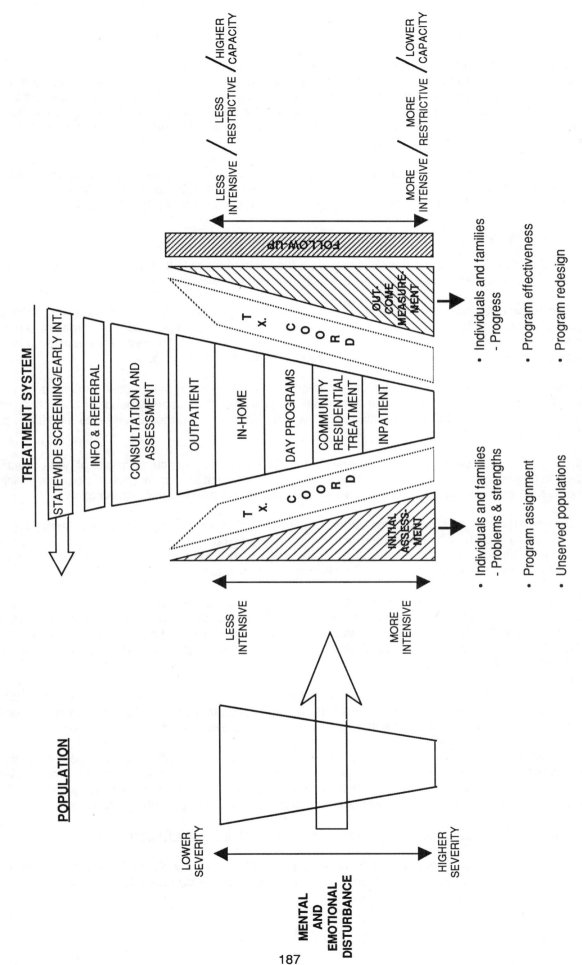

Tx. Coord = Treatment Coordination

From Three -Year Plan. Fiscal Years 1991-1993 (Section 3, facing page 2), by Charles E. Hayward, 1989. Report, State of Delaware, Department of Services for Children, Youth, and Families.

In the figure, case management refers to the role of client monitoring, both for length of stay and transition. The shaded triangles of intake assessment and outcome measurement symbolize the differing quantities of assessment information that will be required at entry to and exit from the various levels. Initial assessment should constitute a minimal barrier to the less restrictive, community-based services, and it should be a substantial procedure, giving a considerable fund of information with which to evaluate admissions to the high restrictive settings.

Finally, the statewide early screening box represents the outreach component, the component that is not passive. Presently the division looks to collaborative activity with Delaware's efforts to implement PL 99-457 and to benefit from California's progress toward universal early screening.

Trainee Background

In a word, the background and the skills that we will seek in trainees is that of applied empiricism. We will look for trainees whose central interest is the translation of research into action.

We look to build a system that does not rely on approaches derived from work with a few well-socialized neurotic Victorian children, because so few of our clients fit any such description. The majority are poorly socialized children and youth who have disorganized families. Very frequently some question of drug/alcohol involvement and some form of neuropsychological dysfunction exist.

The perspective of developmental psychopathology as an overarching perspective (Achenbach, 1988) is particularly desirable. Developmental psychopathology alone offers some ground for prediction through its recognition of risk and protective factors and their relationships. Further, it furnishes a basis for policy, priorities, and program design.

In the assessment area, clearly the awareness of multiple systems, particularly those of neuropsychology (brain integrity) and family are vital. It is high time, for example, that the significance of closed head injury or the presence of an alcoholic family member were recognized in the design of intervention.

Psychological reports, too, must come under scrutiny for their validity and utility. Most referrers are hardly enlightened to read that "Johnny approached the testing situation carelessly dressed in sneakers and jeans. He fidgeted and had a difficult time attending to the examiner and seemed distractible and nervous. His eye contact was poor and he often seemed uncertain."

In intervention, trainees should see therapy as but one particular portion of the realm of interventions. Intervention should be selected on the model of treatment of choice (What has actually been shown to work in this situation?). The question "why a one-to-one approach?" should be asked, rather than the converse "why not?", and the issues of generalization of treatment effects to the environment should be a criterion of intervention design.

In a system such as ours the trainee should always ask, "Why am I personally needed rather than someone else?" Background skills, then, should emphasize supervision, teaching, and the design of interventions because the psychologist will work with a variety of other people in a variety of other systems.

Given the special environment of children, youth, and families, and the difficulties imposed by the litigious nature of society, a special sensitivity to legal issues is necessary. Along with that, the ethical issues of resource use (example: what are the ethical issues of spending more on one chronically mentally ill child who is not improving than on the entire state outpatient budget?) are particularly pressing.

Between the Pits and the Fleshpots: Staying Effective in Public Sector Settings

The professional life of a psychologist who would serve the severely emotionally disturbed in a state system--whether on contract or state entity--is essentially life in a curious middle ground. On the one hand, in the pits, as it were, and under great pressure, there are the underpaid, overworked social welfare caseworkers. Their lives are characterized by having to make on-the-spot decisions about removing children from their families, knowing that no decision satisfies everybody and that some errors are occasionally mortal ones. Psychologists have some difficulty appearing useful and not grossly overpaid to the caseworker.

On the other hand, there are psychologists and psychiatrists who have opted for life in the corporate and private practice sector, and whose income, environment and life-style are startlingly affluent. Their professional lives are oriented to such things as cultivating and safeguarding the stream of referrals and maximizing billings per unit time. Against such a backdrop, public sector psychologists have difficulty not appearing to be poor cousins who lack the verve, often a euphemism for competence, to go private.

Many centuries ago, a psalmist lamented the problems of singing the songs of home in a strange land. In more recent times, Zimbardo (1972) has illustrated how easy it is for decent people not only to forget their own songs, as it were, but actually to adopt with great vigor and enthusiasm the songs that are absolutely alien to their own values.

Slipping Into the Constraints of Other Cultures

Sundberg, Taplin, and Tyler (1983) recognized five general perspectives, Everyday, Psychopathology, Learning, Developmental, and Ecological. The everyday or folk perspective has developed a language, a "pidgin human service" whose oversimplifications are counterproductive and dangerous, for example:

> "Delivering service" --Human service is not a commodity to be delivered as the postman delivers mail. The term leads us to feel we have something to distribute rather like bringing baskets to the poor and leads us away from the ends we desire, such as increased skills and competencies in an enabled individual or family.

> "Placement" suggests that something is known, certain, and being done, when in fact the problem, the mode and the goal are not specified. Admission to a mental hospital acquires a pseudoparity with a short stay in a foster home.

> "Meeting the needs"--When psychologists--or any human service professional--resort to this language, professional progress in classification, description, understanding, and objectivity is thrown out in favor of utter subjectivity of content and of reference. Every worker becomes an expert with the godlike goal of defining and meeting supposed needs of an again-passive client.

The effective psychologist must have the skills to interact with colleagues in fields of education, retardation, developmental disabilities, juvenile justice and child welfare, translating into and out of their languages and terminologies while putting into practice the key values of specialized psychology training.

Slipping Into the Constraints of Fee-Driven Assessment and Intervention Design

Psychologists in settings such as ours must be free in thinking to design programs and interventions that are not limited by the general constraints of the fee-for-service perspective.

Taplin (1987) outlined a number of the pitfalls of third-party fee-for-service reimbursement in outpatient services for children, youth, and their families. These pitfalls include, most obviously, a 50-minute hour-billable-service-in-the-office mentality, but more subtly, assumes the "doctor must do it," interventions should be pathology oriented, and that skills and competencies are not the legitimate province of the psychologist. Interventions, moreover, should have ethnic sensitivity, a dimension rarely encouraged in reimbursement systems.

The Delaware state system gives an opportunity to design and evaluate services without the constraint of having to secure third-party reimbursement, so our designs should be free of such limitations.

We hope to attract interns who can appreciate just how much of our thinking has been driven by the reimbursement machinery. The question for our interns should be: "Given that you are paid for your time, what kind of useful intervention would you design?"

In summary, Delaware hopes to attract and train tolerant catalysts who patiently repeat psychological concepts and research results in a not always easy environment and who will guide the formulation and evaluation of well-specified interventions and programs.

In our potential training we hope to emphasize the skills needed to give the fullest possible psychological contribution in this middle ground. Remembering the important songs of psychology, such as empiricism, outcome, development, and systems in the face of other cultures or pressures is at least as important as the original training syllabus, for excellence forgotten is no more useful than excellence never learned.

References

Achenbach, T.M. (1988, May). Developmental psychopathology as a conceptual framework for training in multiple settings. Paper presented at National Conference on Clinical Training in Psychology, Improving Psychological Services for Children and Adolescents with Severe Mental Disorders, Washington, D.C.

Behar, L.B., & Kayyes, P.T. (1987, October). The public sector's responsibility in serving chronically disturbed children and adolescents. Paper presented at the meeting of the American Academy of Child and Adolescent Psychiatry, Washington, D.C.

Friedman, R.M., & Stroul, B.A. (1986). A system of care for severely emotionally disturbed children and youth. Child and Adolescent Service System Program. Washington, DC.

Gutstein, S. (1987). Family reconciliation as a response to adolescent crises. Family Process, 26, 475-491.

Johnson, Eric M. (1988, May). Juvenile justice treatment programs: Opportunities for subspecialization in child clinical psychology. Paper presented at National Conference on Clinical Training in Psychology, Improving Psychological Services for Children and Adolescents with Severe Mental Disorders, Washington, D.C.

Sundberg, N.D., Taplin, J.R., & Tyler, L.E. (1983). Introduction to clinical psychology - Perspectives, issues, and contributions to human service. Englewood Cliffs, NJ: Prentice-Hall.

Taplin, J.R. (1987). Third-party fee-for-service in children's mental health: Limitations and suggestions. Journal of Community Psychology, 15, 79-89.

Zimbardo, P. (1972). Pathology of imprisonment. Trans-Action, (9), 4-8.

SECTION IX

DETAILED RECOMMENDATIONS FROM WORK GROUPS

GROUP 1 RECOMMENDATIONS:
PREDOCTORAL INTERNSHIP

1. Because of the importance of the family context, clinical child psychology internships should emphasize family assessment and interventions, as well as those focused more on the child as an individual. It would therefore be desirable to designate internship as "child/family," rather than just "child."

2. Because cultural factors are important considerations in the functioning of all children, internships should emphasize the understanding of children in their cultural context, especially with respect to ethnic and socioeconomic characteristics.

3. In 1-year child/family internships, a minimum of two-thirds of the internship experience should be devoted to child- and family-related activities.

4. One or more didactic training seminars should be part of the clinical child internship program and should include topics in child assessment, child intervention/treatment, and professional issues.

5. It is recommended that clinical child psychology internships provide both didactic training and supervised clinical experience in child assessment. Training should include assessment experience with a broad clinical population of exceptional children, diverse with respect to age, gender, presenting problem, source of referral, ethnic origin and socioeconomic status, in their cultural context.

6. A clinical child psychology intern should be provided with experience leading to the development of basic skills in behavioral observations, intellectual assessment, other specialized abilities assessment, behavioral assessment, personality assessment, and assessment of involvement with substances. Familiarity with assessment techniques appropriate for the various age levels (including infancy through adolescence) as well as the response capabilities/limitations of the child is recommended. Emphasis should be placed on the interpretations and integration of test results, as well as training competence in oral and written communication of the results to parents and professionals.

7. Both didactic training and supervised clinical experience in child treatment/intervention techniques would be expected in a clinical child psychology internship. Training sites should strive to provide intervention experience with a broad range of children, diverse with respect to gender, developmental level, type and severity of presenting problem, ethnic origin, and socioeconomic status. This should include oral and written communication of the interventions employed.

8. Clinical child psychology interns should be supervised in the use of a variety of intervention methods, exposed to multiple supervisors employing varying theoretical orientations to treatment, and trained in the selection and application of therapeutic techniques appropriate for an individual patient/client.

9. Supervised training in treatment/intervention with adults who present as patients/clients is recommended, in addition to training in the treatment of the adult parent or family member of the referred child.

10. Experience and training in consultation is essential in the clinical child psychology internship. Training in consultation with teachers and school personnel, physicians and medical personnel, community and social service agencies, and legal/judicial agencies is recommended during the internship.

11. Clinical child psychology interns should receive training in the ethical and legal responsibilities of professionals involved in clinical service delivery. Training and/or experience with the juvenile court system, child advocacy, and divorce/custody issues is recommended.

12. The primary focus of the internship is on the development and refinement of clinical skills. However, in keeping with the scientist-practitioner model of training, we recommend that research experience be provided during the internship, either by modest data collection and/or literature reviews relevant to ongoing clinical experience.

13. Exposure to normal children with a range of individual differences and responses to stress, as well as training and experience in methods of prevention (including anticipatory guidance, parent education,and preschool screening) is highly desirable during the internship year.

14. It is recommended that improved liaison mechanisms between graduate programs and internship sites be formed to improve the collaborative effort toward training clinical child psychologists. Clear communication from the internship site regarding expectations for preinternship preparation, realistic appraisal from the graduate program of the trainee's level of knowledge, clinical skills, and professional development, and regular evaluation of the intern's progress are recommended.

GROUP 2 RECOMMENDATIONS:
POSTDOCTORAL TRAINING

Postdoctoral training in clinical child psychology should be designed to provide significantly more advanced clinical, administrative, and/or research competence than is feasible at the predoctoral level. It is at the postdoctoral level that most of the advanced subspecialty competencies associated with clinical child psychology should be taught, such as pediatric psychology, forensic child psychology, family systems interventions, services to minorities, child neuropsychology, residential treatment, and public administrative service. This is also the level at which advanced research training should be provided for those who wish to pursue careers emphasizing research.

Our recommendations concern two general models for postdoctoral training. One is a 1-year postdoctoral experience that continues the predoctoral clinical internship training at a more advanced level in order to prepare the trainee for clinical practice and to complete the supervision requirements needed for licensure, although the function of this postdoctoral experience would not be merely to prepare for licensure. The second is a 2- to 3-year postdoctoral experience that would also typically include enough supervised clinical experience for licensure, but that would prepare people for clinical, administrative, and/or research leadership in advancing the field of clinical child psychology. These two models are described in more detail below.

1. <u>1-Year Postdoctoral Training</u>. (These recommendations were adapted from the Division I "Guidelines for Postdoctoral Training in Clinical Child Psychology," by D. Drotar, M. Friedman, K. Hodges, and T. Ollendick.) This level of postdoctoral training would be viewed on a continuum with predoctoral internship training. It should be designed to provide clinical training to produce an <u>advanced</u> level of competence in clinical child psychology and would embrace the scientist-practioner model of training. As such, we have viewed clinical child psychology as a scientifically based discipline that is continually evolving as new findings emerge. Postdoctoral training would be specifically geared toward producing professionals who are adept at both clinical practice and research.

All postdoctoral trainees should be called "Fellows" in order to differentiate them from predoctoral interns or residents and to acknowledge their elevated status. In general, all postdoctoral training programs in clinical child psychology should occur in the context of an organized program that is institutionally recognized. Basic standards for postdoctoral training include: (a) the postdoctoral training program should be directed by psychologist who is licensed and certified in the states in which he/she is practicing <u>and</u> who has specialty training in clinical child psychology; (b) a minimal number of postdoctoral fellows (at least two) should be involved in the training program; and (c) there should be a written brochure describing the expectations and responsibilities of the training program. Moreover, the programs should specify the amount and nature of supervision provided. Although specific guidelines regarding the size and diversity of the training faculty are difficult to specify, a goal of all postdoctoral training programs should be to expose the postdoctoral Fellow to multiple supervisors from diverse backgrounds, including, but not limited to, psychology, psychiatry, and pediatrics. Given the early stage of postdoctorates in clinical child training, the priority for funding should be for innovative training in service and research with the populations most in need.

As a general guideline, the postdoctoral training program should provide approximately 50% time in clinical activities to include both consultative and preventive activities, approximately 25% time in clinical research, and approximately 25% time in supervision (direct supervision, cotherapy, collaborative clinical or research work with the supervisor). Variations within these guidelines should be tailored to the needs of the individual.

Postdoctoral training in clinical child psychology should be provided in both a didactic and experiential format and should address the following areas by building upon, and not simply replicating, previous levels of didactic and experiential training:

1. developmental theory and, in particular, developmental psychopathology;

2. interview, diagnostic, and assessment practices;

3. methods of intervention specific to clinical child psychology;

4. consultation to auxiliary services and settings;

5. principles and practices of prevention;

6. ethical, cultural, and legal principles as they relate to the practice of clinical child psychology;

7. research methods specific to the populations, problems, and settings served;

8. supervision of other professionals;

9. program development.

In all cases, it should be recognized that such didactic and experiential training may be achieved in a number of ways, including, but not limited to, lectures, seminars, workshops, readings, direct clinical practices, and research presentations and publications. Because of the critical needs of underserved populations, a priority should be placed on innovative training to meet the needs of these populations. Rigid guidelines should not be required, other than to ensure that these substantive areas be addressed.

2. 2- to 3-Year Postdoctoral Training. Postdoctoral fellows in 2- to 3-year programs would generally be regarded as representing the cutting edge of advancement in the field. They would be viewed as faculty-level professionals who will begin making significant contributions to the treatment and understanding of severely disturbed children during their postdoctoral years. Because this form of postdoctoral training would be the main vehicle for developing highly specialized skills and preparing people for making major research, clinical, and/or administrative contributions to helping severely disturbed children, NIMH support should be provided on the basis of the innovative and creative potential of the postdoctoral experience to be provided by faculty mentors in offering the necessary resources to accomplish the program's specific goals.

Funding should be designed to support the stipends of the postdoctoral fellows and a portion of the relevant faculty salaries, research expenses, and institutional overhead needed to operate the postdoctoral program.

GROUP 3 RECOMMENDATIONS:
FACULTY DEVELOPMENT AND CURRICULUM DEVELOPMENT

NIMH should focus on valid clinical training needs. Social and behavioral science training needs are significant, and an exclusively neuroscience perspective is not desirable.

It is of initial importance that NIMH develop standing review committees for clinical training to provide continuity in evaluation of proposals, as opposed to a string of ad hoc review committees. The continuity of standing committees would also be better than ad hoc committees to encourage program development and improvement of proposals over time.

Encourage a uniform policy across disciplines to either support trainees or faculty. State specifically in the guidelines what types of expenses are legitimate (e.g., staff salaries versus trainee stipends, or both).

Faculty Scholar Announcement

The current faculty scholar announcement is not well suited to psychologists; revisions in the program are needed. A wider variety of more flexible options is needed to reflect the realities of the professional lives of academic psychologists. For example, shorter interval training programs might be possible. Recipient agencies would have to include nonacademic departments, such as internship agencies. The announcement should permit and encourage work on development of clinically relevant innovative multiagency service programs such as those being developed by the CASSP model, rather than simply research-focused programs.

1. Faculty retraining option: to get developmental or other types of research psychology faculty into clinical areas by supporting them to obtain clinical training, including internship.

2. Make it possible to apply for faculty scholars in service delivery sites to develop new comprehensive intervention programs.

3. Sabbatical support options to permit faculty, including research psychologists, to go from their university to a community training or service setting for a year, supplementing the 6 months' pay they often obtain from their own universities for sabbaticals.

Options and Recommendations for Faculty and Curriculum Development

1. Need to recruit and retain minority faculty
   a. need to support such people
   b. use of atypical tenure ladders to recognize special skills
   c. see Utah conference on how to support minority faculty members

Curriculum Development Issues

Provide funding to develop new ways of training service providers and/or new types of exportable model curricula or service programs. Include explicit priority on prevention. The NIMH small grants mechanism could perhaps be used as a model, here: small amounts of funds, quick review, flexibility.

There should be a high priority on training to work with minority ethnic populations.

GROUP 4 RECOMMENDATIONS:
UNIVERSITY/DOCTORAL TRAINING

1. We recommend that the NIMH funding for training for university-based programs with student stipend support be provided for the basic training of psychologists in child mental health in those programs demonstrating each of the following:

A. Attention to the Hilton Head Conference to recommendations for training clinical child psychologists at the predoctoral level.

B. Opportunities for supervised clinical experience with SED children and their families. This exposure to SED problems should include a variety of settings and population types. However, clinical child training should not be exclusively with the SED population.

C. Opportunities for interdisciplinary interactions in training and service delivery. Interdisciplinary should be more broadly defined than typically recognized to include: pediatrics, law, special education, community and city planning, juvenile justice, social welfare,schools, applied anthropology, human development, nursing, political science, and other professional disciplines.

D. Attention to issues of ethnic minorities, gender differences, and cultural diversity, and preparation for service delivery recognizing these issues.

E. Attention to developmental perspectives.

F. Attention to prevention concepts.

G. Involvement of program faculty and students in state human service systems.

H. Integration of research in clinical training.

I. Social policy and system intervention.

J. Service delivery in the public sector.

2. We strongly encourage that better linkages be established between university programs and the internships their students attend in order to better coordinate training. NIMH support should be available for this university-internship interaction.

Furthermore, we recommend that predoctoral and postdoctoral internships recognize the need for and provide greater opportunities to conduct meaningful clinical research with regard to SED children, especially for program development and evaluation and research in the identification of, etiology of, and service delivery for SED children and their families. Interdisciplinary, collaboration, and multisites or systems for clinical-empirical investigations should be utilized.

3. The objectives of these recommendations are twofold:

A. Increase the number of personnel qualified to research and serve SED children and their families and, more importantly,

B. Train those personnel to make better use of the research literature developed through federal leadership, which promotes integrated services that are consistent with the concepts of least restrictive environment, culturally and gender-sensitive services, family-oriented approaches, and cost-effectiveness in therapeutic interventions. This orientation assumes that some reorganization is required in training and service modalities, adding to traditional disciplined-based training more innovative and responsive training that is more oriented to multidisciplinary and multisite approaches.

This philosophy matches the SED children found in the public sector who are in need of mental health services as identified by the state human services systems, described by Federal commissions, and recognized by mental health professionals.

We seek to enhance active involvement of NIMH program-funded students and faculty in state mental health systems, social welfare and social services agencies, juvenile justice systems, education and special education settings, recreational programs, and vocational rehabilitation centers.

Training should be organized through collaborations of universities, state governments, and the private sector, as well as in an enhanced interdisciplinary interaction. Training priorities should include experimentation and innovation with this interdisciplinary training and service delivery.

Based on these assumptions, we further make the following recommendations. There should be NIMH-directed recommendations for training programs that give:

1. increased attention to training of subdoctoral levels of training and service delivery;

2. increased attention to training in the public administration of children's services;

3. increased development of alternative internship sites to meet the identified needs of SED children;

4. new attention to career ladders for public sector service providers to advance their training, their competencies for meeting SED children's needs, and their careers;

5. support for sabbaticals for personnel in governmental children's services (state and local) to spend a year learning from and consulting (teaching) to universities responding to this initiative.

Any NIMH training grant funds to the university for this purpose should be matched by state or locally generated funds.

In order to enhance and establish Federal-state-local and university collaboration, we strongly recommend that NIMH encourage state CASSP coordinators to establish linkages with clinical child training programs in their states through economic incentives for such cooperation.

We further recommend that NIMH provide funds to states to provide opportunities for faculty to collaborate in system programs, planning, training, implementation, and evaluation. This concept should enhance public agency-academic community partnerships.

NIMH should encourage collaboration between universities to identify, research, and train for particularly underserved populations of SED children. This multiuniversity collaboration might include, for example, such areas as: prevention interventions, interventions for children and adolescents at particular risk for AIDS because of a number of factors, in-home services, alternative school placements, juvenile and family court interactions, therapeutic foster care servicers, and services for preschool handicapped children (e.g., for implementing PL 99-457).

We suggest that NIMH experiment with the interdisciplinary structure of grant review panels combined with the education of these panels regarding the training models of the psychology disciplines and the nature of interdisciplinary training and service delivery. These should include the Hilton Head and Section I guidelines. Members of these experimental panels need to have had experience in successful interdisciplinary collaborations.

APPENDIX A

A National Conference on Clinical Training in Psychology: Improving Psychological Services for Children and Adolescents with Severe Mental Disorders

Time: May 18-20, 1988

Place: Ramada Renaissance
                                        Herndon, VA (Dulles Airport Area)

Coordinator: Phyllis R. Magrab, Ph.D.
                                        Georgetown University Child Development Center

Background:

One of the highest priorities of the NIMH clinical training program is the training of mental health professionals to provide comprehensive services to seriously emotionally disturbed children and adolescents, specifically, those with severe mental disorders or who are in need of services of NIMH's CASSP program. Professional education programs should systematically improve the effectiveness of their training programs, and, ultimately, improve the competence of their professional trainees, including psychologists, who will provide services to seriously emotionally disturbed children and adolescents, many of whom still lack adequate services.

Of NIMH's priority areas for clinical training, the field of psychology is making significant contributions in the area of child mental health. Last year, 26 out of the 48 clinical training grants in psychology were in the child area.

Nevertheless, all is not well. Many training program directors believe that NIMH funding for psychology in the child area should continue to support student stipends instead of being redirected to faculty development. If funding can be continued to support student stipends, new questions would then arise about the best use of the limited NIMH clinical training in psychology funds in the complex matrix of possible students/trainees to support.

Overall Purpose, Specific Objectives, and Desired Outcomes of the Washington Conference:

1. The overall purpose of the conference is to make recommendations to help guide NIMH clinical training policy for seriously emotionally disturbed children and adolescents.

2. Specific objectives:

    a. To review the state of the art in child mental health and psychology's potential contributions, including both unique (research) and nonunique contributions (case management, treatment).

    b. To identify good training programs as models and worthwhile program directions.

    c. To identify obstacles in the development of training programs for seriously emotionally disturbed children and adolescents.

3. Desired outcomes of conference:

    To assess options and to recommend <u>actions</u> in four areas:

    a. Academic training programs at the master's level and the doctoral level.
    b. Predoctoral and postdoctoral internship training programs.
    c. Faculty development and curriculum development.
    d. Retraining/continuing education programs.

Agenda:

A. To review the state of the art in psychology as a part of an interdisciplinary team.

    The first step is to systematically review the state of the art, and the contributions made by psychologists, social workers, psychiatrists, psychiatric nurses, and others.

B. Academic-State Linkages

    What are appropriate models of academic-state linkage in psychology? The recent book <u>Interdisciplinary Collaboration Between State Mental Health and Higher Education</u> will be required reading for all conference participants.

C. The Case for Doctoral Training Programs

D. Predoctoral and Postdoctoral Internship Training Programs

    Is interning at one level or another level (or both) preferred? In February, 1987, the National Conference on Psychology Internships strongly recommended that by 1995 all new practicing psychologists have two years of accredited internship, one predoctoral year (now required) and one postdoctoral year (new requirement). Clinical psychology's move to improve its own standards coincides nicely with NIMH's recognition of needed personnel to serve the needs of seriously emotionally disturbed children and adolescents. However, much more specification of the postdoctoral internship standards is necessary.

E. Faculty Development and Curriculum Development

    First, are specific programs in faculty development and curriculum development necessary at this point in time? Are there existing programs of faculty development for clinical psychology faculty in this area? If not, what would one look like? What would be the preferred models: long-term individual, short-term institutional, or other? Should such faculty development in psychology be unidisciplinary, multidisciplinary, or interdisciplinary? Should <u>separate efforts</u> be made in curriculum development, or should the curriculum development be tied to faculty development?

F. Retraining/Continuing Education Program

    Should such programs be planned in each region of the country, or each state, to enhance the capabilities of psychologists caring for seriously emotionally disturbed children and adolescents? How should such programs be funded: federally, by states, or other?

G. Development of Assessment Methodology to Evaluate Training Programs

    The assessment of trainees' clinical competencies will be described. The experts at this conference will be asked for their judgments on the most important clinical competencies in diagnosis, treatment, and case management at three levels of training: master's, doctoral,and postdoctoral.

H. The Interface of Clinical Training and Research

Topics will include: research training and clinical training in the same programs.

I. Summary and recommendations for action

- By NIMH
- By APA or other organizations
- By others

AGENDA

**NATIONAL CONFERENCE ON CLINICAL TRAINING IN PSYCHOLOGY:
IMPROVING PSYCHOLOGICAL SERVICES FOR CHILDREN
AND ADOLESCENTS WITH SEVERE MENTAL DISORDERS**

WEDNESDAY, MAY 18: DAY ONE: BIG PICTURE: GENERAL ISSUES AND TASKS

11:30AM - 12:30PM   Pre-conference informal lunch.
Renaissance Room East

12:30 - 12:45   Introduction and Overview - Phyllis Magrab
Dulles D Room

12:45 -   2:00   Part I: Dimensions and Complexities of the Service/Needs of Children and
Dulles D Room   Adolescents with Severe Mental Disorders

Moderator: Phyllis Magrab

NIMH's Role - James Stockdill (10 min.)
CASSP's Role - Ira Lourie (10 min.)
Psychology Education's Role - Paul Wohlford (10 min.)
National Service Needs - Leonard Saxe (15 min.)
State Mental Health Needs and Adequacy of Personnel to Meet These Needs -
Jerome Hanley (South Carolina)/Gary De Carolis (Vermont) (20 min.)
Discussion (10 min.)

2:00 -   3:30   Part II: Psychology's Role in Providing Trained Personnel to Meet These Needs
Dulles D Room
Moderator: Phyllis Magrab

Developmental Psychopathology and Prevention - David Ricks (15 min.)

Background and Recent History of Improving Psychological Services for Children
- Milton Shore (10 min.)

Standards for Training Psychologists to Provide Mental Health Services to
Children and Adolescents - June Tuma (10 min.)

Significance of Recommendations of 1987 National Conference on Psychology
Internships - Norine Johnson (10 min.)

Significance of Task Force on Accreditation Criteria - Jill Reich (10 min.)

Developing Measures of Clinical Competence - Georgine Pion (10 min.)
Discussion (25 min.)

3:30 -   3:45   Coffee Break

3:45 -   5:15   Discussion Groups (1): To discuss not only Parts I and II, but implications for
establishing specialty training standards for Clinical Child Psychology.

Group I: Dulles D
Group II: Executive Board Room I
Group III: Executive Board Room II
Group IV: Salon (TBA)

6:00 -   7:00   Dinner
Renaissance Room East

7:00 -   8:45   Part III: Achieving Quality Training in the General Area of Clinical Child Psychology
                         and its Several Subspecialties

                         Moderator: Marilyn Erickson

                         Standards for Training Clinical Child Psychologists - Marilyn Erickson (15 min.)

                         Systematic Training Across Settings: Family, School, Clinic, etc. - Thomas
                         Achenbach (15 min.)

                         Pediatric Psychology and Clinical Child Psychology - Carolyn Schroeder (15 min.)

                         Developmental Disabilities, Learning Disorders, School Psychology and Clinical
                         Child Psychology - Nadine Lambert (15 min.)

                         The Legal System, the Social Welfare System and Clinical Child Psychology -
                         Murray Levine (15 min.)

                         Discussion (30 min.)

THURSDAY, MAY 19:   DAY TWO: SPECIFIC ISSUES: NUTS AND BOLTS OF TRAINING
                        PROGRAMS - HOW MUCH CAN BE TAUGHT OR LEARNED IN A FINITE PERIOD

7:00 -   8:15AM   Breakfast
Renaissance Room East

8:30 -   9:30   Part IV: Breadth and Depth of Training in Basic Developmental Psychology,
Dulles D Room   Family Psychology and Clinical Child Psychology

                        Moderators: Thomas Achenbach/Marilyn Erickson
                        Presentors: Robert Zucker/Gary Stollak (12 min.)
                                       Gloria Leon (12 min.)
                                       Robert Emery (12 min.)
                                       Sandra Russ (12 min.)
                        Discussion   (12 min.)

9:30 -   10:30   Part V: Breadth and Depth of Training in Applied Developmental Psychology,
Dulles D Room   Developmental Disabilities, School Psychology, and Clinical Child Psychology

                        Moderator: Nadine Lambert
                        Presentators: Lynda Geller (Mental Retardation) (12 min.)
                                       Pat Bricklin (School Psychology) (12 min.)
                                       Jill Reich (Applied Developmental) (12 min.)
                                       Howard Knoff (School Psychology) (12 min.)
                        Discussion: (15 min.)

207

10:30 - 10:45	Coffee Break

10:45 - 12:00
Dulles D Room

Part V: Breadth and Depth of Training Pediatric Psychology, Childhood Psychoses, and Other Very Severe Disorders

Moderator: Carolyn Schroeder
Presentors: Lee Marcus (Childhood Psychoses) (12 min.)
Donald Routh (Pediatric Psychology) (12 min.)
Gerald Koocher (Pediatric Psychology) (12 min.)
Conchita Espino (Other Severe Disorders) (12 min.)
Robert Friedman (Other Severe Disorders) (12 min.)
Discussion: (15 min.)

12:00 - 1:00
Renaissance Room East

Lunch

1:00 - 2:00
Dulles D Room

Part VI: Breadth and Depth of Training in the Interface of Juvenile Justice System, Social Welfare System and Clinical Child Psychology

Moderator: Murray Levine
Presentors: Gary Melton (Children's Rights) (15 min.)
Alexander Rosen (Delinquency) (15 min.)
Eric Johnson (Treatment Programs) (15 min.)
Discussion: (15 min.)

2:00 - 2:45
Dulles D Room

Part VII: Model Training Programs Designed to Meet the Personnel Needs of State and Local Mental Health Service Systems: Models that are Working and Models for Future

Moderator: Shiela Pires
Presentors: The Vermont Model - John Burchard (15 min.)
The Delaware Approach - Julian Taplin (15 min.)
Discussion: (15 min.)

2:45 - 3:00

Coffee Break

3:00 - 4:15
Dulles D Room

Part VIII: Training Programs Designed to Meet the Needs of Culturally Diverse Groups

Moderator: Jerome Hanley

Training to Meet the Needs of Hispanic Children, Youth and Families - Martha Bernal (15 min.)

Training to Meet the Needs of Black Children, Youth and Families - Bernadette Gray-Little (15 min.)

Training to Meet the Needs of American Indian Children, Youth and Families - Damien McShane (15 min.)

Training to Meet the Needs of Asian American Children, Youth and Families - Jean Chin (15 min.)

Discussion: (15 min.)

4:15 - 5:15   Discussion Groups (2) (continued)
                     Group I: Dulles D
                     Group II: Executive Board Room I

6:00 - 7:00   Dinner
Renaissance Room East

7:00 - 9:00   Discussion Groups (3) (continued)
                     (See above for room assignments)

FRIDAY, MAY 20:   DAY THREE:

7:00AM - 8:30   Breakfast
Renaissance Room East

8:30 - 12:00   Part IX: Recommendations for Action/Strategies for Implementation

                     Moderators: Marilyn Erickson, Al Cain

12:00 - 1:00   Lunch
Renaissance Room East

   1:00 -2:30   Part IX: Recommendations for Action/Strategies for Implementation - Continued.

NATIONAL CONFERENCE ON CLINICAL TRAINING IN PSYCHOLOGY: IMPROVING PSYCHOLOGICAL SERVICES FOR CHILDREN AND ADOLESCENTS WITH SEVERE MENTAL DISORDERS

Participant List

Richard Abidin
320 Terrell Road, West
Charlottesville, VA 22901

Thomas M. Achenbach
Department of Psychiatry
University of Vermont
1 S. Prospect Street
Burlington, VT 05401

LaRue Allen
Department of Psychology
University of Maryland
College Park, MD 20742-1144

Allan G. Barclay
School of Professional Psychology
Wright State University
221 N. Grand Boulevard
Dayton, OH 45435

Martha E. Bernal
Department of Psychology
Arizona State University
Tempe, AZ 85287

Patricia M. Bricklin
General Washington Road
Wayne, PA 19087

John Burchard
Department of Psychology
John Dewey Hall
University of Vermont
Burlington, VT 05405

Albert C. Cain
Department of Psychology
University of Michigan
580 Union Drive
Ann Arbor, MI 48109

Karen Cammuso
3315 Wisconsin Avenue, NW #608
Washington, DC 20016

Jean Chin
Director, Mental Health
South Cove Community Health Ctr.
885 Washington Street
Boston, MA 02111

Martin Cohen
Deputy Director
The Robert Wood Johnson Foundation
  Program for the Chronically
  Mentally Ill
Massachusetts Mental Health Center
74 Fenwood Road
Boston, MA 02115

Jan Culbertson
Child Study Center of Children's
  Memorial Hospital
University of Oklahoma
  Health Science Center
1100 N.E. 13th
Oklahoma City, OK 73117

Gary De Carolis
CASSP Coordinator
Department of Mental Health
103 South Main Street
Waterbury, VT 05676

Robert Emery
Department of Psychology
102 Gilmer Hall
University of Virginia
Charlottesville, VA 22903

Marilyn T. Erickson
Psychology Department
Virginia Commonwealth University
806 W. Franklin Street
Richmond, VA 23284

Conchita Espino
Commission on Mental Health Service
Child and Youth Service Adm.
1536 U Street, N.W.
Washington, DC 20009

Michael Frazier
Howard University Mental Health Clinic
502 College Street, N.W.
Washington, DC 20060

Robert Friedman
Florida Mental Health Institute
1330 N. 30th Street
Tampa, FL 33612

Lynda Geller
Dept. of Psychiatry & Behavioral
Science
South Campus-Putman Hall
SUNY-Stony Brook
Stony Brook, NY 11794-8790

Bernadette Gray-Little
Department of Psychology
University of North Carolina
Chapel Hill, NC 27514

Jerome Hanley
Director
Division of Child & Adolescent Services
Department of Mental Health
P.O. Box 485
2414 Bull Street, Room 309
Columbia, SC 29202

Ira Iscoe
Department of Psychology
Mezes Hall
University of Texas
Austin, TX 78712

Eric Johnson
Morrison Center for Children and
Family Services
3355 SE Powell Blvd.
Portland, OR 97202

Norine G. Johnson
111 Willard Street, Suite 2B
Quincy, MA 02169

Rose Johnson
8241 14th Avenue, #302
Hyattsville, MD 20783

Judith Katz-Leavy
NIMH, CASSP
5600 Fishers Lane
Parklawn Building
Rockville, MD 20857

Thomas J. Kenny
Pediatric Psychologist
Walter P. Carter Center
630 West Fayette Street
Baltimore, MD 21201

Howard Knoff
Associate Professor
Psychological and Social Foundations
University of South Florida
FAO 268
4202 East Fowler Avenue
Tampa, FL 33620

Gerald Paul Koocher
Department of Psychiatry
Children's Hospital
300 Longwood Avenue
Boston, MA 02115

Nadine Lambert
School of Education
University of California - Berkeley
Berkeley, CA 94720

Gloria Rakita Leon
Department of Psychology
University of Minnesota
N. 438 Elliot Hall
Minneapolis, MN 55455

Murray Levine
Department of Psychology
State University of New York - Buffalo
Buffalo, NY 14260

Ray Lorion
Department of Psychology
University of Maryland
College Park, MD 20742

Ira Lourie
Director, CASSP
Community Service Systems Branch
National Institute of Mental Health
5600 Fishers Lane, Room 7-C-14
Rockville, MD 20857

Robert D. Lyman
Executive Director
Brewer-Porch Children's Center
Department of Psychology
University of Alabama
P.O. Box 2968
Tuscaloosa, AL 35487

Phyllis R. Magrab
Georgetown Child Development Center
CG-52 Bles Building
3800 Reservoir Road, N.W.
Washington, DC 20007

Lee Marcus
Clinical Director
Piedmont TEACCH Center
TEACCH Division
CB-7180 Medical School, Wing E, 228H
University of North Carolina
Chapel Hill, NC 27514

Elizabeth McCauley
Department of Psychology
and Behavioral Science
Children's Orthopedic Hospital
and Medical Center
P.O. Box C5371
Seattle, WA 98102

Gary B. Melton
Department of Psychology
209 Burnett Hall
University of Nebraska
Lincoln, NE 68588

Georgine Pion
Institute of Public Policy Studies
Vanderbilt University
1208 18th Avenue South
Nashville, TN 37212

Shiela Pires
Deputy Commissioner
District of Columbia Dept. of Human
Services
Randall Building
1st and I Streets, S.W.
Washington, DC 20024

Roberta Ray
Deputy Director
Division of Child Mental Health Services
Division of Services for Children, Youth
and Families
330 E. 30th Street
Wilmington, DE 19802

Jill Reich
Graduate School
Loyola University
6525 North Sheridan
Chicago, IL 60626

David F. Ricks
Department of Psychology
University of Cincinnati
Cincinnati, OH 45221

Michael Roberts
Professor of Psychology
Department of Psychology
University of Alabama
P.O. Box 2968
Tuscaloosa, AL 35487

Cynthia A. Rohrbeck
Assistant Professor of Psychology
(Clinical)
Department of Psychology
George Washington University
2125 G Street, N.W.
Washington, DC 20052

Alexander J. Rosen
Department of Psychology
University of Illinois - Chicago
P.O. Box 4348
Chicago, IL 60680

Donald Routh
Department of Psychology
University of Miami
P.O. Box 248185
Coral Gables, FL 33124

Sandra W. Russ
Department of Psychology
Case Western Reserve University
Cleveland, OH 44106

Leonard Saxe
Director
Center for Applied Sciences
Boston University
232 Bay Street
Boston, MA 02215

Carolyn S. Schroeder
Pediatric Psychologist
Chapel Hill Pediatrics
901 Willow Drive, Suite 2
Chapel Hill, NC 27514

Milton F. Shore
1370 Lamberton Drive
Silver Spring, MD 20902

Sam Silverstein
10826 Margate Road
Silver Spring, MD 20901

James Stockdill
Director
Division of Education and Service
 Systems Liaison
National Institute of Mental Health
5600 Fishers Lane, Room 11-C-26
Rockville, MD 20857

Gary Stollack
Department of Psychology
Michigan State University
Psychology Research Building
East Lansing, MI 48824

Jim Sucichi

Julian Robert Taplin
Director
Division of Child Mental Health Services
Division of Services for Children,
 Youth and Families
330 E. 30th Street
Wilmington, DE 19802

June M. Tuma
Department of Psychology
Louisiana State University
Baton Rouge, LA 70803

Brian Wilcox
Public Interest
American Psychological Association
1200 17th Street, N.W.
Washington, DC 20036

Paul Wohlford
NIMH
5600 Fishers Lane
Parklawn Building
Rockville, MD 20857

Robert A. Zucker
Department of Psychology
Michigan State University
Snyder Hall
E. Lansing, MI 48824

Resource List

Lenore B. Behar
Div. of MH/MR/SAS
Department of HR
325 North Salisbury Street
Raleigh, NC 27611

Orion Bolsted
Morrision Center for Children and
 Family Services
3355 S.E. Powell Boulevard
Portland, OR 97202

Jo Anne Callan
CSPP - San Diego
6212 Ferris Square
San Diego, CA 92121

Mary Campbell
Social and Ethical Responsibilities
American Psychological Association
1200 17th Street, N.W.
Washington, DC 20036

Patrick DeLeon
c/o Senator Inouye
722 Hart Senate Office Building
Washington, DC 20510

David Goodrick
Director
National Technical Assistance Center
 for Mental Health Planning
COSMOS Corporation
1735 Eye Street, N.W., Suite 613
Washington, DC 20006

Susan Harter
Department of Psychology
University of Denver
2040 S. York Street
Denver, CO 80208

Joseph Hasazi
Department of Psychology
University of Vermont
John Dewey Hall
Burlington, VT 05405

Susan Igneizi
CASSP Director
Ohio Department of Mental Health
30 East Broad Street, Suite 2475
Columbus, OH 43215

Mareasa Isaacs
Child/Youth Services Administrator
Commission on Mental Health
1875 Connecticut Ave., N.W.
Suite 1130
Washington, DC 20009

Kathy Katz
Department of Psychology
Georgetown University
Child Development Center
3800 Reservoir Road, N.W.
Washington, DC 20007

Ronald Kurz
5401 Westbard Avenue
Bethesda, MD 20816

John C. Masters
Institute for Public Policy Study and
Department of Psychology
Vanderbilt University
134 Wesley Hall
Nashville, TN 37240

Damian A. McShane
Department of Psychology
VMC 28
Utah State University
Logan, UT 84322

Sally Roger
University of Colorado
Health Sciences Center
J.F.K. Center
C-234, 4200 East 9th Avenue
Denver, CO 80262

Alan O. Ross
Department of Psychology
State University of New York
Stoney Brook, NY 11794

Lee Sechrest
Department of Psychology
University of Arizona
Tuscon, AZ 85721

Ruby Takanishi
Director
Carnegie Council on Adolescent
  Development
11 Dupont Circle, N.W., Suite 900
Washington, DC 20036

Richard A. Weinberg
Department of Educational Psychology
N 548 Elliot Hall
University of Minnesota
Minneapolis, MN 55455

Diane J. Willis
Child Study Center of Children's
  Memorial Hospital
University of Oklahoma Health Sciences
  Center
1100 N.E. 13th
Oklahoma City, OK 73117

Logan Wright
Wright Foundation
Golden Valley Ranch
2701 60th Avenue, N.W.
Norman, OK 73072

Edward F. Zigler
Department of Psychology
Yale University
New Haven, CT 06520

APPENDIX B

The Effects of Projected Loss of NIMH Support on
Clinical Training for Mental Health in Psychology

Murray Levine
State University of New York at Buffalo

Cutbacks in funding from the National Institute of Mental Health (NIMH) for clinical training have now reached the point where the NIMH program will be phased out entirely unless Congress restores support. Those arguing for phasing out clinical training emphasize that training programs have continued to grow despite cutbacks in federal funds. However, that argument looks at overall figures and does not evaluate training needs in specialty areas such as work with children and adolescents. Documentation of the need for trained workers in the child and adolescent field may be found in the Report of the President's Commission on Mental Health (1978) and in policy reviews by Namir and Weinstein (1982), Knitzer (1984), and Levine and Perkins (1987). What effects will cutbacks in funding have on training in child clinical psychology, an area of critical national shortage?

Method

In order to evaluate the effect of loss of NIMH funding on training in child clinical psychology, in February 1987 a questionnaire was distributed to the directors of all 26 programs receiving NIMH support for training in child clinical psychology Nineteen of the 26 programs responded. Of the 19 respondents, 9 were from clinical training centers and 10 were from programs based in psychology departments.

Results

Responses to the questionnaire showed that 284 persons were in training in the 19 child clinical programs during the 1986-1987 academic year. Of these, 75 (26 percent) were supported by NIMH funds. Of those supported by training funds, 54 percent were in their first year of training. Most of the NIMH money was going into trainee support. Seventy-four percent of the programs reported that they spent 90 percent or more of the funds they received on trainee stipends. The few programs that spent less were in clinical centers where the training funds went for staff support for supervision. The fact that most of the money goes to support trainees foretells the area of cutback with the loss of funds.

The 19 programs reported that they graduated 292 persons in the previous 5 years (1982-1986). Of these, 233 (79.6 percent) entered public service in their first position, 12.6 percent went into private sector positions, and 7.5 percent were listed as "unknown" or "other." The figures are somewhat deceptive. Training directors included among the 12.6 percent who went into private sector positions those who accepted employment in child and family service agencies or in community-supported child guidance clinics. Included under "other" were those who went into postdoctoral training or those who went into academic positions. It is clear that most of those in child clinical psychology supported by public funds are obtaining employment in public sector agencies where they apply their skills in an area of critical shortage.

The questionnaire called for program directors to indicate the benefits flowing from the training grant. Most responded with more than one benefit. The totals exceed 19 for that reason. Ten of 19 program directors indicated that the funds helped them to attract a higher-quality student or that the stipends enabled lower-income and minority students to accept full-time training opportunities. Nine of 19 mentioned that the NIMH training funds enabled them to create new programs, to expand existing programs, or to avoid cuts in existing programs. Important for the purposes of the NIMH program, 9 of 19 program directors indicated that training funds enabled them to control the field placements of students to practicum agencies where students could get experience with hitherto underserved populations such as members of minority groups, low-income families, and adolescents. Training directors indicated they would be less able to direct the placement of students in community agencies without training funds.

In addition to attracting better students, 8 of 19 program directors pointed out that the grant enabled them to make more supervisory time available. They said that their programs were enriched by having outside consultants who conducted workshops for them and by the opportunity to use supervisors in field agencies serving low-income and minority populations.

Several mentioned additional benefits. They reported a spread of effect to community agencies. In a number of instances, the presence of students and the interaction of faculty and agency personnel created new opportunities for interdisciplinary efforts, for new clinical programs, and for research. Staff members of practicum agencies attended in-service training programs sponsored by the agency holding the NIMH grant and benefited in that way. Moreover, students sometimes alerted agency personnel to new approaches, enriching and updating the clinical facility's program. Some reported a spread of effect to other faculty not directly involved with the NIMH training program who benefited from their contacts with students involved in the program or from NIMH-funded in-service training events.

None of the program directors expected new funds from state or local agencies to replace lost funds, although a few are negotiating with other agencies for suport. The few who mentioned it are pessimistic about raising private foundation money for training. Program directors do not expect to lose other funds they presently use to support training programs, but most did not expect to be able to generate additional funds from within their own agencies. Because they do not expect replacement funds either from within or from external sources, most of the program directors indicate they will cut back between 25 and 40 percent on the number of trainees they accept for training.

In addition to the reduction in the number of trainees, almost all training directors said the quality of the program will be harmed by loss of training funds. The training directors say they will have less control over the field placements of the trainees in the program. They will be less able to place students in agencies serving minorities or low-income families. Students will have to engage in more income-generating activities. Moreover, students who accept support from teaching or research assistantships will have less freedom to use their time for clinical training with children and adolescents. Supervising faculty and agency staff will also reduce the amount of time devoted to supervision because they too will have to engage in income-generating activities if training funds do not underwrite training activities. The constructive links that have been forged between clinical and academic centers will be broken.

Some mention a long-range problem of institutional support. Training directors believe that they are able to leverage NIMH support within their institutions. Seventy-four percent of trainees are supported by other than NIMH funds. They note that many administrators gauge the quality of programs by the amount of external funds the program generates. If no external funds are forthcoming, training directors foresee an erosion of their position within their own institution, with eventual loss of the support they presently enjoy.

Training directors have mixed views of the effect of loss of funds on length of time to complete training programs. Those in internship or postdoctoral centers do not foresee any increment in time to complete training because their programs are for fixed 1- to 2-year periods. However, those in academic settings do foresee an increase in length of time to complete programs because students will have to take outside jobs to support themselves, reducing their commitment to academic training. NIMH stipends provide summer money for students. Students who will have to work at other jobs will be at a disadvantage in that they will not be able to use the summer months to take courses, do research, or obtain relevant clinical experiences.

Discussion

NIMH training funds are well spent. They are used primarily for student support. NIMH funds are leveraged in that three quarters of the students in child clinical psychology training programs are supported by other funds allocated to the child clinical training program. The funds allocated for a specific training program give training directors control over student experiences and make it possible to attract students of high quality into areas of work that have not been attractive in the past.

Training directors report that the vast proportion of graduates take their first position in public sector agencies. These results indicate that the congressional purpose in providing the funds, to attract high-quality students into an area of critical national shortage, is being met.

The loss of funds will slow down progress in overcoming the shortage of clinical psychologists trained to work with children, adolescents, and families. Training directors predict they will cut their programs from 25 to 40 percent. Those in academic settings believe that training time will be prolonged in the absence of funds to support full-time training. They also fear that the infrastructure that has been built will be lost because administrators set their priorities not by national need, and often not by program quality, but by the ability of a program to generate external funds. Program directors fear that their ability to seek additional institutional funds to support training in child clinical psychology will be adversely affected by the loss of external, federal support.

Program directors also noted a number of other benefits that will be eroded with the loss of federal funds. Relationships between academic institutions and training facilities will again become more distant. Less time will be available for supervision and for in-service education. Interdisciplinary understanding will be eroded as training programs reduce their efforts and do not have the resources to support interchange with community agencies.

It is apparent that our national effort to meet the critical shortage in well-trained child mental health workers will be affected by the loss of federal funds. Training directors do not anticipate that funds from other sources will replace lost federal support. Training directors indicate they will accommodate the loss of funds by reducing the size of their programs, and they anticipate a loss of quality as well. The amount of NIMH funds for clinical training in psychology is minuscule in the federal budget as a whole, and it clearly buys benefits of use to the nation. Congressional failure to restore clinical training funds would be a grievous error, with potential long-term consequences for our training infrastructure in chid and adolescent mental health.

References

Knitzer, J. (1984). Mental health services to children and adolescents: A national view of public policies. American Psychologist, 39, 905-911.

Levine, M., & Perkins, D.V. (1987). Principles of community psychology: Perspectives and applications. New York: Oxford University Press.

Namir, S., & Weinstein, R.S. (1982). Children: Facilitating new directions. In L.R. Snowden (Ed.), Reaching the underserved: Mental health needs of neglected populations. Beverly Hills, CA: Sage.

President's Commission on Mental Health. (1978). Report to the President (Vol. I-IV). Washington, DC: U.S. Government Printing Office.